STRATEGIC COMMUNICATION IN CRISIS MANAGEMENT

STRATEGIC COMMUNICATION IN CRISIS MANAGEMENT

Lessons from the Airline Industry

Sally J. Ray

Q

QUORUM BOOKS
Westport, Connecticut • London

Library of Congress Cataloging-in-Publication Data

Ray, Sally J., 1961–
    Strategic communication in crisis management : lessons from the
airline industry / Sally J. Ray.
        p.   cm.
    Includes bibliographical references and index.
    ISBN 1–56720–153–9 (alk. paper)
    1. Aircraft accidents.   2. Airlines—Communication systems.
3. Crisis management.   4. Communication in management.   I. Title.
TL553.5.R36   1999
658.4'056—dc21   98–41664

British Library Cataloguing in Publication Data is available.

Library of Congress Catalog Card Number: 98–41664
ISBN: 1–56720–153–9

First published in 1999

Quorum Books, 88 Post Road West, Westport, CT 06881
An imprint of Greenwood Publishing Group, Inc.
www.quorumbooks.com

Printed in the United States of America

The paper used in this book complies with the
Permanent Paper Standard issued by the National
Information Standards Organization (Z39.48–1984).

10   9   8   7   6   5   4   3   2   1

Contents

Acknowledgments

Many people have offered assistance and guidance, as well as support and encouragement, in the process of working on this project. I am sincerely appreciative of everyone's help.

My interest in exploring crisis communication in the airline industry began as a doctoral student at Wayne State University in Detroit, Michigan. The crash of Northwest Airlines Flight 255 at Detroit Metropolitan Airport in August 1987 raised my awareness of the many complexities associated with major airline disasters, particularly the communicative aspects. I wish to thank Matthew W. Seeger for his guidance in the initial phase of this research.

At a time when there is much cynicism about our government, the National Transportation Safety Board (NTSB) is an agency in which the American people can take pride. Its outstanding achievements are noted worldwide. I am indebted to NTSB Chairman Jim Hall, who granted me permission to interview NTSB aviation officials. I cannot express enough thanks to Jim Danaher, retired Chief, Operational Factors Division, NTSB Office of Aviation Safety, who hosted me when I visited the Board in Washington, D.C., and set up appointments with the key people I interviewed and put additional energy into assisting me with the chapter on the NTSB to ensure factual accuracy. Special thanks to Al Dickinson, NTSB Senior Air Safety Investigator, for his insights and comments on the TWA case, as well as for his encouragement. I wish to thank additional individuals in the NTSB's Office of Aviation Safety who gave me their time and shared their personal experiences with major airline disasters: Senior Air Safety Investigators Robert Benzon, Greg Feith, and Robert MacIntosh; John Drake, Chief, Aviation Engineering Division; Nora C. Marshall, Survival Factors Division; Barry Strauch, Chief, Human Performance Division; and Peter Goelz, NTSB Managing Director.

I would also like to thank all my colleagues in the Department of Communication at Western Kentucky University for their interest and encouragement. Special thanks to my colleague, mentor, and friend, Judith D. Hoover, for suggesting that I write this book. Thanks are also due Larry J. Winn for insights on the subject of crisis, as well as his support and encouragement, and to Mary Schneider for her assistance and continuous enthusiasm for this project. Through the years a number of graduate students have assisted me in researching this subject. I wish to thank Andy Poklad, Stephanie Franklin, Doug Morey, and especially Lihong Zhao for their work.

Thanks also go to Sam Willett for his interest, support, and opening the necessary doors, and to my colleague and friend, Roger D. Vincent, for his dialogue, insights, and suggestions.

Finally, I wish to thank my family for their patience and understanding. Mother and Arthur, whenever I have experienced my own crises you have always been there for me. Your support and encouragement did much to make this book possible.

Introduction

Strategic Communication in Crisis Management: Lessons from the Airline Industry examines organizational crises in the context of the airline industry and the communication strategies employed by airlines when responding to various issues associated with a major air-carrier crash. Airline accidents illustrate the industry's high level of vulnerability to crisis and capture the complexities of crisis management and communication. Because of its vulnerability, the industry is well-prepared to handle a crash at a moment's notice. But the unpredictable nature of crisis can challenge even the most prepared organizations. Major air-carrier crashes are large-scale events that involve numerous stakeholders, receive considerable media coverage, and are characterized by surprise, threat, uncertainty, time pressures, and extreme emotions. Critical issues which emerge following a crash may result in an airline contending with accusations of blame, irresponsibility, or inadequacy. Under these conditions a company must provide appropriate and effective responses. For this reason, the airline industry has much to teach crisis managers in other industries. The case studies in this book demonstrate both the successes and failures of the airlines and the industry as a whole when responding to crisis.

Major aviation accidents fuel concern about safety. After a well-publicized plane crash, airlines expect an increase in cancellations. Naturally, when the industry encounters two or three crashes in a year's time, the public forms the impression air travel in general is suddenly unsafe. The fact the industry may go years without a major crash usually goes unrecognized.

Despite its vulnerability to aviation accidents, the aviation community has achieved some compelling statistics where safety is concerned. The airline industry operates under a distinctive public standard of zero major accidents—in other words, no accidents. To the public, one accident is one too many. In the 1995 Annual "Site" Lecture to the Wings Club of New York (Wings Club, 1995), two striking facts regarding airline safety were highlighted: (1) The United States accounts for about one-half the world's air travel, but only 8 percent of fatalities on airlines around the world since 1990, and (2) the United States has had about 12,600 fatalities during the entire history of commercial aviation, comparable to the average number of highway-related fatalities over a three- to four-month period. Members of the aviation community continuously strive to achieve an even higher level of safety.

One might think the increased growth consequent to deregulation would escalate the number of airline accidents; however, a 1992 Federal Aviation Administration (FAA) study regarding the impact of deregulation on commercial aviation operation shows otherwise. Since the enactment of the 1978 Airline Deregulation Act, there has been no statistical evidence indicating deregulation has adversely affected the safety of U.S. carriers. The study suggests that while annual total fatal accident rates fluctuated for Part 121 carriers, there was a general downward trend between 1978 and 1989. The accident rate for major carriers has been stable at low rates for over twelve years and, despite dramatic growth and change, the accident rate has also declined sharply for commuter air carriers (Wings Club, 1995). This remarkable safety record is primarily due to technological advancements in several fields and the knowledge gained by accident investigations and subsequent research.

U.S. SAFETY SYSTEM

The enviable safety record of the U.S. commercial aviation industry can be credited to many dedicated safety professionals. Foremost, the airlines are to be commended for their continuous efforts to maintain a safe system. It is the day-to-day management of the industry, as well as the professionalism of employees, that keeps everything going. In addition, numerous other groups influence the safety system for U.S. commercial aviation—the Federal Aviation Administration, under the supervision of the Department of Transportation (DOT), the National Transportation Safety Board (NTSB), associated labor groups, manufacturers of aircraft and equipment, Congress, the National Aeronautics and Space Administration (NASA), the National Weather Service (NWS), as well as various consumer and industry safety advocates. All matters related to aviation in the United States are regulated and administered by the FAA. Although it is not a regulating agency, the NTSB plays a significant role in the aviation safety system. The NTSB is the federal government's transportation investigator and "watchdog" of transportation safety. An independent federal agency, the NTSB functions to determine the "probable cause" of transportation accidents and formulate safety recommendations to improve transportation safety. Aviation is the largest section of the

Board's divisions. The NTSB investigates hundreds of accidents annually, including all air-carrier accidents, all in-flight collisions, fatal general-aviation accidents, and all air-taxi/commuter accidents. The agency is responsible for reporting the conditions and circumstances relating to accidents and making accident reports public. The major share of the Board's air-safety recommendations are directed to the FAA. These recommendations, vital to accident prevention, serve as a mechanism to prompt safety changes and improvements to the country's transportation system.

Progress in the areas of airframe and engine reliability, onboard automation, knowledge of human factors, training simulation, and air traffic control and technology have contributed to the industry's overall safety record. Accident investigations have served as a principal tool for improving cabin safety and the ability to survive a crash and the resulting fire and smoke. For example, in 1989 a United Airlines DC-10 crashed in Sioux City. Though 111 persons died in the accident, 185 persons survived what previously would have been typed a "nonsurvivable" crash.

Through the years, airline accidents have expedited government actions concerning safety. Following World War II, the industry entered into a period of unreadiness. Technology was unable to keep up with the rapid growth of air travel and budgetary restrictions further limited the placement of long-range radars. Consequently, a number of midair accidents occurred en route which increased public and government concern. In June 1956, a TWA L-1049 collided at 21 thousand feet in midair with a United DC-7 over the Grand Canyon, killing 128. At the time, the Grand Canyon accident became the deadliest in history, shocking the public and increasing concern about air safety. This concern accelerated funding for additional long-range radars for air traffic control and, in 1958, the passage of the Federal Aviation Act which created the Federal Aviation Agency. In 1960, when a United DC-8 collided with a TWA Constellation on approach to Idlewild and LaGuardia, killing 133, the focus moved from en-route collisions to terminal collisions.

These accidents prompted actions and developments which eventually revolutionized the air traffic control system. Today, midair collisions involving large commercial aircraft are extremely rare events. When a Delta Airlines L-1011 crashed on approach to the Dallas–Fort Worth International Airport after encountering wind shear in 1985, government efforts regarding the development and implementation of Doppler radar were expedited. On July 11, 1988, the Doppler radar successfully demonstrated its ability to provide warning of dangerous microbursts when it helped to avert a potentially fatal airline accident at Denver's Stapleton Airport.

AIRLINE SAFETY AND PUBLIC OPINION

Crashes tend to increase apprehension about the safety of specific carriers or types of carriers. After USAir (now US Airways) encountered a series of accidents in 1994, for example, the public referred to the carrier as "US-Scare." The issue of smaller commuter planes being less safe than larger major aircraft emerged following the 1994 American Eagle accident near Roselawn, Indiana, which killed all sixty-eight passengers, and again in January 1997, when Comair crashed near Detroit, killing all twenty-nine passengers and crew. Questions concerning the safety of low-fare airlines followed the ValuJet crash in May 1996. Contrary to public opinion, the FAA has argued ranking airlines according to safety is virtually impossible. Though there may be distinct differences among air-carrier safety records at any particular time, it is impossible to predict airlines' future safety performance (FAA, 1997).

The number of accidents and the death toll for 1996 were the highest yet, with 1,187 fatalities on commercial flights worldwide. The highly publicized crash killing Commerce Secretary Ron Brown in April, the ValuJet crash in May, and the TWA disaster in July increased public concern about safety and those charged to guarantee safety. A 1997 FAA report, "Issues Related to Public Interest in Aviation Safety Data," indicated the flying public placed more trust in the individuals who affect the safety of flying (pilots, controllers, maintenance workers) than the public and private institutions that provide and ensure safety. Subsequently, the White House Commission on Aviation Safety, chaired by Vice President Gore, was formed to improve aviation security and safety. To further alleviate public concern, the FAA announced, in January 1997, it would begin a public education campaign designed to emphasize the overall safety of aviation. In an effort to make aviation safety data more available and accessible to consumers, the information is posted on the World Wide Web.

AIRLINE ACCIDENTS

The NTSB classifies accidents according to four categories: Damage, Injury, Serious, and Major (NTSB, 1997). Accidents classified as "Damage" are least severe and have no fatalities or severe injuries, but there is substantial damage to any Part 121 aircraft. "Injury" accidents are nonfatal and there is no substantial damage to the aircraft, but there is at least one serious injury. These accidents may occur during abrupt maneuvers, turbulence, or evacuation. An accident qualifies as "Serious" when one of two conditions is met: one fatality but no substantial damage to a Part 121 aircraft, or at least one serious injury and substantial damage to the aircraft. Accidents deemed "Major" occur when a Part 121 aircraft was destroyed, or there are multiple fatalities, or there is one fatality and aircraft destruction.

Rarely is an accident caused by a single factor. Most accidents involve multiple causes or a chain of events. Aircraft component failures, weather factors, traffic environment, unpredictable events (terrorism or sabotage), and human errors are often cited.

While accidents receive varying degrees of interest from media and public, a major accident attracts the greatest attention. From an organizational perspective, a crash represents a threat to the airline's legitimacy, image, and financial situation. Some airlines never recover from a crisis caused by such a crash, as learned from Air Florida following its 1982 crash into the Fourteenth Street Bridge in Washington, D.C. In other instances, a crash and its subsequent investigation ignite a crisis for the entire industry. Investigators' findings following the crash of American Airlines Flight 191 in May 1979 raised questions about the DC-10. Eventually, the FAA ordered an indefinite grounding for all DC-10s operated by U.S. airlines, creating chaos and financial loss throughout the industry.

While recognized as the nature of the industry, a crash is never expected. Following an accident, there are primary concerns for safety, humanity, and public relations. An airline experiences uncertainty with regard to cause, blame, response, public perception, and resolution. In addition, airlines encounter general legal concerns, such as enforcement proceedings against individuals, certificate limitations, or revocation proceedings against the company. In order to survive the crisis, the airline must strategically communicate to victims and/or their families, the media, the public, other airlines, manufacturers, government agencies, stockholders, officers, employees, and future customers.

REFERENCES

Federal Aviation Administration (FAA). (1992). *Annual report on the effect of the airline deregulation act on the level of air safety.* Washington, DC: U.S. Government Printing Office.

Federal Aviation Administration (FAA). (1997). Issues related to public interest in aviation safety data. [http://nasdac.faa.gov/SA.../SafetyPaperComplete.htm] February 15, 1997.

National Transportation Safety Board (NTSB). (1997). *Improved classification system for airline accidents.* Washington, DC: NTSB.

Wings Club of New York. (1995). Annual "site" lecture, May 5, given by David R. Hinson, FAA Administrator, New York City.

Part I

Context

Chapter 1

Context for Crisis:
The Airline Industry

Major airline accidents are compelling events that capture the attention of the industry, government, media, and public. A large number of fatalities in a single event is devastating and leaves an indelible impression on those it affects. We have sympathized with anguished families over their losses, listened with a morbid curiosity as NTSB investigators attempt to explain why such a tragedy occurred, and perhaps even questioned whether we would want to fly again. The industry has demonstrated how some good can come from bad in the wake of an airline disaster. With accident investigation as a principal tool, safety continues to improve. The U.S. commercial airline industry has compiled an outstanding safety record thanks to technological advancements and the knowledge gained through accident investigations. Today, air travel remains one of the safest forms of transportation.

Despite the industry's efforts to reduce factors that lead to accidents, such crises are inevitable because of the complexity of modern technologies, human factors, and the highly interdependent nature of the industry. Crashes have occurred since the dawn of aviation, but the growth of the industry combined with the lightning speed of mass communication and technology have made airline disasters larger in size, highly visible, and extremely complex to manage. An airline crash results in a crisis that threatens the legitimacy of the airline, its image, and its financial situation. Moreover, it has the tendency to resonate throughout the industry, affecting not only victims and the airline in crisis, but other stakeholders as well.

Communication, critical to the control of a crisis, serves to either manage the situation or create further confusion. In order to competently manage the crisis, the organization must organize and act to protect its long-term corporate interest and public image; therefore, an effective communication plan becomes critical. This book examines organizational crises and the communication strategies available to organizations in crisis and the factors that influence their effectiveness. No organization is immune to a crisis; however, one industry and one form of crisis is the focus of this examination. Limiting the focus to major airline crashes allows for a deeper understanding of strategic communication in a particular crisis situation. In addition, it captures the specific phenomena associated with the management of these disasters.

"Crash Management" may seem an appropriate title for this book; however, Pauchant and Mitroff (1992) are quick to distinguish between "crisis management" and "crash management," the latter referring to reactive actions. Crisis management refers to a proactive as well as reactive approach to crisis. It involves a recognition of the physical and symbolic dimensions of a crisis prior to and following a crisis.

Crisis management plans do not always include a coherent and well-thought-out strategy of public communication. Crisis communication enables an organization to respond appropriately in order to maintain public confidence and minimize the damage. Managers may assume that all crisis communication has the same objective and all audiences may be approached with the same strategy. It is to their dismay when they realize what works in one situation does not necessarily work in another. Assuming the same orientation in all situations may result in a failure to achieve the desired result, or, worse, compound the crisis for the organization. Situations vary, so it is impossible to prescribe a standardized communication strategy for crisis managers. But by illuminating the complexities associated with a major airline disaster, we can place those who manage this type of crisis in a better position to determine effective communication strategies.

This book is written from two perspectives. First, airline crashes are viewed in terms of phases: pre-crisis, crisis, and post-crisis. The events surrounding an airline crash occur in phases. Each phase contains factors which impact communication efforts in the other phases. By looking at crises in terms of phases, we can better comprehend the numerous variables, characteristics, and events which influence the onset of crisis, its management, and its resolution. This understanding is vital to crisis managers when determining strategic communication.

Second, a crisis cannot be understood in isolated parts, but as a system (Pauchant & Mitroff, 1992). The variables associated with a crisis are interdependent and influence one another, ultimately impacting the whole. A crisis often resonates beyond the organization in crisis. Focusing solely on one entity limits our understanding of crisis and communication. To fully understand the crisis resulting from an airline disaster and the implications for communication, crisis managers must look at the whole picture, not isolated parts. Only then can effective communication strategies be identified.

Understanding how an airline should communicate following a major airline disaster gives rise to a number of questions: What issues or factors influence an airline's communication following a major crash? How do these issues and factors constrain a crisis organization's efforts in restoring its public image and ultimately resolving the crisis? Which communication strategies are the most effective? What variables influence the effectiveness or ineffectiveness of communication strategies? How can airlines prepare for managing their communication to the public following a crash? These are just a few of the questions addressed in this book.

While an air-carrier crash tends to be the most visible form of crisis, it is not the only type of crisis the industry encounters. The highly complex, competitive, and interdependent nature of the industry places airlines in a chronic crisis phase. The competitive nature of the industry often induces sudden market shifts. Competitive airfares stimulate fare wars, threatening smaller carriers and, in some instances, forcing them out of business. Financial problems pressed both TWA and Continental into Chapter 11 bankruptcy. Top-management succession may create a crisis, as was the case when legendary Frank Lorenzo took over Continental and Eastern airlines in the 1980s. Mergers may also give rise to crises. Northwest's merger with Republic Airlines in 1986 created labor disputes, vandalism, and service problems for the company (Houston, 1987).

Union strikes can potentially devastate an airline. Even the threat of a strike negatively impacts an airline, as observed with American Airlines and its pilots' union during February 1997 (CNN Interactive, 1997). American Airlines pilots' union, at odds with the airline over a new labor contract, threatened a potentially devastating strike at the nation's number-two carrier. Prior to the strike deadline, President Clinton intervened and imposed a "cooling off" period. Analysts noted that prior to President Clinton's intervention, the airline reported losses of over $40 million per day. In an effort to win back loyal customers, American drastically reduced its fares. Government dictates may also create varying degrees of crisis. Obstacles such as taxations and regulations, which increased labor costs, contributed to the industry's $13 billion loss in the early 1990s (Heppenheimer, 1995).

Air piracy presents another form of crisis. In 1971, D. B. Cooper took control of a Northwest Airlines 727, gathered up $200 thousand in ransom, and disappeared along with four parachutes out the rear door of the aircraft, never to be seen again (Heppenheimer, 1995). Prior to the notorious Mr. Cooper, adverse international events prompted instances of air piracy. In the 1960s, skyjackings resulting from the conflict surrounding Castro's Cuba made Havana a potential destination for flights. In 1970, two members of the Popular Front for the Liberation of Palestine hijacked a Pan Am 747 to Cairo. Subsequent hijackings in the Middle East prompted the FAA to tighten its rules on suspicious passengers and install metal detectors.

Flight crews have increasingly experienced problems with passengers when flying. The nature of these incidents is alarming. In-flight crimes and other offences are not uncommon. Numerous cases of flight attendants being physically or verbally assaulted by drunken or irate passengers while performing their duties have recently received media attention. One of the most crude incidents occurred in 1996, when a United Airlines passenger on an international flight relieved himself on a food cart and threatened a flight attendant because he was refused another drink (Crew Member Crime Victims' Advocacy Outreach, 1997). Unruly passengers not only create inconvenience, but threaten the safety of everyone on board.

Sudden market shifts, finances, top-management succession, mergers, strikes, government dictates, air piracy, adverse international events, and inflight crimes create many crises for airlines. These events may not rise to the level of public scrutiny and concern accorded major airline crashes, but they are generally unpredictable and have potentially negative consequences which may significantly damage the public perception of an airline.

We move to a consideration of organizational crises and crisis communication in Chapter 2. Subsequent chapters are divided into three parts according to the simplified model of crisis stages: pre-crisis, crisis, and post-crisis. This organizing pattern provides the reader with a comprehensive understanding of significant factors and issues which influence crisis, communication, and resolution. Pre-crisis identifies variables that lead to airline crashes, illuminates factors and/or issues that may later compound efforts at crisis management, and considers the process of contingency planning. The crashes of Northwest Airlines Flight 255 and American Flight 191 are examined to demonstrate the complexity of these issues. Crisis considers the concerns that characterize the crisis stage and presents two studies of crisis response by Delta Airlines and Trans World Airlines. Post-crisis discusses the post-crisis investigation. Studies of Pan Am Flight 103, USAir Flight 427, and ValuJet Flight 592 are offered to illustrate the diverse issues encountered during the post-crisis phase. A final chapter reflects on the lessons learned from the preceding chapters.

REFERENCES

CNN Interactive. (1997). Stakes high for American Airlines as strike talks stall. [http:\\www.CNN.com/US/97.erican.strike.index.html] February 12, 1997.

Crew Member Crime Victims' Advocacy Outreach. (1997). *Inflight assault of flight crewmember*. Roanoke, TX: Author.

Heppenheimer, T. A. (1995). *Turbulent skies: The history of commercial aviation*. New York: John Wiley & Sons.

Houston, P. (1987, September 28). Steve Rothmeier's Northwest looks good on paper. *Business Week*, pp. 58–59.

Pauchant, T., & Mitroff, I. (1992). *Transforming the crisis-prone organization: Preventing individual, organizational, and environmental tragedies*. San Francisco: Jossey-Bass.

Chapter 2 ———————————————————

Organizational Crisis and Communication

Crisis! It is a word that evokes feelings of uneasiness, fear, or panic in those companies and individuals who have survived its effects. For others fortunate enough to not have had the experience, the term may be somewhat of an enigma. A crisis can occur at any time and place and happen to any organization. No company is immune to a crisis. As our world continues to become increasingly complex, the potential for crisis escalates. One only has to read a newspaper or watch television to recognize that crises are occurring more frequently and becoming larger in scope.

The frequency of organizational crises has spawned numerous studies intended to provide insight into this complicated phenomenon. Crisis research identifies a multitude of guidelines and recommendations designed to assist those responsible for managing what may initially seem an unmanageable event. To effectively deal with the effects of crisis, managers should understand its nature, managerial prescriptions, and communication implications. Such an understanding provides a sense of predictability, should a crisis occur. This chapter considers the crisis phenomenon and communication strategies available to an organization that finds itself in a threatening situation.

CONCEPTUALIZING ORGANIZATIONAL CRISIS

Most agree a crisis is an unpredictable event which disrupts an organization's routine pattern of day-to-day life. While we may use the words "crisis" and "disaster" interchangeably, the research literature makes a clear distinction. Disasters are generally viewed as large-scale community events (tornadoes, floods, earthquakes, etc.) managed by community, government, or social groups. A crisis tends to be triggered by organizational errors, oversights, or deficiencies (Quarantelli, 1988). From this perspective, a major air-carrier crash is both a crisis and disaster, in that it is often caused by organizational inadequacies and managed not only by the airline, but by the community in which it occurs and government agencies.

Pauchant and Mitroff (1992) distinguish between incident, accident, and crisis, the demarcating factor being the magnitude of the event. An incident is an event which affects a "self-contained" part of a larger system. An accident physically disrupts a system as a whole. A crisis "physically affects a system as a whole and threatens its basic assumptions, its subjective sense of self, its existential core" (p. 12). When amplified by other variables in the system, incidents can evolve into accidents and, possibly, crises. Following the ValuJet crash in May 1996, reports surfaced indicating the airline's lax attitude toward safety had resulted in a number of prior safety incidents. The airline failed to consider the seriousness of this prevailing attitude, as well as the amplifying effect of another variable, a subcontractor's faulty handling and labeling of oxygen generators.

A systems perspective further suggests a crisis impacts an entire industry. The Three Mile Island accident heavily damaged the reputation of, and public confidence in, the whole nuclear power utility industry. In the case of an air-carrier crash, not only is the airline jolted, but its effects resonate to other airlines, the aircraft manufacturer, the engine manufacturer, the FAA, and other industry groups. In many cases, the determination of the probable cause(s) of a crash implicates organizations beyond the airline, often creating a crisis for that particular group.

Causes

Crises occur as a consequence of the organization's imperfection and vulnerability to its environment. They have been explained as "large scale intelligence failures" or "failures in foresight" (Turner, 1976). In other words, the events leading up to a crisis accumulate because internal and/or external factors were overlooked or misinterpreted as a result of false assumptions, poor communication, cultural lag, and misplaced optimism (Turner, 1976). Organizations become particularly vulnerable to crisis when they have low control over their external environment. When external factors (competitors, suppliers, customers or clients, regulators, society, owners and boards of directors, and natural disasters) negatively combine with internal factors (executive characteristics, experience and history, demographics, and attributes), a crisis may occur. The likelihood of an organization experiencing a severe crisis is highest when it has low control over the environment and a high level of susceptibility due to internal factors. The Bhopal accident became a crisis when internal technological problems negatively combined with environmental conditions outside the plant. The plant, under pressure from Union Carbide to make profits, was located in a city totally unprepared to handle a major industrial accident (Shrivastava, 1987). The consequences were devastating.

Communication failures may also play a key role in causing crisis. Communication climates that discourage open communication about problems and breakdowns and disruptions of coordination often contribute to crisis (Seeger, Sellnow, & Ulmer, 1998). Cushing (1994) examined how miscommunication plays a role in airline disasters. Communication breakdowns between pilots and air traffic controllers as well as misunderstandings due to accent and technical jargon have contributed to numerous aircraft disasters.

Crisis Typologies

Organizations experience a variety of crises. Typologies classify complex phenomena and provide insights into crisis planning. Meyers (1986) identified nine types of business crises: crises in public perception, sudden market shifts, product failures, top-management succession, finances, industrial relations, hostile takeovers, adverse international events, and regulation and deregulation. Crises can be distinguished by their underlying structural similarity: breakdowns or defects in products, plants, packages, equipment, and people; extreme antisocial acts directed at corporations, products, consumers, executives, employees, and employees' families; external economic attacks such as extortion, bribery, boycotts, and hostile takeovers; external information attacks such as copyright infringements, loss of information, counterfeiting, and rumors; and environmental accidents (Mitroff, 1988). Crises may also be typed as strategic, performance, or liquidity (Muller, 1985). A strategic crisis results from the failure of an organization to build or maintain its foundations in the marketplace; a performance crisis arises when a firm consistently fails to meet its goals; and a liquidity crisis occurs when a firm can no longer meet its obligations.

Another way to classify crises is to place them into two broad categories of violent (immediate, usually cataclysmic, and involving loss of life or property) and nonviolent (Newsom, Turk, & Kruckeberg, 1996). Subcategories contained within these two general categories are acts of nature, intentional acts, and unintentional acts. Violent acts of nature include earthquakes, storms, and floods. A nonviolent act of nature would be an epidemic, such as AIDS. Violent intentional acts are those which lead to death or destruction, such as terrorism or product tamperings. Nonviolent intentional acts include threats of a bomb or product tampering, hostile takeovers, and insider trading. Explosions and fires would be considered violent unintentional acts. Violent unintentional acts are those which may result in loss of life due to product or process problems, such as Chernobyl (Newsom, Turk, & Kruckeberg, 1996).

Coombs's Typology

Coombs (1995) explains crisis situations according to stakeholders' perceptions. "Stakeholder" refers to any group or public impacted by the organization's operation (employees, consumers, stockholders, suppliers, competitors, unions, special interest groups, government, media, and local community). In a crisis, managers must communicate to multiple stakeholders who may perceive the situation differently. Stakeholders' perceptions of a crisis are based on whether the cause was internal or external to the organization, a constant or random event, and an intentional or unintentional act. An organization is perceived responsible for the crisis when the cause is internal to the organization, a consistent presence, and an intentional act. The public does not view the organization as responsible if the cause is external to the organization, an infrequent occurrence, and an unintentional act. The bombing of Pan Am Flight 103 was an intentional act by an international terrorist. Pan Am, however, was perceived responsible for the disaster because of its weak security system, the fact that its security operation had been inadequate for some time, and because the airline was in the position to control security risks. Based on a combination of the internal–external and intentional–unintentional dimensions, Coombs specifies faux pas, accidents, terrorism, and transgressions as crisis situations.

Faux pas refers to unintentional acts (initially considered appropriate by the organization) challenged by an external group or person. For example, a faux pas occurs when a company is challenged by an outside group concerning the appropriateness of its product advertising. Accidents are unintentional events which occur during organizational operations. An accident may be a natural disaster or influenced by human error. Acts of nature tend to receive a less negative public response due to the minimal control which can be exercised over such acts. Nevertheless, there is the expectation that the organization must effectively cope with acts of nature. A transgression is an event where an organization "knowingly" places others at risk—the organization is clearly responsible. A company that knowingly sells defective or dangerous products has committed a transgression. Terrorism is an intentional act by an outside group intended to do direct or indirect harm to the organization. The organization is often perceived a victim. In addition to the crisis situation, Coombs (1995) suggests the public's perception of a crisis is influenced by the accuracy of evidence, the degree of damage associated with the triggering event, and the organization's performance history. Media are critical in influencing these perceptions.

The typologies specified by researchers provide us with a way of identifying and categorizing the varied events which lead to crisis situations. The particular crisis situation becomes influential in determining strategic communication.

Characteristics of Crises

While every crisis is unique, there are common characteristics. A crisis situation can escalate in intensity, receive intense scrutiny from media or government, interrupt a company's normal operating procedures, threaten a company's image, and damage its bottom line (Fink, 1986). Crises are generally characterized by surprise, insufficient information about the problem, stress (which may impact the effectiveness of decision makers), threat (to the organization's profitability, viability, and legitimacy), and limited response time, and require immediate decision making, problem solving, and communication (Hermann, 1963). Even with contingency planning, organizations are surprised by a triggering event and have minimal time in which to respond. The unexpected nature of an event, for example, may result in a delayed response to the situation. NASA's Challenger explosion was so unanticipated that for a brief time Mission Control maintained normal procedures before announcing there had been a "major malfunction" (Brown, 1990).

Crisis situations generally involve a high level of uncertainty with regard to cause, blame, response, public perception, resolution, and other possible consequences. A lack of information creates the potential for crisis, as well as influencing the resolution of the crisis. The severity of a crisis is often dependent on the level of uncertainty. The greater the uncertainty about resolving a situation, the more severe the crisis. The acquisition of critical information places the organization in a stronger position to plan for and manage the crisis. Information is necessary to determine the nature of a response, understand the probabilities, and recognize the values of a loss. The severity of a crisis may also be determined by perception (Billings, Milburn, & Schaalman, 1980). A situation is a crisis only if it is perceived as such by the decision makers.

During a crisis, decisions must be made about how to manage the crisis, allocate resources, interpret information, and respond to groups, issues, and possible allegations. The stress, pressure, and limited information associated with a crisis often prevents sound decision making. Faulty decision making may occur in one of two ways. First, crisis management teams may be unable to produce sound decisions because of disagreements and conflicts. Second, the team may be so cohesive that there is an absence of independent critical thinking, what Janis (1982) refers to as "groupthink." Groupthink, a situation in which a cohesive decision-making group suppresses disagreement and the appraisal of alternatives, has been associated with such crises as NASA's Challenger disaster (Gouran, Hirokawa, & Marz, 1986). In a crisis situation, decision makers may "react" rather than "reflect" on the situation, which may compound the crisis (Gouran, 1982).

Consequences

As with most conflicts, crisis can result in negative or positive consequences. The effects of crises may be caused or extenuated by multiple stakeholders. Crisis can bring about two effects in an organization (Hermann, 1963). A crisis can lead to behavior that is destructive to the organization and seriously limits its continued viability. The *Exxon Valdez* catastrophe in March 1989 became America's worst oil spill disaster. Exxon handled the crisis badly by delaying its response, downplaying the incident, and responding offensively to the media. The company severely damaged its image and reputation. A crisis may further threaten an organization's legitimacy, reverse its strategic mission, and distort people's subjective world (Pauchant & Mitroff, 1992). On the other hand, a crisis may create closer integration of the organization, the appropriate innovations for meeting the crisis, and the clarification of relevant values. Johnson & Johnson's handling of the 1982 Tylenol crisis reinforced its image as a caring and trustworthy company. The company's response became an exemplary model for crisis management (Fink, 1986).

While a crisis generally presents a threat, opportunities may be introduced. A crisis focuses attention on one concern, calls for cooperation, and gives the company a chance to demonstrate its capabilities and concern for people affected and for the interests of the community involved (Stephenson, 1982). Further, it provides managers who deal with the crisis and resolve it a chance to demonstrate problem-solving capability. Meyers (1986) suggests seven potential advantages of crisis: heroes are born, change is accelerated, latent problems are faced, people can be changed, new strategies evolve, early-warning systems develop, and new competitive edges appear.

Modeling Crises

Modeling a crisis helps us to recognize and understand the numerous variables, characteristics, and events which influence the situation. Fink (1986), for example, identified four phases of a crisis: prodromal, acute, chronic, and resolution. The prodromal crisis phase is what Fink labels the warning period. This stage consists of elements signaling an impending crisis, which may or may not be recognized. A prodrome may be as obvious as a phone call warning of a bombing. In some crises, a warning stage may be absent. The actual damage occurs in the acute crisis phase, a brief and intense period which Fink describes as "the point of no return" (p. 22). The organization controls the aftermath of a crisis in the chronic or clean-up phase. This is a time for self-analysis, recovery, investigations, explanation, and blame, and may also be a turning point in the crisis. Resolution is the goal during the preceding stages. At this point, the crisis is over and the organization seeks to return to normal operations. These phases may occur over a relatively short period or over an extended period of time.

Turner (1976) offers a more differentiated model of crisis stages. Stage I is the conceptually normal point, with initial culturally accepted beliefs about the world and its hazards and associated precautionary norms set out in laws, codes of practice, mores, and folkways. For example, the negative health effects of tobacco were not initially known. In fact, early European physicians held to the Native American belief that tobacco had healing powers. In the early twentieth century, however, the initial beliefs concerning the positive medicinal value of tobacco changed as science and medical journals began reporting on the negative effects of cigarette smoking. Subsequent to a 1952 *Reader's Digest* article (Norr, 1952) detailing the dangers of smoking, other reports began to appear prompting smokers to take notice. Cigarette sales soon declined. The changes in the belief structures surrounding cigarette smoking resulted in a dramatic change in the accompanying norms and practices. The tobacco industry responded by mass marketing filtered cigarettes and low-tar formulations which promised a "healthier" smoke. The public responded and sales increased.

Stage II (Turner, 1976) is the incubation period where the accumulation of an unnoticed set of conflicting events occurs. The events are either unknown, not fully understood, or not communicated in meaningful ways to capture decision makers' attention or trigger an action. Whatever the reason, managers fail to foresee potential dangers. Stage III is the precipitating event. While difficult to define, the crisis cannot be ignored. Stage IV is where the immediate consequences of the failure become apparent. Stage V is the rescue and salvage and the first stage of adjustment. This is where a company will likely activate its crisis plan. Stage VI is full cultural readjustment. An inquiry or assessment is carried out and beliefs and precautionary norms are adjusted to fit the newly gained understanding of the world. Following Stage VI, an organization returns to Stage I, suggesting crises are cyclical.

A more simplified model of crisis proposes three overlapping stages. These include pre-crisis, crisis, and post-crisis (Meyers, 1986). In the pre-crisis phase, signs of crisis may be perceived. This is equivalent to Fink's prodromal phase and Turner's Stage II. The primary impacts of crisis are experienced in the second stage, crisis. This phase corresponds to Fink's acute phase and Turner's Stages III and IV. Post-crisis is a period of recovery and assessment and a point where unique opportunities may be created or additional negative effects occur. Post-crisis equates with Fink's chronic phase and comprises Turner's Stages V and VI. The duration of each stage varies and is characterized by varying levels of stress, threat, surprise, and limited response time. The transition from the pre-crisis stage to the crisis stage is generally marked by an accumulation of events resulting in a "triggering event."

CRISIS MANAGEMENT

Crisis management functions to provide accurate information as quickly as possible to organizational stakeholders (Schuetz, 1990). It provides a systematic, orderly response to crisis while enabling the organization to continue its daily business. Organizational threat is controlled and opportunities become available with effective crisis management. The stress, threat, uncertainty, and time pressure associated with an unpredictable event create extreme challenges for those charged with managing a crisis. The process of crisis management involves organizational design, personnel selection, team development, environmental auditing, contingency planning, and the management of the actual crisis. The goal is resolution, return to normal operations, and repair of any damage.

Organizations attempt to deal with uncertainty surrounding a crisis by developing contingency plans. With timely and appropriate responses, the perceived seriousness of a threat may be lessened. Smart (1985) suggests, "At a minimum, the impact of surprise associated with a threat can be reduced by contingency planning, but one must first have some indication about the direction and change before these contingency plans can be developed" (p. 11). Planning in advance for a crisis reduces the perceived risk and uncertainty associated with a given situation, thereby allowing the organization to exert more control. An effective plan presets certain key decisions on aspects that rarely vary, leaving the organization free to manage the content portion of the crisis. The effectiveness of coping actions, however, depends on the decision maker's perception of the situation (Tjosvold, 1984). Coping actions are generally more effective when the decision maker views the situation as a challenge rather than as a threat. Issues regarding crisis management and contingency planning are discussed in depth in subsequent chapters.

CRISIS COMMUNICATION

Throughout the various phases of crisis, the organization must organize and act to protect its own long-term corporate interest and public image; therefore, open and accurate communication is critical to the control of a crisis. Heath (1994) has defined crisis communication as "the enactment of control (at least in its appearance) in the face of high uncertainty in an effort to win external audiences' confidence, in ways that are ethical" (p. 259). In addition to resolving the crisis and returning to normal operations, crisis management seeks to maintain or restore an organization's image, the public perception of the organization. Union Carbide, NASA, and Exxon have demonstrated how ineffective communication in a crisis can further damage the image of an organization.

Organizations respond to a crisis in one of three ways: (1) deny a crisis exists and refuse to cooperate with media and government agencies; (2) provide partial, inaccurate, or delayed information; or (3) establish and maintain open and accurate communication channels with external constituents (Wilcox, Ault, & Agee, 1986). Most analysts agree on the importance of the latter response (Fink, 1986; Ramee, 1987; Ressler, 1982; Stephenson, 1984).

Functions of Communication

Crisis communication is necessary to influence public perception of the organization. Sturges (1994) contends that crisis communication should maintain the present positive opinions about a company's image from the negative aspects associated with a crisis. On July 18, 1984, James Huberty invaded a

McDonald's restaurant in San Ysidro, California, and shot forty people, killing twenty-one and wounding nineteen before he was shot and killed from a nearby rooftop by a member of the San Diego Police Department's SWAT team. Though a victim itself, McDonald's communicated openly with the media and the public, paid hospital bills, flew in victims' relatives for the funerals, and provided counseling for victims' families. The company's response reinforced its positive image.

Communication should direct stakeholders' physical responses, psychological responses, and impressions about the organization. Insufficient and inaccurate information may give rise to myths, false alarms, and heightened perceptions of harm (Shrivastava, Mitroff, Miller, & Miglani, 1988). While open and accurate disclosures may be damaging initially, they reduce the risk of rumors, leaks, drawn-out media coverage, and the perception of dishonesty. Ethical behavior benefits both the organization and the public. Responses which are candid, prompt, honest, and complete may further bolster the organization's reputation and integrity.

An open and honest posture may enhance image, but it often conflicts with legal strategies designed to limit organizational liability (Fitzpatrick & Rubin, 1995). Legal constraints may keep a company from communicating as freely as it would like. Liability may determine how a company responds to victims or victims' relatives. Some airlines, for example, have been accused of assisting victims' relatives after a major plane crash for the sole reason of soliciting information for litigation purposes.

In addition, persons, groups, events, values, beliefs, attitudes, documents, facts, images, interests, and motives may place a constraint (positive or negative) on the crisis organization's efforts in restoring its public image. These constraints may also present opportunities or liabilities to a company in restoring its image. Following a major air-carrier crash, an airline's communication may be constrained by the NTSB's investigation. The NTSB constrains the airline to conforming to a rational, systematic, and orderly process; assisting in fact finding, technical support, and staff support; and complying with recommendations. In the context of these constraints, the airline must provide an appropriate response to its stakeholders.

In many cases communication between organizations, from organizations to the public, and from the public to the organizations becomes problematic (Quarantelli, 1988). While communication may reduce uncertainty and threat and help to resolve a crisis, the reverse is also true. By speculating, a company may contribute to rumors and cause additional confusion, serving to compound the crisis and prolong its resolution.

Communication and Culture

Corporate culture directly influences how a company communicates. An organization's culture reflects the company's consistent values, basic assumptions, attitudes, and norms. Because culture dominates management's thinking, it will directly influence managerial perceptions and actions. The "fit" of the organization's culture with the culture of its external stakeholders is critical (Heath, 1994). By failing to understand its stakeholder's culture, a company may cause further damage. Heath notes that corporate culture influences how a company responds to the issue of blame. Some may accept blame and atone for responsibility, while others may attempt to redirect blame to another source. Organizations must be sensitive in responding to their unique audiences. The global nature of the airline industry, for example, presents a direct challenge to crisis management and underscores the significance of sensitivity to crosscultural communication differences. Cultural implications for communication cannot be ignored.

Pinsdorf (1991) identified the complexity of crisis communication in the airline industry by arguing that to effectively sustain a company's positive public image following an airline crash communication must reflect diverse cultural values. Pinsdorf contrasted the response of Japan Air Lines (JAL) following its most fatal crash, August 12, 1985 (520 fatalities), with Pan Am's Flight 103 explosion over Lockerbie, Scotland, December 21, 1988. JAL's response to the crash clearly illuminated Japanese culture. The Japanese airline adhered to an elaborate protocol, emphasizing its sense of humanity and responsibility. Personal apologies, requests of forgiveness, admissions of responsibility, and offers of resignation were given by JAL's President Yasumoto Takagi, who at the memorial service bowed low and long to victims' families and again to a wall bearing victims' names. The maintenance chief committed suicide. While Pan Am showed care and concern over the crisis, CEO Thomas Plaskett was not quite as demonstrative in showing his feelings of responsibility and grief. According to Pinsdorf, these differences in response clearly reflected the nationalistic, paternalistic, and anti-individual society of the Japanese and the capitalistic side of the American culture.

STRATEGIC COMMUNICATION

Following a crisis event, organizations offer apologies, explanations, excuses, and justifications to different audiences in an effort to remove the threat to legitimacy and restore image. Public-relations experts have clarified general ways in which organizations should communicate with stakeholders, including media. In my own field, speech communication, the rhetorical tradition of apologia, corporate advocacy, and impression management have offered insights into communication strategies available to organizations in crisis. Heath (1996), for example, argues that an organization's (as well as others engrossed in the event) crisis response involves the telling of a story. Thinking in terms of narrative provides practitioners with a consistent and organized way of viewing crisis planning, management, and communication.

The airline industry greatly depends on the traveling public's perception that it is safe. A major plane crash tends to shatter this perception. Generally, the airline is immediately perceived to be responsible for the tragedy. Following a major crash, an airline may find itself battling allegations of blame, irresponsibility, or inadequacy. A crash may also create concerns about the general safety of the airline. When image is threatened, the organization must engage in defense strategies (Benoit, 1995). The public's perception of the crisis and the company involved is influenced by communication. Defending an image involves altering the public's perceptions of responsibility for a tragedy or impressions of the organization itself (Coombs, 1995).

Strategic Alternatives

When confronted with a crisis, what or how should an organization communicate? Strategic communication focuses on the design of the message. The following discussion identifies general communication strategies which provide a guideline for responding to various issues associated with a crisis. These strategies function to defend an organization's image.

Communication theorists have identified various response strategies which function to repair an organization's image in times of crisis (Allen & Caillouet, 1994; Benoit, 1995; Coombs, 1995). The communication strategy alternatives identified and applied to the cases in this book were selected from this theoretical foundation. Organizations essentially have five different options when communicating during crisis: deny responsibility, hedge responsibility, ingratiate the organization with its stakeholders, make amends, and elicit sympathy.

Deny Responsibility

Organizations may choose to deny any association with or responsibility for the cause of an event. Four tactics serve to deny responsibility: directly deny, expand denial, redirect blame, and aggression. Direct denial is a simple statement denying any accountability for the event. Expansion of denial goes further by explaining why the organization is not responsible for the event. An organization may redirect blame to another source as a method for denying responsibility. In situations where an accuser wrongly places blame, an organization may choose more aggressive tactics, such as confronting or attacking its accuser.

Hedge Responsibility

A more viable alternative may be to hedge or evade responsibility for the event. Hedging responsibility allows the organization to distance itself from the crisis, or "duck" responsibility. Four tactics function to dodge responsibility:

excuses, scapegoating, pleading ignorance, and refuting evidence. An organization may offer excuses, which explain extenuating circumstances or justify some action. Scapegoating enables the organization to place primary responsibility on another. An organization may plead ignorance by stating there was a lack of significant information about the situation. Or the organization may be in a position to refute or argue conflicting evidence to reduce responsibility.

Ingratiation

Ingratiation tactics are designed to win stakeholders' support for the organization and reduce negative feelings toward the organization. One ingratiation tactic is to accentuate the positive. The organization must identify and reinforce positive aspects of the organization. A second tactic is to create an identification between the organization and its stakeholders. Organizations attempt to become identified with symbols, values, or institutions which have a strong base of public acceptance. A third tactic is to positively acknowledge others. Positively acknowledging another generally gains approval from the acknowledged recipient, and may possibly leave a positive impression on other stakeholders.

Make Amends

Organizations may choose to make amends in an effort to win forgiveness for the event. This is done in three ways: apologize, remunerate, and right the wrong. An apology expresses regret over the event and requests forgiveness. Organizations may remunerate victims with money or other services in an effort to reduce negative feelings toward the organization. Finally, by righting the wrong the organization demonstrates concern and regret by correcting the problem. Necessary changes are made to prevent the recurrence of the event.

Elicit Sympathy

A final strategic option is to elicit sympathy. This approach portrays the organization as an innocent victim. Sympathetic stakeholders tend to be less critical and the organization is likely to be placed in a positive light.

Considerations for Employing Strategic Alternatives

Each of these strategies has the potential to successfully influence stakeholders' perceptions of an organization following a crisis. When considering strategic communication options in the context of crisis, companies must remember the importance of creating the perception that they are in control. This requires speaking with a credible and unified voice (Heath, 1994). The crisis situation determines the crisis communication strategy (Coombs, 1995).

The crisis situation, then, must be the crisis manager's framework when communicating following the onset of a crisis. Determining appropriate and potentially effective strategies involves a consideration of the particular target audience, type of crisis, available evidence, severity of damage, company performance history, legal issues, as well as other key variables and events characterizing a particular crisis.

Appropriate strategic choices calm and do not offend stakeholders. When choosing a strategy, companies must make sure their choices fit the damage done by the crisis (Coombs, 1995). Deaths, injuries, or property destruction requires some effort to make amends. It is important to remember that efforts to make amends often provide closure for victims and nonvictims (Coombs, 1995).

An organization's performance history will likely influence the effectiveness of strategic communication. A company which has a positive performance history or initial image, for example, has greater credibility among its stakeholders than a company with a history of problems. Consequently, stakeholders may be more willing to "forgive" the organization that possesses credibility. Furthermore, stakeholders are likely to accept claims made by a credible company. Strategies of denial, hedging responsibility, ingratiation, and eliciting sympathy tend to be more effective when supported by credibility. Coombs (1995) notes that a positive history often functions as a halo effect for an organization, casting a positive image on its actions. When a company has experienced similar crises in the past, the perception is that they are responsible for the crisis in the present. The cause is attributed to the organization.

CONCLUSION

This chapter has provided an overview of what academics and practitioners have learned about organizational crisis and communicating in crisis. Understanding the nature of crisis and considerations for management and communication helps managers to anticipate the difficulties and challenges which will likely arise in crisis. No crisis is identical to another. While guidelines and recommendations offered in the crisis literature provide some direction, managers ultimately must stay aware (as much as possible) of the many factors which could possibly influence the resolution of a crisis.

REFERENCES

Allen, M. W., & Caillouet, R. H. (1994). Legitimation endeavors: Impression management strategies used by an organization in crisis. *Communication Monographs, 61*, 44–62.

Benoit, W. L. (1995). *Accounts, excuses, and apologies.* Albany: State University of New York Press.

Billings, R. S., Milburn, T. W., & Schaalman, M. L. (1980). A model of crisis perception: A theoretical and empirical analysis. *Administrative Science Quarterly, 25*, 300–316.

Brown, M. H. (1990). Past and present images of Challenger in NASA's organizational culture. In B. D. Sypher (Ed.), *Case studies in organizational communication* (pp. 111–124). New York: Guilford Press.

Coombs, W. T. (1995). The development of guidelines for the selection of the "appropriate" crisis response strategies. *Management Communication Quarterly, 4,* 447–476.

Cushing, S. (1994). *Fatal words: Communication clashes and aircraft crashes.* Chicago: University of Chicago Press.

Fink, S. (1986). *Crisis management: Planning for the inevitable.* New York: AMACOM.

Fitzpatrick, K. R., & Rubin, M. S. (1995). Public relations vs. legal strategies in organizational crisis decisions. *Public Relations Review, 21* (2), 21–33.

Gouran, D. S. (1982). *Making decisions in groups.* Glenview, IL: Scott-Foresman.

Gouran, D. S., Hirokawa, R. Y., & Marz, A. E. (1986). A critical analysis of factors related to decisional processes involved in the Challenger disaster. *Central States Speech Journal, 37,* 119–135.

Heath, R. L. (1994). *Management of corporate communication: From interpersonal contacts to external affairs.* Hillsdale, NJ: Lawrence Erlbaum.

Heath, R. L. (1996). *Telling a story: A narrative approach to communication during crisis.* Paper presented at the meeting of the Speech Communication Association, San Diego, CA, November.

Hermann, C. F. (1963). Some consequences of crisis which limit the viability of organizations. *Administrative Science Quarterly, 8,* 61–82.

Janis, I. L. (1982). *Groupthink: Psychological studies of policy decisions and fiascoes.* Boston: Houghton-Mifflin.

Meyers, G. C. (1986). *When it hits the fan: Managing the nine crises of business.* New York: Mentor.

Mitroff, I. (1988). Crisis management: Cutting through the confusion. *Sloan Management Review,* Winter, 15–20.

Muller, R. (1985). Corporate crisis management. *Long Range Planning, 18* (5), 38–48.

Newsom, D., Turk, J., & Kruckeberg, D. (1996). *This is PR: The realities of public relations* (6th ed.). Belmont, CA: Wadsworth.

Norr, R. (1952, December). Cancer by the carton. *Reader's Digest, 61,* 7–8.

Pauchant, T., & Mitroff, I. (1992). *Transforming the crisis-prone organization: Preventing individual, organizational, and environmental tragedies.* San Francisco: Jossey-Bass.

Pinsdorf, M. K. (1991). Flying different skies: How cultures respond to airline disasters. *Public Relations Review, 17,* 37–56.

Quarantelli, E. L. (1988). Disaster crisis management: A summary of research findings. *Journal of Management Studies, 25,* 373–385.

Ramee, J. (1987, February). Managing a crisis. *Management Solutions, 32,* 25–29.

Ressler, J. A. (1982). Crisis communications. *Public Relations Quarterly, 3,* 8–10.

Schuetz, J. (1990). Corporate advocacy as argumentation. In R. Trapp and J. Schuetz (Eds.), *Perspectives on argumentation: Essays in honor of Wayne Brockriede* (pp. 272–284). Prospect Heights, IL: Waveland Press.

Seeger, M. W., Sellnow, T. L., & Ulmer, R. R. (1998). Communication organization and crisis. In M. E. Roloff (Ed.), *Communication Yearbook, 21,* 231–276. Thousand Oaks, CA: Sage.

Shrivastava, P. (1987). *Bhopal: Anatomy of a crisis*. Cambridge, MA: Ballinger.

Shrivastava, P., Mitroff, I., Miller, D., & Miglani, A. (1988). Understanding industrial crises. *Journal of Management Studies, 25*, 285–303.

Smart, C. F. (1985). Strategic business planning: Predicting susceptibility to crisis. In S. J. Andriole (Ed.), *Corporate crisis management* (pp. 9–20). Princeton, NJ: Petrocelli Books.

Stephenson, D. R. (1982). How to turn pitfalls into opportunities in crisis situations. *Public Relations Quarterly, 22*, 11–15.

Stephenson, D. R. (1984, June). Are you making the most of your crises? *Public Relations Journal, 40*, 16–18.

Sturges, D. L. (1994). Communicating through crisis: A strategy for organizational survival. *Management Communication Quarterly, 7*, 297–316.

Tjosvold, D. (1984). Effects of crisis orientation on managers approach to controversy in decision making. *Academy of Management Journal, 27*, 130–138.

Turner, B. A. (1976). The organizational and interorganizational development of disasters. *Administrative Science Quarterly, 21*, 378–397.

Wilcox, D. L., Ault, P. H., & Agee, W. K. (1986). *Public relations strategies and tactics*. New York: Harper & Row.

Part II

Pre-Crisis Stage

Chapter 3

Existing in a Perpetual Pre-Crisis Phase

Crises evolve according to different phases. The inability to effectively manage any one of these phases may result in the actual occurrence of a crisis, its escalation, or irrevocable damage to the organization. An organization's actions in the pre-crisis phase, for example, often determine whether a crisis is avoided, what issues arise in a crisis, or how well a crisis is managed. The airline industry is perhaps one of the few industries in the world completely vulnerable to crises. Technological complexity, human factors, and the interdependent nature of the industry place airlines in a perpetual pre-crisis phase. Airlines operate in an environment characterized by conditions which can give rise to crisis.

A perpetual pre-crisis stage requires organizations to constantly monitor both their internal and external environments in order to stay aware of the threatening signs and symptoms which compromise the safety of an air carrier and may lead to crisis. By recognizing pre-crisis conditions, companies are in a stronger position to prevent, prepare for, and manage accidents. This chapter discusses the pre-crisis stage in the context of the airline industry.

PRE-CRISIS STAGE

Fink (1986) refers to the pre-crisis stage as the prodromal or warning stage, which in some cases only becomes apparent after the actual crisis has occurred. This phase may or may not include signs of an approaching crisis. Turner (1976) considers the pre-crisis period in the first two stages of his six-stage model. Crises result from "some inaccuracy or inadequacy in the accepted norms and beliefs" (p. 380). Stage I is a normal period with culturally accepted beliefs about the world and its hazards. Precautionary norms are established in laws, codes of practice, mores, and folkways. In Stage II, the incubation period, an unnoticed set of events which conflict with accepted beliefs about hazards and precautionary norms begin to accumulate. In some instances, the events are known and understood, but they are not communicated in meaningful ways that receive the attention and action of decision makers. Warning signs may be difficult or impossible to recognize. In other situations, signs are evident and it is possible to avoid the crisis if properly managed. Even if a crisis cannot be avoided, recognition aids in preparation. As Fink (1986) states, "If you look out into the distance, and you see a storm coming, you can batten down the hatches" (p. 22).

FACTORS CONTRIBUTING TO CRISIS

Internal and external factors create pre-crisis conditions. Defects within organizations themselves, threatening factors in an organization's environment, or a combination of both can cause a crisis. Turner (1976) posits that crisis-provoking events accumulate because internal and/or external factors have been overlooked or misinterpreted as a result of false assumptions, poor communication, cultural lag, and misplaced optimism.

Internal Factors

Intraorganizational factors may contribute to an organization's susceptibility to crisis. Strategic factors which create certain internal pressures on operations, as well as operating policies and procedures that determine safety variables, may precondition organizations to crisis (Shrivastava, 1987). Inaccurate perceptions of organizational decision makers can contribute to crisis. Organizational decision makers select what they observe and make interpretations in light of their current goals, methods, and competencies (Starbuck, Greve, & Hedberg, 1985). Defects within the organization may distort interpretations. Organizational defects manifest themselves in the form of choices and actions. Starbuck, Greve, and Hedberg argue that crisis-prone organizations tend to be extreme in their choices and actions. For example, they may apportion too much influence to high-level management; rigidly comply with formal procedures, formalized communications, and standardized programs; possess a false sense of security; hold unrealistic beliefs; and initiate unwise procedures. Perceptual distortions can contribute to crisis by influencing an organization to either take no action or the wrong action.

External Factors

The organization's external environment is viewed as the source of events and changing trends which create opportunities and threats (Lenz, 1980).

According to Katz and Kahn (1978), all organizations exist and adapt to five environments: cultural, political, economic, technological, and ecological. Crises occur as a result of an organization's inability to cope with changes and challenges presented by these various environments. The quality of the industrial infrastructure may affect the likelihood of an accident occurring and possibly escalating into a crisis (Shrivastava, 1987). Organizations are prone to accidents when technological systems are supported by a weak infrastructure. This infrastructure also influences the ability of stakeholders to respond effectively to a crisis. In order to survive and succeed, organizations must be externally oriented.

Uncertainty

Organizations become vulnerable to crisis when they have a high level of environmental uncertainty. Fundamentally, the environment is a source of uncertainty for the organization. Milliken (1987) identifies three types of environmental uncertainty experienced by an organization. These types—state, effect, and response uncertainty—correspond roughly to types of information shortages. State uncertainty is the uncertainty about the state of the environment; that is, how components of the environment are changing. Effect uncertainty is an inability to predict what the nature of the impact of a future state of the environment, or environmental change, will be on the organization. It involves a lack of understanding of cause–effect relationships. Response uncertainty suggests lacking knowledge of response options and/or an inability to predict the likely consequences of a response choice. This is experienced in the context of a need to make an immediate decision. Pfeffer and Salancik (1978) note that uncertainty becomes a problem when it involves an element of critical organizational interdependence.

Environments create uncertainty for the organization with increased competition, rapidly advancing technology, and close scrutiny by consumers, government, and public interest groups. Survival depends in part on the organization's ability to adapt and control these uncertainties. Uncertainty creates problems for organizations regarding choices and actions. Various strategies are employed to reduce uncertainty, such as general rules, using rituals, relying on habitual patterns, setting goals, and making plans to reach goals (Turner, 1976). While these methods reduce uncertainty for present actions, organizations are never certain if the present actions will be adequate in reaching goals. Organizations may adopt simplifying assumptions about the environment to make action possible.

Generally, uncertainty is seen as being reduced by information. Information about the environment, then, becomes critical to the survival of the organization. An unpredictable environment requires organizations to upgrade their intelligence systems and long-range planning (Smart, 1985). They must constantly monitor the environment for timely and accurate information.

Internal and External Factors

Crises often result from the interaction of internal and external variables. Milburn, Schuler, and Watman (1983) conceptualize organizational crisis by incorporating the antecedents of crises with individual and organizational characteristics. The two major classes of antecedents include the external environment (competitors, suppliers, customers/clients, regulators, society, owners and boards of directors, natural disasters) and the internal environment (executive characteristics, experience and history, demographics, and attributes). The extent to which a component of the external environment becomes an antecedent of crisis is the degree to which it causes an organization–environment mismatch. Aspects of the internal environment determine the organization's susceptibility to crisis.

This discussion underscores the significance of recognizing the pre-crisis stage. The earlier problems are identified, the better the chance to resolve them. Usually, there are signs and symptoms warning of an impending crisis. These signs and symptoms may or may not go unnoticed. Ignoring signs increases the likelihood of crisis. Pauchant and Mitroff (1992) indicate that managers and members in a crisis-prone organization tend to block out crisis signals, whereas in crisis-prepared organizations they have the ability to sense even weak signals.

While this makes much sense, it is easier said than done. Managers are constantly inundated with signals and it is often difficult to distinguish the significant ones from the insignificant ones. However, managers and employees must, as much as possible, stay alert to the signs and symptoms which foreshadow a crisis and take appropriate actions. One way organizations can develop a sensitivity to pre-crisis conditions is to examine factors which have historically led to crises in their particular industry.

PRE-CRISIS: THE AIRLINE INDUSTRY

Airlines are part of a complex, tightly coupled, interactive technological system. The highly interdependent nature of the industry places airlines in a continuous pre-crisis phase. An airline's safety environment is influenced by the organization's culture, its own management and individual workforce, government, manufacturers, and technology. Safety is achieved only when all elements of the aviation system cooperate and accomplish their responsibilities. The industry's infrastructure is strong. Federal aviation regulations, NTSB recommendations, airline safety departments, and new technology control many pre-crisis conditions.

Conditions which give rise to crises are either latent or active. Latent conditions, which lie dormant until exposed by other conditions, are dangerous in that they often go unrecognized until after a crisis occurs. Aviation accident investigations illuminate many conditions which create a pre-crisis stage for airlines. Some of these factors are directly controlled by airlines, while other factors are beyond its control. Accidents rarely occur from a single, isolated cause. Rather, it is usually a consequence of the interaction of human behavior, technology, and the environment. To understand an airline's pre-crisis stage, the following discussion examines some of the factors and conditions which have historically contributed to airline accidents.

Primary Factors in Airline Accidents

Personnel capabilities, traffic environment, aircraft capabilities, weather, and unpredictable events are considered primary factors in aviation accidents (Wells, 1991).

Human Error

In the majority of commercial aviation accidents human error, ranging from mental to physical, is a factor. Flight-crew members, dispatchers, mechanics, and air traffic controllers may experience lapses in attention, poor judgment, inaccurate perception, or inadequate knowledge or motor skills due to environmental (i.e., equipment, managerial practices) or health factors (Wells, 1991). Fatigue and its effects on the human body, for example, is considered a major hazard in aviation safety. Between 1972 and 1995, the NTSB issued eighty fatigue-related safety recommendations (Hall, 1995). Fatigue often results from irregular and unpredictable work and rest cycles (Danaher, 1995). Erratic work schedules may cause insufficient rest on the part of flight crews, which can create unsafe conditions.

Industry efforts have been directed at preventing or minimizing human errors. Rigid employee selection requirements, federal regulations which address airline procedure (pilot flight time, emergency operations, and checklists), air traffic rules (instrument approach and departure procedures, separation standards, weather minimums), and automation (minimizing human workload with technology) are all methods to reduce human error in aviation (Wells, 1991).

Traffic Infrastructure

The air traffic infrastructure is also a primary cause of aviation accidents. Airways, airports, and air traffic can strain the traffic environment. For example, high traffic density will stress the air traffic control system and increase the risk of midair collisions. By installing anticollision equipment and training air traffic controllers, the industry has minimized the risk of catastrophic midair collisions (NTSB, 1995).

Mechanical Failure

Aircraft mechanical failures occur in over 40 percent of airline accidents (Wells, 1991). While components such as engines, structural members, landing gear, control systems, and instruments occasionally fail, they rarely cause serious accidents. Rather, mechanical failure usually results from improper maintenance, design flaws, or operator error.

Weather

Weather is a major concern for aviation pilots. Modern aircraft enable pilots to traverse virtually all kinds of weather; however, insufficient information, human error, or maintenance difficulties during severe weather conditions can prove disastrous. Unpredictable and severe conditions, like wind shear or icing, have contributed to numerous fatal accidents. Between 1970 and 1985, wind shear claimed 575 passengers and crew (NTSB, 1995). In an effort to control wind shear difficulties, major airports have installed low-level wind shear alert systems. Airlines require enhanced wind shear training for pilots to educate them on wind shear conditions and assist them in controlling the aircraft during escape/avoidance maneuvering. Icing on aircraft greatly reduces aircraft performance. At the recommendation of the NTSB, the FAA upgraded deicing/anti-icing requirements for major air carriers and commuters, improving safety during icing conditions (NTSB, 1995).

Unpredictable Events

Unpredictable events, such as sabotage or terrorism, occur randomly. The unexpected nature of such events creates a constant state of uncertainty. Levels of risk are often indicated by actual incidents or accidents. Government and industry have been quick to respond to these events. For example, hijackings during the 1960s and 1970s prompted the installation of metal detectors in all airports. Suspicions that a bomb brought down TWA Flight 800 in July 1996 prompted increased security measures at airports throughout the nation.

Secondary Factors in Airline Accidents

Secondary factors are those which indirectly influence a situation. Flight operations, maintenance, and training, for example, significantly influence the primary factors of traffic environment, aircraft capabilities, and personnel capabilities (Wells, 1991). In addition, airline policy and practices directly influence events. An airline's policies are affected by federal regulatory policy. The FAA establishes standards and conditions for airline practices; however, individual airlines vary widely in their procedures to meet these requirements. FAA inspections ensure airlines comply with Federal aviation regulations.

Factors external to the industry further influence industry policy and practices. Following deregulation, for example, there were concerns that economic pressures would force airlines to skimp on maintenance. There is the belief that economics makes for unsafe conditions. But safety problems do not necessarily equate with economics. Prosperous airlines can have safety problems. Most in the industry have adopted a fundamental philosophy regarding the economics of safety: "If you think safety is expensive, try having an accident." Safety contributes to a company's bottom line. While it appears most airlines have not cut maintenance costs, they have increased contract maintenance, aircraft leasing, and flight operations and have tightened schedules (Wells, 1991). Contract maintenance, unfortunately, lessens an airline's control and gives a critical part of the safety network to an outsider. Deregulation also forced major operating changes in the commercial aviation system. With the growth of the hub-and-spoke system and increased flights, additional pressures and demands are placed on airports, air traffic system equipment, facilities, and personnel (Wells, 1991).

Corporate Culture

Because it exerts a powerful influence over its members, corporate culture plays a major role in aviation safety. Culture refers to "the deeper levels of basic assumptions and beliefs that are shared by members of an organization, that operate unconsciously, and that define in a basic taken for granted fashion, an organization's view of itself and its environment" (Schein, 1985). Culture, therefore, is something an organization is as opposed to something it has. An organization's culture is identified through the observed behavioral regularities of its members' interactions, the norms that evolve in working groups, the dominant values it espouses, the philosophy that guides its policy toward employees and customers, the rules and ropes for getting along, and the feeling or climate conveyed.

Pre-crisis conditions are often created as a consequence of an organization's culture. The presence of arrogance or the lack of common sense in an organization's culture can lead to crisis. A potentially unsafe culture is characterized by management's antagonistic or indifferent views and actions toward employees in safety-sensitive jobs, organizational practices which deviate from industry standards, and inappropriate values and attitudes which create unsafe situations (Hall, 1997). Knowing when an organization has a "good" safety culture is often difficult. While an accident represents a major failure of the organization's safety system, the absence of an accident does not necessarily imply the system is safe. Recently, many airlines have established safety departments with a Director of Safety in order to promote and foster a "safety culture." Because of the relative newness of such departments, some assert their role lacks clear definition. While a safety culture does not necessarily guarantee zero accidents, it does emphasize an important value that creates an awareness and hopefully influences appropriate actions in a risky environment. A culture that values safety anticipates and controls risks which may arise while it also develops and implements safeguards. Complacency is fatal to a safety culture (Reason, 1997).

Safe cultures encourage the facilitation and flow of information. Reason (1997) identifies four critical subcomponents of a safety culture: a reporting culture, a just culture, a flexible culture, and a learning culture. A reporting culture refers to a climate which encourages members to report errors and close calls. A just culture is an environment of trust, where members are encouraged and rewarded for providing significant safety-related information. A flexible culture is one that has the ability to pass control from the hierarchy to task experts. A learning culture has the ability and desire to draw accurate conclusions from its safety information system. The interaction of these four creates an informed culture which, Reason asserts, is a safe culture. To make sound decisions, managers must have information on all aspects of the safety system (human, technical, organizational, and environmental).

In April 1997, the NTSB sponsored a symposium entitled "Corporate Culture and Transportation Safety." During this two-day forum, representatives from government, industry, and academia gathered to explore ways organizational management philosophy and practices directly affect the day-to-day operations of the nation's transportation system. In reviewing a series of accidents across all modes of transportation, NTSB Chairman Jim Hall (1997) identified six cultural factors leading to accidents: overconfidence in technology; disregard for the human role in a highly technical system; the lack of divergent opinions; a management arrogance that believes in its inherent superiority over government regulations and sound operating practices; an overemphasis on revenue; and an organizational culture that discourages communication, divergent opinion, and an appreciation for the importance of safety.

Though accidents and incidents do not necessarily signify a weak safety culture, a managerial climate which encourages (or does not discourage) the violation of rules and regulations and sacrifices safety for profit negatively affects the safety of the airline's operations and ultimately plants the seeds for a crisis. In other words, management actions or inactions can contribute to accidents. In the airline industry, government is responsible for setting guidelines for safety. It is management's responsibility to comply with these guidelines. Establishing safety as a priority value demands commitment from upper-level management. This was a theme repeated throughout the two-day symposium. John Lauber (1997), former Vice President of Corporate Safety and Compliance at Delta Airlines and a former NTSB member, stated, "A corporate safety culture begins in the board room" (p. 1). A commitment to safety at this highest level ultimately influences every pilot, flight attendant, maintenance technician, air traffic controller, dispatcher, and the many others who help to run an airline. When leaders commit to safety, employees will follow.

Communication Factors in Pre-Crisis

Communication is fundamental to all levels of an airline's operations. An open-communication climate, for example, facilitates the flow of information which is necessary in fostering a safe operating environment. The role of communication is often taken for granted. Experience suggests the consequences of ineffective communication can be extreme. Communication has been identified as a direct or indirect factor in many aviation accidents.

There is a reciprocal relationship between organizational culture and communication. An organization's culture is created through communication. Communication, in turn, is influenced by an organization's culture. Contained within organizational cultures are subcultures, with their own unique characteristics and values, which may impact an organization's operations. Subcultural communication problems have been identified in the various areas of an airline's flight operations. For example, accident investigations in the 1960s and 1970s pointed to a negative subculture in the cockpit which contributed to accidents. A perceived status difference among cockpit crewmembers resulted in some members being treated as underlings who should speak only when spoken to. In some cases, this intimidating atmosphere prevented communication of critical information among cockpit crewmembers, which led to accidents (NTSB, 1995). As a result, the concept of Cockpit Resource Management (CRM) emerged. CRM focuses on teamwork, workload management, and communication in the cockpit. Eventually, Cockpit Resource Management became Crew Resource Management, since teamwork extends beyond the cockpit to the cabin crew, dispatchers, maintenance technicians, and ramp agents (Lauber, 1997).

Another problematic example is found in cockpit–cabin communication. Several dramatic accidents emphasized certain deficiencies in cockpit–cabin coordination and communication. According to Chute and Wiener (1995), air carriers are traditionally characterized by two distinct cultures—the cockpit and the cabin—which lead to misunderstandings and difficulties in coordination and communication. Flight attendants have experienced difficulty communicating safety information to the cockpit (Chute & Weiner, 1996). Culture, status differences, past negative experience, and fear of violating Federal aviation regulations are identified as barriers to cabin crew members conveying safety-critical information which could prevent an accident. This division is particularly problematic during abnormal situations, when the cockpit and the cabin must combine their efforts and function as a team. Communication is necessary to create an awareness and understanding of each other's duties and to enable the flight crew to operate at a higher level.

Language presents another communication problem. Cushing (1994) examined air–ground communication problems which arise from voice-mediated language, as well as the various aspects of the communication situation with which the language must interact. The ambiguous nature of language as well as the medium through which a message is conveyed can result in confusion and misunderstanding. Language-related problems have been identified as a key contributing factor in aviation accidents and potential accidents. Cushing offers the Tenerife, Canary Islands, accident as an example of how misunderstanding a phrase can lead to tragedy. The flight crew used the phrase "at takeoff" to mean they were in the process of taking off; however, the control tower interpreted the phrase to mean "at the takeoff point."

CONCLUSION

Crises are generally preceded by warning signals. These signals may or may not be readily identified, and in some situations the signs are recognized but management fails to take the appropriate action. Effective crisis management and communication requires managers to be alert to the many factors and conditions which can trigger a crisis. Crisis-prepared organizations are alert to the signs and symptoms warning of an impending crisis. Pre-crisis conditions generally evolve from internal and external factors and events. It is rare that a single factor causes an accident. Although certain factors may appear nonthreatening, when combined with other factors or circumstances the consequences can be disastrous.

As a result of its strong infrastructure, the airline industry has established a number of measures to control pre-crisis conditions. This chapter by no means provides a comprehensive overview of pre-crisis conditions; however, it does point to the more obvious conditions leading to accidents. Because of the industry's highly interdependent nature, airlines must stay internally as well as externally oriented to factors which could trigger an accident. They must seek information to reduce uncertainty associated with various risks. Pre-crisis factors may also complicate efforts at crisis management and communication. For example, an airline's image or financial status may strongly influence stakeholder perceptions following crisis.

Airlines must constantly stay alert to pre-crisis conditions. A climate of open communication will encourage the flow of information necessary to make the appropriate choices and decisions. While an accident may be unavoidable, a company can be prepared to effectively deal with its consequences.

REFERENCES

Chute, R. D., & Wiener, E. L. (1995). Cockpit-cabin communication: I. A tale of two cultures. *The International Journal of Aviation Psychology, 5*, 257–276.

Chute, R. D., & Wiener, E. L. (1996). Cockpit-cabin communication: II. Shall we tell the pilots? *The International Journal of Aviation Psychology, 6*, 211–231.

Cushing, S. (1994). *Fatal words: Communication clashes and aircraft crashes*. Chicago: University of Chicago Press.

Danaher, J. (1995, November 1–2). Opening remarks. In *National Transportation Safety Board Fatigue Symposium Proceedings* (pp. 11–15). Washington, DC: U.S. Government Printing Office.

Fink, S. (1986). *Crisis management: Planning for the inevitable.* New York: AMACOM.

Hall, J. (1995, November 1–2). Opening remarks. In *National Transportation Safety Board Fatigue Symposium Proceedings* (pp. 3–6). Washington, DC: U.S. Government Printing Office.

Hall, J. (1997, April 24). Remarks of Jim Hall, Chairman, NTSB, before the Symposium on Corporate Culture and Transportation Safety, Arlington, VA.

Katz, D., & Kahn, R. L. (1978). *The social psychology of organizations.* New York: Wiley.

Lauber, J. K. (1997, April 24–25). *Some comments about corporate culture and transportation safety.* Paper presented at the Symposium on Corporate Culture and Transportation Safety, Arlington, VA.

Lenz, R. T. (1980). Environment, strategy, organization structure and performance: Patterns in one industry. *Strategic Management, 1,* 209–226.

Milburn, T. W., Schuler, R. S., & Watman, K. H. (1983). Organizational Crisis. Part I: Definition and conceptualization. *Human Relations, 36,* 1141–1160.

Milliken, F. J. (1987). Three types of perceived uncertainty about the environment: State, effect, and response uncertainty. *Management Review, 12,* 133–143.

National Transportation Safety Board. (1995). *We are all safer: NTSB inspired improvements in aviation safety.* Washington, DC: U.S. Government Printing Office.

Pauchant, T., & Mitroff, I. (1992). *Transforming the crisis-prone organization: Preventing individual, organizational, and environmental tragedies.* San Francisco: Jossey-Bass.

Pfeffer, J., & Salancik, G. R. (1978). *The external control of organizations.* New York: Harper & Row.

Reason, J. (1997, April 24–25). *Corporate culture and safety.* Paper presented at the Symposium on Corporate Culture and Transportation Safety, Arlington, VA.

Schein, E. H. (1985). *Organizational culture and leadership.* San Francisco: Jossey-Bass.

Shrivastava, P. (1987). *Bhopal: Anatomy of a crisis.* Cambridge, MA: Ballinger.

Smart, C. F. (1985). Strategic business planning: Predicting susceptibility to crisis. In S. J. Andriole (Ed.), *Corporate crisis management* (pp. 9–21). Princeton, NJ: Petrocelli Books.

Starbuck, W. H., Greve, A., & Hedberg, B. (1985). Responding to crises. In S. J. Andriole (Ed.), *Corporate crisis management* (p. 155–188). Princeton, NJ: Petrocelli Books.

Turner, B. A. (1976). The organizational and interorganizational development of disasters. *Administrative Science Quarterly, 21,* 378–397.

Wells, A. T. (1991). *Commercial aviation safety.* New York: McGraw-Hill.

Chapter 4

Preparing for the Worst: Contingency Planning

On the night of April 14, 1912, the R.M.S. *Titanic*, the largest ocean liner the world had ever seen, tragically sank into the deep waters of the North Atlantic, claiming over 1,500 lives. For almost a century, many have questioned why the "unsinkable" leviathan plunged to her doom on the maiden voyage. Why did the captain increase the ship's speed when he knew there was heavy ice in her path? Why were the two lookouts in the crow's nest without binoculars? Why did the ship carry only sixteen wooden lifeboats, hardly enough for half the passengers? Why were the boats not filled to capacity?

The tragedy of the Titanic illuminates the consequences of a company's failure to identify its vulnerability to crisis. Management difficulties in recognizing the potential for crisis may result in the actual occurrence of a crisis and, possibly, its escalation. Chapter 3 considered the importance of constantly probing an organization's internal and external environment for warning signs or symptoms of an impending crisis. Recognizing and understanding the factors contributing to a pre-crisis phase is significant to prevention and preparation. Through early detection, some crises can be prevented or at least dealt with effectively. Preparation requires considering the various response options to a crisis and determining the best strategy to handle the crisis. Perhaps the Titanic calamity could have been avoided had decision makers anticipated and adequately prepared for the possibility of a crisis.

Some organizations are naturally more prone to crisis than others. Airlines operate in a continuous pre-crisis stage. Despite the industry's established safety mechanisms, there is not a single day when an air carrier is totally immune to an accident. Human error, technological failures, weather, and sabotage are only a few of the factors which contribute to an air carrier's vulnerability to a crash. Because they recognize the ever-present possibility of a crisis, most airlines have developed carefully prepared plans which can be activated at a moment's notice. The uniqueness of each situation, however, usually prevents a crisis plan from being flawless. Unforeseen circumstances and variables tend to create complications and difficulties for which crisis managers may be unprepared. Following an air-carrier accident, airlines expect public, media, and government scrutiny; interference with normal operating procedures; possible damage to the company image; and a negative impact on profit or revenue.

Crisis planning involves identifying the various types of crises the organization could likely encounter and preparing for each. This chapter will consider the process and aspects of crisis contingency planning by synthesizing the principles, strategies, and methods identified and discussed by scholars and practitioners.

THE PURPOSE OF PLANNING

A contingency plan is a comprehensive plan, developed during a rational and calm period, that deals with how to manage the various aspects of a crisis. The plan serves as a tool or guideline for dealing with various aspects of the crisis. Routine decisions are determined prior to the event so managers can deal more effectively with the unique aspects of the crisis. A crisis plan is not only a tool which enables the organization to manage the crisis, but, as Pauchant and Mitroff (1992) suggest, it further communicates a general mood and set of actions by management. Crisis planning is a way to maximize performance during a critical period. A systematic and orderly response to a crisis enables the organization to maintain its daily and routine activities while simultaneously managing the crisis. While a contingency plan assists an organization in effectively handling a crisis, organizations should never falsely assume that it will take care of every problem. In fact, a crisis plan rarely covers every contingency. However, pre-planning allows the organization to respond to a crisis in a timely and appropriate manner.

Barriers to Planning

Planning seems a logical response to the threat of crisis, but certain barriers prevent some organizations from planning effectively. In their "Onion Model of Management," Pauchant and Mitroff (1992) identify four key factors which influence whether an organization is prepared for crisis: individual defense mechanisms, organizational culture, organizational structure, and organizational strategies. Individual defense mechanisms, considered the innermost layer of the model, refer to the attitudes and character of the organization's membership. For some managers, the thought of a crisis implies the organization is weak, that it is imperfect, and that management may be incompetent (Pauchant & Mitroff, 1992). The easiest line of resistance is to avoid thinking about crisis. Thinking in terms of crisis can create high levels of anxiety, further inhibiting the ability to take action. Because the notion of crisis creates anxiety, management may put up defense mechanisms, which can create additional crises. The response may be "explain the crisis away" or take quick and thoughtless actions.

Pauchant and Mitroff (1992) refer to March and Simon's notion of "bounded rationality," which suggests that human beings have limited capacity to cognitively comprehend the full extent of an issue. Emotionally bounded managers experience difficulty responding to crises and empathizing with the victims of the crisis. They question how their organization could be responsible for a crisis. Emotionally bounded managers fail to recognize the impact of their responses on their employees and customers. It only makes sense that emotionally bounded managers would have difficulty planning for crisis. Crisis-prepared managers are in a better position to handle the anxiety created by the crisis and effectively respond. "Being less bounded emotionally, they are more able to be ethically, emotionally, and cognitively responsible toward themselves, their employees, their business partners, and their surrounding environment" (p. 5).

An organization's culture determines how seriously managers approach preparing for crisis. In their research, Pauchant and Mitroff (1992) identified four general groups of rationalizations: a belief that the organization's characteristics or properties will shield it from crises, a belief that environmental properties will protect the organization if a crisis occurs, a belief that the organization will not be affected due to particular properties of the crisis itself, and a casual attitude toward the organization's susceptibility to crisis. While these beliefs enable the organization to function in its daily operations, they are problematic in light of crisis.

The organization's operating structure can be a potential barrier which can contribute to or inhibit crisis. Organizational strategies refer to the effectiveness of existing plans, mechanisms, and procedures for crisis management.

PREPARING FOR CRISIS

Contingency planning has been described by Littlejohn (1983) as a process of identifying "hypothetical situations and alternative scenarios" which could occur in an organization. Three factors influence the effectiveness of a contingency plan. First, as Pauchant and Mitroff (1992) suggest, a crisis plan is influenced by an organization's culture, management, and structure. A second and somewhat closely related factor is the involvement and commitment of top managers, which is important to the development of a crisis plan. Management involvement and commitment is necessary to convince other organizational members to cooperate. Third, crisis planning is a continuous, ongoing process. Contingency plans must be frequently reviewed, refined, and updated.

Preliminary Steps

Management Structure

Researchers and practitioners have identified the various aspects, methods, and strategies involved in crisis planning. Critical to the effectiveness of any crisis management program is its structure. Littlejohn's (1983) model of crisis management begins with the organization of a crisis management structure. He distinguishes between a functional and matrix structure. A functional structure organizes individual groups according to their particular purpose or role. Though this structure encourages expertise and responsibility, it is expensive because of excessive resources and equipment, inefficient as a consequence of overstaffing, hindered by tedious communication channels, and results in unclear relationships among functional divisions. A matrix structure is more desirable. It consists of a lean, permanent crisis management unit which is supported by technical and administrative staff from functional divisions. It is a flexible structure for responding to shifting circumstances. A matrix structure also offers a variety of expertise. Depending on the crisis issue, relevant personnel are selected by the crisis manager.

Crisis Team

Traditionally, the crisis manager is responsible for designing the crisis management organization, leading the management team in identifying and assessing crisis issues, determining goals and objectives for contingency planning, developing relationships with external constituents for information exchange, and fostering work relationships between the crisis management team and various organizational groups (Littlejohn, 1983). Crisis teams may be organized according to function. One approach is to divide the team into a policy team, a management team, and a liaison team. A crisis team is generally composed of top management, legal counsel, public relations, professionals, and technical experts. Whatever the composition, the team should be cohesive and have a high level of communication, trust, involvement, commitment, and delegation. This team is responsible for organizing and designing the plan for a threatening crisis issue, selecting and assigning individuals to varying crisis units, and conducting training sessions for themselves and other employees (Littlejohn, 1983).

Crisis Audit

The crisis audit is a process of gathering and analyzing information. Crisis auditing involves thoroughly analyzing the internal and external environment, identifying possible issues, considering their potential impact, and prioritizing for the purpose of planning. This step is necessary to develop contingency plans. Information needed to identify crisis issues may be discovered by reviewing existing published data or by gathering statistics on the organization (Littlejohn, 1983). Identified issues should then be analyzed according to their likely occurrence and potential impact on the organization. In determining impact, Littlejohn suggests considering the extent of physical injury, expense to the organization and society, recovery time, future impact, and public response.

Information gathering is a primary task for the management team. To generate ideas and create understanding, there must be a facilitation and exchange of information across all levels of the organization. Such information is required for managers to understand the full range of functions and issues associated with a particular type of crisis and determine fitting responses. Blending ideas is one method to identify novel approaches to handling different crisis scenarios. The more involved members are throughout the organization, the greater the ideas generated, the more thorough the plan, the more committed the members, and the better prepared the organization. The crisis management team coordinates during a crisis, but there are others who may be closer to the situation and are more knowledgeable of the associated crisis factors. It is advantageous to capitalize on the expertise of various members. In addition to gathering internal information, there should be efforts to gather external information in order to determine the organization's vulnerability to crisis.

Developing Contingency Plans

Littlejohn (1983) discusses five general parts of a crisis plan: introduction, objectives, assumptions, trigger mechanism, and actions. The purpose of the introduction is to provide a thorough background of the crisis event. This provides a general understanding as to the type of crisis situation, relevant issues, and groups involved. The objectives of the plan identify and prioritize what the crisis plan hopes to achieve and prevent. Assumptions identify potentially uncontrollable factors which could significantly influence the crisis situation. The triggering mechanism identifies the event which activates the plan. The action component is a series of acts designed to accomplish the objectives. Responsibilities, roles, and back-up roles are defined.

The contingency plan may also include specifics concerning the initial steps in managing a crisis. In a chaotic situation, this ensures the crisis team covers essential steps. For example, a plan usually identifies when to notify internal and relevant external publics that a crisis exists and when to implement the crisis team. Caywood and Stocker (1993) suggest including checklists for furnishing a crisis room and a media center and identifying methods for information collection.

An effective contingency plan is achievable, understandable, comprehensive, approved by those it affects, regularly reviewed, tested, and cost effective (Littlejohn, 1983). Most agree a contingency plan should function as a guideline; therefore it should not be too rigid or heavily detailed (Pinsdorf, 1987; Newsom, Turk, & Kruckeberg, 1996). Crisis team members should be able to easily recall the steps of a plan; and because situations vary, contingency plans should remain flexible. An effective plan should also identify guidelines on how to actually manage the crisis. In other words, it should clearly state the organization's crisis policy or philosophy. This involves identifying and clarifying relevant issues and formulating a policy for each.

The testing of a crisis contingency plan is highly recommended. Through a simulated crisis, areas which need improving can be identified. In addition, the process familiarizes members with the plan and their particular role and responsibilities. Littlejohn (1983) suggests announcing the initial simulation and following up with an unannounced test at a later time.

Developing a Crisis Communication Plan

Managing communication during a crisis is quite different from managing the crisis. Crisis management provides an efficient, planned response to crisis while enabling the organization to continue its daily operations. It involves designing a crisis management structure, selecting personnel, team development, environmental auditing, and contingency planning. Crisis communication, on the other hand, is an effort to avert or ease conflict between the organization and its internal and external stakeholders. Communication reconciles the relationship between an organization and stakeholders. According to Heath (1994), the goal of crisis communication is "to create a single voice that achieves credibility and a timely response" (p. 262). Companies in crisis must convey a controlled, consistent, coherent, and credible message to their relevant stakeholders. Communication should direct stakeholder responses and impressions about the organization.

An effective crisis communication plan identifies communication initiatives to assist the organization in achieving its objectives of controlling a particular crisis, preventing its escalation, and protecting the organization's long-term corporate interest and public image. An effective communication plan involves identifying stakeholders, clarifying strategic issues, identifying communication objectives, developing themes and messages, and determining appropriate communication channels.

Stakeholders

Effective communication is audience centered. Throughout the crisis, the organization must be sensitive and knowledgeable of stakeholder opinions and the issues which characterize the crisis. This is critical to identifying appropriate responses and equalizing difficult situations. The emotional effect of the crisis on identified stakeholders and their perceptions of the organization's responses should be constantly monitored and evaluated by the crisis team. How will their feelings and perceptions influence the organization's strategies? Understanding the company's various stakeholders is a critical component to an effective communication plan. Stakeholders may include employees, manufacturers, customers, consumer interest groups, stockholders, media, industry experts, government groups, the board of directors, community and civic leaders, suppliers, competitors, family members, analysts, and legal groups.

Ten Berge (1990) identified four types of publics or stakeholders: enabling publics, functional publics, normative publics, and diffused publics. Enabling publics provide authority and control resources which enable the organization to exist. This group includes regulatory agencies, shareholders, and boards of directors. Functional publics provide inputs and take outputs from the organization. This group includes employees, unions, suppliers, and customers. Normative publics are those who share similar values or deal with similar problems, such as trade unions, political groups, and professional societies. Diffused publics emerge when organizational activities have external consequences. This audience includes the media, environmentalists, residents, and so on. Ten Berge's typology is useful in identifying an organization's relevant stakeholders.

Primary stakeholders are the victims. The process of communicating to victims' families is complicated, as already discussed. How does an organization, the perceived cause of pain, respond to feelings of shock, confusion, disbelief, loss, anger, frustration, grief, and sorrow? The degree of an organization's concern and respect for humanity is identified by how it responds to these particular stakeholders. Prior planning may define specific procedures for dealing with victims' families. An effective crisis response involves providing information and support and showing compassion, sensitivity, and respect to these individuals. Despite its best efforts, in the context of devastation and grief the company may still be perceived as uncaring and insensitive. In addition, cultural expectations, values, and differences must be taken into consideration.

Another significant stakeholder is the flying public. In the minds of the public, the image of an airline crash immediately creates a negative perception, a perception that is not easily changed with facts. Public fears are increased following a crash and concerns are raised not only about the airline in question but about the general safety of the entire industry. It is common for media to include reports of public anxiety about the safety of air travel in their coverage of a crash. Responding to public fears in the wake of an airline crash is challenging. Communication efforts must be genuine, as stakeholders are quick to label the organization as trustworthy, or not. In addition to victims and the flying public, communication should be directed toward internal stakeholders. Employees have a demanding need for information; therefore an organization's failure to communicate honestly and openly with its employees can create numerous problems. Information must be disseminated throughout the organization to avert problems.

A comprehensive list of stakeholders affected by the crisis should be identified and approaches to communicating with each determined. A detailed communication plan prioritizes the list of key stakeholders for contact (Caywood & Stocker, 1993). A stakeholder analysis, which involves considering the impact the event will have on a particular group, can be a complex task. For example, as a consequence of the global nature of business, there may be unintended audiences, or what Newsom, Turk, and Kruckeberg (1996) refer to as "nimbus publics." These are groups that the organization did not identify as being affected by the crisis and the organization's response.

In addition to unexpected stakeholders, there is the difficulty associated with stakeholder diversity. Pauchant and Mitroff (1992) argue that the various stakeholders involved in a crisis have different frames of reference or basic assumptions. Therefore, crisis managers must recognize and understand the differences and relationships between these varying assumptions. Caywood and Stocker (1993) emphasize the importance of sensitivity to the needs of each audience. They suggest targeting a key contact among each stakeholder group and assigning a crisis team member to maintain contact during periods of noncrisis.

Strategic Issues

A critical part of any communication plan is identification of the organization's strategic crisis issues. Issues are unresolved concerns relevant to the organization, are characterized by a conflict in values, and have at least two points of view. Issues regarding victims, damage, performance history, liability, stakeholders, corporate image, safety, and prevention may emerge in a crisis situation. When considering strategic issues, it is often helpful to phrase them in the form of questions. For example, concern over air-travel safety is common following an airline crash. Simply stating "air-travel safety" does not clarify the issue. It is too vague. The issue is focused by defining strategic questions. Depending on the particular perspective of the company, the strategic question on safety might be, "What actions should the airline take to convince the flying public it is safe to fly?" Another approach is, "To what extent should the airline address concerns about safety?" When phrased correctly, strategic issues imply some form of action. Addressing issues in the form of a question ensures a mutual understanding and keeps everyone focused.

A communication plan should also consider the various positive and negative factors, both internal and external, which may directly influence the organization's strategic management of these issues. Crisis managers should monitor both the internal and external environment for factors which might enhance or inhibit strategic communication choices.

Communication Objectives

Communication objectives do not necessarily arise from the issues you address. Nevertheless, they should directly relate to the issues and must be consistent with the overall crisis plan. Communication objectives generally seek to inform, convince, or move certain stakeholders or audiences to action. The organization should identify its communication philosophy and policies. For example, will the organization be proactive or reactive with its communication? How candid will the company be with information? What is the company's approach to media? How does the company wish to be perceived? Acknowledging the company's position on communication up front provides a framework and guidelines for communicating during a crisis.

Managers must recognize that there is an interdependent relationship between culture and communication. Corporate culture, for example, is reflected in the organization's communication climate. A company's culture (the collective beliefs, values, attitudes, and ways of doing things) exerts a primary influence on its approach to communication; specifically, the strategies it uses and the responses it gives. Culture is the frame of reference used by organizational decision makers in determining what they see as appropriate responses. How the company communicates to its employees, victims, customers, media, government officials, and other significant groups is influenced by its culture. An effective crisis plan requires a culture that is supportive of an effective crisis response, open, and honest.

Culture influences how an organization responds in times of crisis (Heath, 1994). Culture, for example, accounts for how an organization addresses the issue of blame. Some accept responsibility, others offer explanations or excuses, while others pass blame elsewhere. In regard to stakeholders, when a company's culture is comparable and congruous with its stakeholders, the relationship will likely be agreeable (Heath, 1994).

Themes and Messages

Public-relations practitioners argue the importance of identifying themes and organizing messages and information in advance (Newsom, Turk, & Kruckeberg, 1996; Fink, 1986). The organization can place itself in a proactive position by identifying the things it should be prepared to say before the event occurs, enabling the organization to quickly issue statements. This is information that must be communicated early in a crisis. Practitioners agree that an organization in crisis must speak with a single voice (Pinsdorf, 1987; Hearle, 1993; Heath, 1994). Conflicting stories, what Pinsdorf (1987) calls "hydra-headed" messages, create confusion and the image of an organization not in control. Conversely, silence breeds uncertainty, skepticism, and rumors. In order to ensure a consistent message with one voice, Caywood and Stocker (1993) suggest appointing a gatekeeper to centralize and control the flow of internal and external information.

Crisis management teams can identify appropriate themes and prepare some messages ahead of time which will be readily available in the event of a crisis. Themes provide a general overriding idea and are frequently repeated. Themes, for example, may focus on concern for safety, humanity, or future prevention. Information should be available on the organization's services and processes, its employees, company policies, current safety and instruction manuals, recent inspection reports, personnel lists and benefits, and a history of the organization. Biographies on all employees, particularly for high-level executives, are suggested (Fink, 1986; Newsom, Turk, & Kruckeberg, 1996). This information can be prepared in the form of a crisis background kit given to media (Fink, 1986). Information must be updated regularly.

Crisis communicators often find themselves in conflict with legal counsel over what should or should not be said. Lawyers are sensitive to protecting the company from lawsuits and reducing long-term liabilities. "No comment" is generally the preferred response. Crisis communicators, on the other hand, argue that such a response only raises questions and the best response to protect corporate image is to be open and honest (Newsom, Turk, & Kruckeberg, 1996). Managers should involve legal counsel in communication planning to determine, as much as possible, acceptable and nonliable statements.

Communication Channels

Messages may be communicated through press releases, speeches, press conferences, and interviews. Planning for communication entails determining appropriate communication channels to reach each audience. Channel refers to the means through which a message is communicated. It is often useful to determine the best channel prior to a crisis. In identifying ways to reach each audience, Caywood and Stocker (1993) suggest first determining who is responsible to reach a particular audience and the appropriate channel for communicating. In addition, planners should consider various crisis scenarios and prioritize communication channels for each, confirm that the necessary facilities and abilities to use the various channels are available, ensure that audiences have means to communicate back to the company, and establish a mechanism to gather audience information.

Selecting the spokesperson is perhaps one of the most critical aspects to crisis planning, because it is the spokesperson who sets the tone and style for handling the crisis and is the key contact for all media (Newsom, Turk, & Kruckeberg, 1996). The spokesperson should be an individual perceived by the public as knowledgeable and credible. Pinsdorf (1987) describes an effective spokesperson as "cool, level-headed, articulate, knows how the media works, and can make swift decisions" (p. 44). This person must also have full authority to speak on behalf of the organization. Usually the spokesperson is a member of the crisis team. The public generally expects the chief executive office (CEO) to represent the company; however, this person may not be the most effective communicator. In that case, the crisis team must select someone who can effectively communicate to represent the organization (Rogers, 1993). The spokesperson should be trained to work with the media to ensure the person's effectiveness when a crisis arises.

Managers must recognize that frontline employees often function in the role of spokespersons. These are employees who come into contact with customers, media, and others. Because stakeholder perceptions are influenced by these individuals, they should be recognized as a critical part of the crisis plan. Media do not necessarily limit themselves to official spokespersons. They may target employees at the crisis scene who can more clearly and thoroughly explain the situation. Employees may disclose information that conflicts with the "organizational voice," which may be perceived as harmful to the organization. Heath (1994) explains that managers must recognize, like it or not, that the organization's employees are a critical and valuable part of the communication network. Management is wise to take advantage of their worth and prepare them to share in the responsibility of managing the crisis. By empowering employees with such great responsibility, they indirectly foster a culture of crisis avoidance.

Media Relations

A crisis organization's primary vehicle for communication is the media. Whether or not an organization makes effective use of this communication vehicle depends on its approach to the media. Public-relations representatives generally serve as the media contact. Pinsdorf (1987) explains that organizations can take one of two approaches to media relations. The first approach is a "take-charge" position. This is a proactive approach which enables the organization to tell its story first, generally ensuring that the story will be told accurately. The second approach, what Pinsdorf calls a "sit-on-it" mindset, delays the inevitable and risks the organization's story being distorted. It is important in the planning process to identify the organization's media policy and clarify the rules and procedures regarding media inquiries. Executives, managers, and other members of the crisis team should then be trained in handling the media in light of the organization's policies.

Crisis communication should occur prior to a crisis when the organization can establish good will and relations with media (Fink, 1986). If an organization establishes a positive rapport with media before a crisis, the task of communicating with the media during a crisis is generally less difficult. Pinsdorf (1987) suggests that media preparation involves knowing and understanding how reporters work, viewing the organization the way outsiders do, planning for media chaos, and getting the house in order. Organizations can prepare for media by anticipating the types of questions media would ask and then developing the appropriate background material (Hearle, 1993). By providing a list of credible, reliable, and trusted people the media can refer to who can supplement information during a crisis (i.e., industry experts, financial analysts, manufacturers), the organization further controls the flow of information (Caywood & Stocker, 1993). "Getting the house in order" suggests that unethical or questionable events should be dealt with honestly and up front, particularly since media tend to have a way of discovering such information.

CONCLUSION

A contingency plan is a useful tool for dealing with the complexities of crisis. It presets certain philosophies, policies, approaches, and actions to which a company will adhere during turbulent times. A crisis-prepared organization plans for both crisis management and crisis communication.

When planning for crisis, practitioners emphasize some general but important considerations. Those in charge of communication during a crisis must have immediate access to authority as well as commitment from senior-level management. A crisis is characterized by limited response time, so difficulties accessing authority and obtaining executive support can prove detrimental. Also, managers must be knowledgeable of government rules, regulations, and laws for a particular type of crisis and comply with such requirements. Violating these requirements will only serve to compound the organization's crisis. Finally, contingency plans must be communicated to employees prior to a crisis. Failure to discuss and review crisis response procedures with employees will likely defeat the planning process.

REFERENCES

Caywood, C. L., & Stocker, K. P. (1993). The ultimate crisis plan. In J. A. Gottschalk (Ed.), *Crisis response: Inside stories on managing image under seige* (pp. 409–427). Detroit: Visible Ink Press.

Fink, S. (1986). *Crisis management: Planning for the inevitable*. New York: AMACOM.

Hearle, D. G. (1993). Planning for crisis. In J. A. Gottschalk (Ed.), *Crisis response: Inside stories on managing image under seige* (pp. 397–406). Detroit: Visible Ink Press.

Heath, R. L. (1994). *Management of corporate communication: From interpersonal contacts to external affairs*. Hillsdale, NJ: Lawrence Erlbaum.

Littlejohn, R. F. (1983). *Crisis management: A team approach*. New York: American Management Association.

Newsom, D., Turk, J., & Kruckeberg, D. (1996). *This is PR: The realities of public relations* (6th ed.). Belmont, CA: Wadsworth.

Pauchant, T., & Mitroff, I. (1992). *Transforming the crisis-prone organization: Preventing individual, organizational, and environmental tragedies*. San Francisco: Jossey-Bass.

Pinsdorf, M. K. (1987). *Communicating when your company is under siege*. Lexington, MA: Lexington Books.

Rogers, R. (1993). Anatomy of a crisis. In J. A. Gottschalk (Ed.), *Crisis response: Inside stories on managing image under seige* (pp. 123–139). Detroit: Visible Ink Press.

ten Berge, D. (1990). *The first 24 hours: A comprehensive guide to successful communications*. Cambridge, MA: Basil Blackwell.

Chapter 5

Northwest Airlines Flight 255

Organizations which have a credible image prior to a crisis are in a stronger position to positively influence stakeholder opinion in a crisis. Conversely, organizations with a negative image tend to have greater difficulty with crisis communication. Such difficulties were evidenced by Northwest Airlines. The crash of Northwest Flight 255 in August 1987 culminated almost a year of problems that plagued the airline following its merger with Republic Airlines. As a result of its merger-related problems, Northwest struggled to defend its position after the accident. This chapter examines the crash of Northwest Airlines Flight 255 and considers how a negative image prior to a crisis can complicate a company's efforts at crisis communication.

PRE-CRISIS

Northwest Airways was founded in September 1926 by a group of businessmen from Detroit, Minneapolis, and St. Paul. Under the leadership of Colonel Lewis Brittin, the carrier began providing airmail service the following month between Minneapolis and Chicago (Northwest Airlines, 1998). A year later, it was carrying passengers. In 1928, Northwest became the first U.S. airline to offer coordinated airline and railroad service. The company expanded westward, achieving the transcontinental route to Seattle. In 1934, the carrier was reincorporated as Northwest Airlines, Inc.

Northwest began service to the Far East in 1947, and extended the Great Circle route to Tokyo, Seoul, Shanghai, and Manila (Northwest Airlines, 1998). As a result of the costly Boeing 377 Stratocruisers used on trans-Pacific flights and a series of fatal accidents, the company experienced financial struggles in the early 1950s. Donald W. Nyrop became Northwest's president in 1954 and the airline's financial situation soon improved with his prudent management. Between 1968 and 1970, Northwest led the U.S. airline industry in net profit. When Nyrop retired in 1978, Northwest Airlines had the highest profit margin in the industry. M. Joseph Lapensky succeeded Nyrop. Under Lapensky's leadership the carrier continued to profit. Following deregulation, Northwest launched trans-Atlantic service and entered new routes to more than twenty U.S. cities (Northwest Airlines, 1998).

Steven Rothmeier was named president and CEO in 1985. The following year, Northwest purchased Minneapolis rival Republic Airlines for $884 million (one of the largest U.S. airline mergers ever), making Northwest the fifth largest U.S. airline and increasing its debt to $1.6 billion (Houston & Payne, 1986). Northwest almost doubled its workforce overnight, expanding from less than 17 thousand to more than 33 thousand (Northwest Airlines, 1998). The carrier was now the dominant hub airline at Detroit, Minneapolis–St. Paul, and Memphis. New cities were added to its route system.

The merger, unfortunately, created labor dispute, vandalism, and service problems for Northwest. Labor unrest resulted from the failure to solve merger-related problems among workers. In addition, great antagonism existed toward Northwest's CEO, Steven Rothmeier (Houston, 1987). In January 1987, the FBI confirmed it was investigating reports of tampering with Northwest planes at the Minneapolis–St. Paul Airport ("Problems nag airline," 1987). There was widespread suspicion that luggage was being purposely misrouted, and mechanics were accused of staging a slowdown to cut on-time flight performance. Rothmeier reported that 15 percent of the airline's daily flights were behind schedule ("Problems nag airline," 1987). Before the merger, Northwest had one of the lowest complaint records in the industry, but with flight delays, lost luggage, and computer difficulties customer complaints increased. Passengers now referred to the carrier as "Northwest Disorient" and "Northworst Airlines" (Marbach, Turque, Springen, & Cohn, 1987). The magnitude of Northwest's service problems became apparent when the carrier had the second-highest complaint rate during July 1987 (Houston, 1987).

Previous Accidents

Along with labor problems, two accidents drew public attention to Northwest Airlines in the year following its merger. In March 1987, a twenty-two-seat Northwest Airlink flight crash-landed at Detroit Metropolitan Airport, killing nine and injuring thirteen ("Problems nag airline," 1987). In August, a Northwest DC-9 aborted takeoff from Palm Beach County International Airport after the pilot noticed a gas tank leak. Seventy-five gallons of fuel were dumped on the runway when a valve in the wing tank malfunctioned ("Problems nag airline," 1987).

CRISIS

On Sunday, August 16, 1987, Northwest Flight 255 prepared for takeoff at the Detroit Metropolitan Wayne County Airport (Detroit-Metro). Flight 255 was a regularly scheduled passenger flight between Saginaw, Michigan, and Santa Ana, California, with en route stops at Detroit and Phoenix (NTSB, 1988). The pilots, both experienced, had flown earlier in the day. Prior to takeoff there was confusion as to which taxiway Flight 255 was to use. The ground controller instructed the aircraft to taxi to runway 3C, the shortest of the three available runways, but during the taxi out the captain missed the turnoff at taxiway C. He was redirected by the ground controller to a new taxi route to the runway. As a result of the confusion, the pilots reportedly grew irritable with the control tower (Marbach et al., 1987).

At 8:44 P.M., Flight 255 was cleared for takeoff. The plane, a McDonnell Douglas DC-9-82, was fully loaded with 36 thousand pounds of baggage, 149 passengers, and six crew members (NTSB, 1988; Stengel, 1987). Following liftoff near the end of the runway, the wings of Flight 255 rolled to the left and the right, about 35 degrees in each direction, and collided with obstacles northeast of the runway. The left wing struck a light pole located 2,760 feet beyond the end of the runway, subsequently striking other light poles and the roof of an Avis car rental facility. The aircraft then broke up as it slid across the ground, with post-impact fires erupting across the wreckage path, and slammed into a concrete embankment. The wreckage, distributed over a 3,000-foot crash path, covered a railroad embankment, an overpass, and two interstate highway overpasses (NTSB, 1988). Destroyed by impact forces and fire were three occupied vehicles on a road adjacent to the airport and numerous vacant vehicles in a rental car parking lot (NTSB, 1988).

POST-CRISIS

Search and Recovery

The local controller in the tower immediately notified the airport fire department of the accident. The Wayne County Sheriff's Deputies arrived at the site and took command of the scene (Johnson, 1987b). A major command post was established at the site (NTSB, 1988). Within fifteen minutes, the airport and surrounding roads and interstates were closed and the crash site was sealed off (Johnson, 1987b). Passengers on planes waiting to take off were told there would be a delay and those in the air were rerouted to other airports. Police controlled the traffic, crowds, and looters. Sixteen arrests were made (Johnson, 1987b).

Airport fire department personnel and fire departments throughout western Wayne County, Michigan State Police, surrounding police departments, and the Health Emergency Medical Services began rescue and fire-fighting operations. The rescue work centered on accounting for the dead. On Flight

255, 148 passengers and 6 crew members were killed. One sole survivor, a four-year-old girl, was found ("Amid wreckage," 1987). On the ground two persons were killed, one person seriously injured, and four persons suffered minor injuries (NTSB, 1988).

A temporary morgue was set up in a hangar where pathologists, investigators, and forensic experts worked to identify victims. It was six days before the last victim was identified (Bunting & Colt, 1988). Toxicological tests were conducted on the pilots. Autopsies were not performed on the victims in view of the obvious injuries which caused instantaneous death. The cause of death was severe blunt force trauma (NTSB, 1988).

Investigation

Within four hours of the crash the NTSB go-team, a group of thirteen investigators, left Washington for Detroit. By dawn, they were investigating the wreckage. The NTSB followed standard procedures in its investigation of the crash. The investigation involved more than 100 investigators from the NTSB, FAA, Northwest Airlines, McDonnell Douglas (the aircraft manufacturer), Pratt & Whitney (the engine manufacturer), Air Line Pilots Association (ALPA), National Air Traffic Controllers Association, International Association of Machinists, the International Brotherhood of Teamsters' Airline Division, the Wayne County Sheriffs Department, and the Detroit-Metro Wayne County Airport (NTSB, 1988). Investigative groups were formed for operations, air traffic control, witnesses, meteorology, survival factors, structures, powerplants, systems, digital flight data recorder (DFDR), maintenance records, cockpit voice recorder (CVR), airplane performance, and human performance (NTSB, 1988). Each group attempted to determine the facts, conditions, and circumstances relating to their area of investigation which could have a bearing on the probable cause of the accident. Evidence was examined both on-site and in NTSB laboratories.

At the crash site, the NTSB attempted to document and develop a comprehensive record of what remained and what was seen and heard. Eyewitnesses, air traffic controllers, and friends and families of the crew were interviewed. The structures group charted and photographed the wreckage path (Bunting & Colt, 1988). Much of the wreckage was found between the light pole and the forward fuselage section. The fuselage structure had disintegrated and was scattered throughout the wreckage path. Following each day's investigation, investigative groups met to discuss their findings, with press conferences being held afterward.

Much of the investigative work occurred off-site. The DFDR and CVR, which recorded the final seconds before the crash, were recovered from the wreckage and immediately flown to the NTSB lab in Washington. Significant information needed to explain the cause of the crash was expected to come from the newly designed DFDR, which recorded fifty-two functions on the aircraft ("Jet rose," 1987). Flight 255 was the first commercial airliner to crash with the design on board. The NTSB, however, experienced difficulty decoding the tape and eventually sent it to the manufacturer to be decoded. Various parts recovered from the wreckage considered significant in determining the cause of the crash were sent to NTSB and other laboratories.

Preliminary Findings

The NTSB explored various factors which could have caused the crash, such as meteorological, airplane, and aerodrome difficulties. Investigators thoroughly examined meteorological conditions at the time of the accident. According to the National Weather Service (NWS) radar observation at Detroit-Metro, at the time of the crash the airport was in an area partially covered by thunderstorms with very heavy rain showers, but according to a NWS radar observer at Selfridge Air Force Base, Michigan, there were no thunderstorms in the Detroit-Metro area (NTSB, 1988). The Detroit Edison Company's lightning detection system had not recorded any lightning activity in Wayne County between 8:00 P.M. and 9:00 P.M. Only one pilot had reported moderate turbulence five miles west of Detroit at 8:06 P.M. The Detroit-Metro wind shear alert system recorded winds at thirteen to fifteen knots at the time of the crash (NTSB, 1988, p. 5). Based on these factors, meteorological conditions were discounted as a causal factor.

Conditions and circumstances associated with the plane itself were investigated. Because Northwest Airlines experienced problems following its merger, questions of sabotage arose, but no evidence was found to support this notion ("Jet rose," 1987). Other factors examined by investigators included the plane's history, maintenance, engine, and flight planning and operation. The aircraft, a McDonnell Douglas DC-9-82, was manufactured in 1981 and delivered to Republic Airlines the following year. Northwest acquired the aircraft in its takeover of Republic. There were no discrepancies or malfunctions found in the flight and maintenance logbooks which would have contributed to the accident. According to maintenance records, the airplane was maintained and operated in accordance with applicable Federal aviation regulations and company operations specifications rules and procedures. Aside from the possible failure of the takeoff warning system, there was no evidence of any preexisting malfunctions or failures of any airplane structures or systems which would have contributed to the crash.

The possibility of a faulty engine was suggested after witnesses testified they thought they saw the engine aflame (Witkin, 1987). The aircraft's two Pratt & Whitney engines were examined, but the NTSB stated there was no immediate evidence that any parts of either engines penetrated their outer covers, nor was there any evidence of an in-flight fire. The flames seen by witnesses were attributed to the plane hitting the light pole, which ripped open a wing fuel tank. The left engine torched after it ingested the fuel (Witkin, 1987). The plane's CVR indicated the crew was not aware of engine problems ("Jet rose," 1987). Catastrophic engine failure was ruled out, as was the possibility of an engine explosion.

Investigators explored whether the airline had erred in planning and operating the flight. The tower supervisor has the primary responsibility to determine which runways are designated as active runways based on wind conditions, weather forecasts, wind shear alert indications, availability of lighting and electronic navigational aids, and runway and taxiway closures. The decision to change Flight 255's runway configuration was based on the tower supervisor's judgment that the wind direction was changing from southwest to northwest. His decision was accomplished in accordance with published Air Traffic Control procedures (NTSB, 1988). Based on these data, the Safety Board concluded the supervisor's decision was reasonable. Airport conditions were investigated, since the crash occurred on takeoff, but investigators found no contributory factors to the crash.

Probable Cause

As the investigation progressed, human error and equipment difficulties became the focus. The DFDR indicated that the slats and flaps on the front and rear edges of the wings, which enable the aircraft to rise rapidly at a slow speed when extended, were in a retracted position (Wilkerson, 1987). Failure to extend them for takeoff would critically restrict the jet's ability to climb. The DFDR indicated the jet traveled 6,000 to 6,500 feet on the 8,500-foot-long runway before lifting off the ground and rose only forty-eight feet before it went down (Wilkerson, 1987). Witness accounts, indicating the flaps were extended, contradicted the Board's findings and raised questions about the accuracy of the newly designed DFDR.

Investigators determined whether the retracted flaps and slats were due to faulty instruments or human error. Mechanical failure was ruled out since there were no findings of problems with the hydraulic or electrical systems that control the wing surfaces (Wilkerson, 1987). Analysis of the CVR, however, indicated the pilot and first officer neglected to confirm that they had properly set the high-lift flaps and slats on the wings, a routine procedure, during the required pre-flight checklist before taking off (Marbach et al., 1987; "NTSB evaluates factors," 1987). The taxi checklist required the pilot and first officer to call out, then verify, the different settings to ensure the airplane's systems were ready for takeoff. Northwest procedures clearly defined the flight crew's duties and responsibilities pertaining to the checklist in the Standard Operating Procedures section of the Airline Pilots Handbook (APH). The APH stated consistent and proper checklist usage, which is reliable and fosters predictable and standardized crew member interaction, is a requirement of good cockpit management (NTSB, 1988).

Human-performance investigators immersed themselves in the lives of the captain and first officer in hopes of finding answers as to why a veteran crew failed to accomplish such a routine procedure. The fifty-seven-year-old captain had thirty-two years' experience and the first officer had nine years' experience (NTSB, 1988). Investigators reviewed training records and medical records and talked to the flight crew's relatives and colleagues. The NTSB found the flight crew and cabin crew of Flight 255 qualified in accordance with applicable Federal and Northwest regulations and procedures to operate the plane (NTSB, 1988). There were no unusual revelations found in the flight crew's training records nor in their personal background and actions during the two to three days prior to the crash. The captain's spotless record and level of experience raised questions surrounding human error as the cause. He was type rated on seven different airplanes and had served as an FAA-designated check airman in the B727, DC-9, and DC-9-82 (NTSB, 1988). His colleagues described him as a competent and capable pilot who always used the airplane checklist and would not tolerate any deviation from standard procedure. The first officer was also described in favorable terms.

The Board theorized, but could not determine conclusively why the first officer failed to lower the flaps. Because the captain is not required to advise the first officer, it was likely the Flight 255 captain assumed his first officer had accomplished the task. The Board believed the crew members made themselves more susceptible to distractions or memory lapses by not adhering to standard operating procedure, thereby increasing their vulnerability to the problems associated with conducting checklists during taxi operations (NTSB, 1988). While there had been potentially distracting factors present during Flight 255's departure, the Board believed they did not represent unusual circumstances (NTSB, 1988).

In addition to the flight crew's failure to extend the flaps, analysis also confirmed that the Central Aural Warning System (CAWS), a computerized vocal warning horn designed to alert the crew of problems, did not sound. Furthermore, the warning light on an overhead cockpit panel which alerts the pilot when the CAWS is not functioning properly had not worked due to a power failure. The CAWS had been tested in Santa Ana that morning and had functioned properly twice earlier in the day (Gruley, Martin, Smith, & Warren, 1987).

Public Hearing

A four-day public hearing convened November 16, 1987, in Romulus, Michigan. The FAA, Northwest Airlines, McDonnell Douglas, and the ALPA were all represented (NTSB, 1988). More than 250 crash investigators, liability attorneys, families, aviation lawyers, insurance officials, photographers, and others attended (Kerwin, 1987b, November 17). Issues covered included the Flight 255 crew, the failure of the CAWS to alert the crew that the flaps and slats were not set for takeoff, and the miraculous survival of the four-year-old girl (Gruley et al., 1987). Twenty-seven witnesses testified during the four-day hearing (Witkin, 1987). The witnesses included the chief investigator for the NTSB; a McDonnell Douglas performance manager; a Northwest MD-80 training manager; and two senior Northwest pilots ("Hearing opens," 1987; Gruley et al., 1987; Warren & Smith, 1987).

Two psychologists were interviewed about the influence automation has on flight-crew performance (crew complacency). A consequence of the increasing technological advancements of the cockpit is the flight crew's dependence on computers to tell them what is wrong. The influence of interpersonal relationships between flight-crew personnel on the flight crew's performance of cockpit duties was also discussed (NTSB, 1988). A NASA psychologist stated the effect of role structure among the cockpit crew was very well defined and significantly reduced ambiguity about responsibilities. He further testified that research indicated highly effective crews had more task-oriented communication. With regard to checklist procedures, while it was rare to see a checklist completely ignored, it was possible. He suggested that checklist use was directly related to the number of errors made by the flight crews. Those who go by the book tend to perform more effectively (NTSB, 1988).

Questions were also raised concerning the height of the light pole struck by Flight 255 after a McDonnell Douglas witness testified that the plane would have eventually gained sufficient altitude during liftoff with its flaps and slats retracted had its left wing not clipped the forty-two-foot-high light pole (Gruley et al., 1987). While the light pole was 2.2 feet higher than the FAA approved forty-foot height, it did not constitute an obstruction to air navigation (NTSB, 1988). The NTSB determined the pole's additional height was not a causal factor. With only its wing slats extended, the airplane would have cleared the light pole by 500 feet (NTSB, 1988).

Much of the fact-gathering phase of the investigation was brought to a close with the NTSB hearing. Although there were no new revelations, much of the information gathered prior to the hearing was substantiated (Smith, Martin, & Warren, 1987).

Conclusions and Recommendations

Based on an analysis of the information gathered during the fact-finding phase, the NTSB formally described its findings and offered recommendations at a public meeting on May 10, 1988. The NTSB ruled the probable cause of the accident was the flight crew's failure to use the taxi checklist to ensure that the flaps and slats were extended for takeoff. A contributing factor to the accident was the absence of electric power (for which a reason could not be determined) to the airplane takeoff warning system, which did not warn the flight crew that the airplane was not configured properly for takeoff (NTSB, 1988, p. 68).

The analysis of the Northwest Flight 255 crash resulted in recommendations to the FAA directed toward technical aspects, operating procedures, and flight-crew training. The failure of the CAWS to alert the flight crew of problems prompted the NTSB to recommend an investigation of the reliability of circuit breakers. The NTSB also recommended that the FAA require the modification of the DC-9-80 series airplanes to illuminate the CAWS fail light in the event of a power loss, and develop and disseminate guidelines for the CAWS design that includes the warning, its criticality, and the degree of system self-monitoring.

While the Safety Board could not determine whether the accident crew's performance was representative of other carriers' flight crews, they recommended the FAA require operators and operations inspectors to emphasize the importance of standard operating procedures; specifically, adherence to the prescribed checklist procedures (NTSB, 1988).

Finally, the issue of individualized crew-member training, raised during the analysis, received suggestions. The NTSB recommended the FAA expedite the issuance of guidance materials for operators in the implementation of team-oriented flight-crew training techniques. It was also recommended that an Air Carrier Operations Bulletin directing principal operations inspectors to emphasize initial and recurrent training programs on various recovery tactics be issued. The NTSB recommended all large air carriers review initial and recurrent training programs to ensure they include simulator or aircraft training exercises which involve cockpit resource management and active coordination of all crew-member trainees, which would permit evaluation of crew performance and adherence to crew coordination procedures (NTSB, 1988, p. 69).

Industry Response

In the initial phase of the investigation, findings which suggested the flight crew failed to include the wing flaps and slats in their pre-flight check and the failure of the takeoff warning system to alert them of the problem prompted immediate responses from the ALPA and the FAA. The ALPA stated it was premature to assume pilot error was the cause of the crash, since information had not been confirmed by other means (Bohy, Martin, & Smith, 1987). The association suggested that even if the flaps had not been lowered, other factors could have been responsible. They also stated their long-standing concern that aircraft such as the MD-80 should have a three-member crew rather than a two-member crew, since there were times when the workload was too heavy for only two people.

In late August, the NTSB reported that physical evidence recovered from the wreckage and further examination of data from the flight recorders supported their initial belief about flight-crew error. The FAA immediately responded to this information by calling a meeting at which its chief said that the aviation community must restore public confidence in airline safety. He said pilot training was his top priority. The meeting was a huge media event and consisted of pilots and industry representatives reading prepared statements about safety being their top priority and their successes with pilot training (McGinley, 1987). A Delta executive, for example, acknowledged recent pilot errors by his company, but stated the company was determined to live up to its advertising slogan, "Delta gets you there with care" (McGinley, 1987).

After the NTSB identified and made public the failure of the CAWS to alert the pilots to the problem, McDonnell Douglas and the FAA responded with appropriate actions. On September 1, 1987, McDonnell Douglas issued a telex to all DC-9-80 operators recommending the airplane checklist be changed to include a check of the takeoff warning system prior to departing the gate on each flight. On September 23, 1987, a memorandum was issued by the FAA creating a special team to investigate all takeoff warning systems on air carriers and the procedures used by maintenance and flight-crew personnel to check them (NTSB, 1988).

Media Coverage

Media provided both factual and sensational coverage of the crash of Northwest Flight 255. Factual reports relayed what occurred based on information provided by the NTSB. Media often supplemented this information with their own theories as to what caused the crash. After the first week of the investigation, media reported the Northwest flight crew's failure to set the flaps and slats correctly and complete the pre-flight checklist before takeoff and the failure of the CAWS to alert the crew to the problem as the likely cause of the crash (NTSB evaluates factors in Detroit MD-82 crash, 1987). Coverage of the NTSB investigation was combined with reports of the deteriorating service among commercial airlines. Aside from covering the crash and the investigation, there were reports on liability and the miraculous survival of the four-year-old girl.

Reports continued to focus on the declining confidence in air safety. In the summer of 1987, crowded skies, multiple reports of near collisions, overworked air traffic controllers, and indifferent maintenance created extreme public concern about air safety. These concerns were magnified with the crash of Flight 255. The crash created a crisis of public confidence in air safety. Following the accident, the *New York Times* reported the Flight 255 crash had served to increase the public's anxiety about flying ("Rise in fear," 1987). A Gallup poll in November 1987 indicated that Americans, by a two-to-one margin, thought air travel was less safe than five years earlier ("Airlines' safety trend assailed," 1987, November). Reasons for the perceived decline in air safety included the Northwest crash.

There were reports of various stories and incidents associated with the crash. For example, one incident concerned a Roman Catholic priest who counseled victims' relatives following the crash and was later discovered to be an im-postor soliciting cases for a lawyer ("Priest at Detroit crash," 1987). There were emotion-packed stories about victims and their survivors ("New York GM plant honors," 1987; Johnson, 1987a) and those who missed the flight ("Six who missed ill-fated flight," 1987). Following the on-site investigation, media coverage on the Flight 255 crash decreased.

CRISIS COMMUNICATION:
AN ANALYSIS OF NORTHWEST'S COMMUNICATION

The crash of Northwest Flight 255 exacerbated an already critical situation for the carrier. Northwest topped the list of consumer complaints for August and this trend continued through December ("NWA unit tops," 1987; "Con-sumer gripes," 1987; "Gluttons for punishment," 1987; "Delay data," 1987; Cranshaw, 1988). The airline also experienced a decline in its stock. The largest decline in Northwest stock occurred immediately following NTSB reports of evidence pointing to pilot error. Northwest's stock declined over twelve points ("Market focus," 1987). Three lawsuits were filed by victims' families less than a week after the crash (Gest & Seamonds, 1987). It was estimated the crash would cost aviation insurers approximately $200 million for losses for the craft and in passenger liability claims (Diebolt, 1987). North-west indicated it had adequate insurance to cover any claims.

In addition to financial and legal concerns, Northwest faced two serious charges following the Flight 255 accident. First, critics accused the airline of providing an inadequate response immediately after the accident. Second, NTSB findings indicated the Northwest Flight 255 pilots were responsible for the accident. These charges further damaged the airline's image. The analy-sis which follows examines Northwest's defense against these charges.

Northwest's Immediate Response

Northwest Airlines activated its crisis plan immediately after the crash (Kerwin, 1987a). Phone lines were set up to handle calls from the public while managers were personally assigned to assist victims' families (Kerwin, 1987a). Within six hours of the crash, a plane carrying a team of twenty ex-ecutives and medical and technical experts left for Detroit. Northwest offered to pay families' travel expenses, funeral costs for victims, and medical care for the injured (Kerwin, 1987a). Condolences were sent by Northwest's CEO, Rothmeier. The airline offered other customers full refunds if they wanted to cancel flight plans.

Despite its efforts to assist families and communicate with the media following the crash, Northwest was pounded with criticism. Crisis experts and media blasted the airline for failing to establish a "take-charge" posture, for not providing suffi-cient information, and for not using a top executive as a spokesman after the crash (Kerwin, 1987a). Northwest's efforts to assist victims' families after the crash was perceived as an effort to obtain information for use in liability suits (Peterson, 1987). Northwest vehemently denied ulterior motives.

Initially, Northwest looked to the NTSB to supply appropriate responses to questions. The company did not speculate as to a cause nor did it release the passenger list out of respect for the victims' families (Gest & Seamonds, 1987). Northwest's refusal to speculate on a cause or release the passenger list to protect family privacy angered local officials, foreign consuls, news organizations, and others (Kerwin, 1987a; Gest & Seamonds, 1987). The Society of Professional Journalists and the American Society of Newspaper Editors were quick to express their frustration with the airline ("Airline is still refusing," 1987). They argued that withholding names served no useful purpose and created false hopes for the relatives and friends. Northwest was creating a crisis of confidence and damaging their own credibility.

An antagonistic relationship existed between Northwest's media relations director and the media. Northwest's media relations director was quoted as saying, "The media thinks we're obligated to furnish them with information on every little irregularity on every little airplane. That's the province of the National Transportation Safety Board" (Kerwin, 1987a, p. A1). The media criticized Northwest for its media relations director's antagonistic position. The *Detroit News* listed unflattering examples of the comments made by the director which were quoted in press reports after the crash ("Northwest comments," 1987).

The Issue of Blame

The assignment of blame placed the airline in a defensive position. Northwest's primary defense strategy was denial. The company further employed the tactics of expanding denial, redirecting blame, and aggression in an effort to reduce the degree of responsibility associated with blame and ultimately to defend its image. Northwest responded to findings of pilot error by providing evidence contradicting the Safety Board's findings. In a letter sent to the Safety Board prior to the public hearing, Northwest denied the fact the pilots neglected to confirm the setting of the flaps and slats (Witkin, 1987). The airline offered evidence to support its position and disprove the Board's findings. Included along with the letter was a report of a reanalysis of the CVR tape, in which consultants from a Virginia firm hired by the airline stated, while the tape is not perfectly clear, they could hear words like "flaps" and "flaps set." The NTSB replied it did not prove they actually accomplished the checklist or the flaps and slats did not malfunction somehow and retract before takeoff (Witkin, 1987).

During the investigation Northwest's primary accuser, McDonnell Douglas, contended the Flight 255 crew may have deliberately pulled a circuit breaker which impaired the CAWS. Northwest attacked its accuser by arguing McDonnell Douglas was aware of the problems with the circuit breakers and failed to deal with the problem (Martin, 1988). The airline redirected blame to the aircraft manufacturer. Northwest contended, throughout the investigation, that the cause of the crash was due to a poorly designed computer warning system by McDonnell Douglas. The airline pressed the problem with the circuit breaker, since there had been a history of problems with the type of circuit breaker used on many systems aboard several McDonnell Douglas planes (Smith, 1987). In turn, McDonnell Douglas placed blame on poor pilot performance and defended itself against charges that a faulty circuit breaker caused the failure of the CAWS. The ALPA, siding with the airline, also attributed the cause of the crash to the failure of the takeoff warning system to alert the crew (Martin, 1988).

Public Hearing

All parties generally agreed that the plane's performance indicated the slats and flaps were retracted, but there was no agreement on how to account for it. The airline continued to deny its pilots were responsible. Northwest and the ALPA argued the crew's lack of warning, due to a power failure, caused the crash. The airline and the union submitted the computer-enhanced version of the CVR tape during the hearing. The NTSB, however, refused to listen to "a copy of a copy" (Martin, 1988). The original tape had been listened to twice and all members agreed to what was heard on tape. Northwest further argued that had it not been for the forty-two-foot light pole, the plane would have eventually gained sufficient altitude during liftoff.

McDonnell Douglas contended Flight 255's CAWS had been tested the morning of the accident in Santa Ana and had worked properly. According to the manufacturer, the power interruption may have been caused by the pilot deliberately pulling the circuit breaker. A McDonnell Douglas spokesman further argued that the warning system is not a substitute for good professional practices and that other checks would have alerted the crew to the malfunction (Gruley et al., 1987; "Hearing opens," 1987).

Media reports criticized Northwest and its constituents during the public hearing. The *Detroit News* observed, "Instead of providing a conduit for new insights into the crash, the hearing had become a forum for Northwest, Douglas, and the ALPA to plead their innocence and try to pass responsibility for the tragedy onto one of the other parties" (Smith, 1987).

NTSB Final Report

Prior to the NTSB's announcement of its conclusions, Northwest, McDonnell Douglas, and the ALPA submitted reports in an attempt to persuade the NTSB to adopt their versions of the probable cause and thereby minimize damage to their reputations and weaken the many lawsuits filed by the victims' families (Martin & Gruley, 1988). In a sixty-seven-page report which presented evidence in its defense, Northwest contended the cause of the crash was due to McDonnell Douglas' poorly designed computer warning system. The airline charged McDonnell Douglas with being aware of the problem with the circuit breakers and failure to deal with the problem (Martin, 1988). By redirecting blame to Douglas, Northwest attempted to minimize the negative effects associated with blame.

EVALUATION OF STRATEGIES

The effectiveness of Northwest's communication following the Flight 255 crash was influenced by three factors: the severity of the crash, evidence of human error, and the airline's prior negative image. First, the crash claimed 156 lives and injured six. At the time, the crash was the second deadliest in U.S. aviation history (Marbach et al., 1987). The crash also ended a two-year period without a single fatal accident involving a major domestic carrier. Second, the crash was caused by human error. The fact that it was an accident implied the crash was an irregular and unintentional event; however, the fact that it resulted from human error suggested the accident was preventable. Stakeholders are more likely to react negatively to events which are considered controllable than noncontrollable. Third, Northwest's image prior to the crash left the airline without a bank of goodwill. There was little public sympathy for Northwest, due to merger-related problems. At the time of the crash, Northwest had the highest complaint record in the industry. Simply put, the airline lacked credibility. These three factors significantly influenced stakeholder perceptions of Northwest's efforts to manage and communicate following the crisis and to defend itself against the assignment of blame.

Northwest's Immediate Response

Criticism concerning its response to the crash is indicative of Northwest's difficulties in communicating after the crash. The lack of goodwill, a direct result of merger-related problems, influenced stakeholder perceptions of the airline's actions immediately after the crash. Efforts to assist families were perceived as a bribe to offset liability. Actions considered protocol by the industry (e.g., not releasing the passenger list prior to family notification) received extreme criticism. Because of its preexisting negative image, stakeholders were less willing to believe the company's actions were sincere. Consequently, Northwest's poor image made it virtually impossible for ingratiation strategies to work. Furthermore, the severity of the situation along with the company's negative image made the choice of denying ulterior motives where families were concerned an antagonistic strategy.

In light of the factors influencing Northwest's crisis, it appears the airline's strategic options were limited. Given Northwest's position, strategies to make amends would have been the most appropriate choice. Messages which atone for the perceived inadequacy of its response as well as efforts to improve its response to families and media would likely have been effective.

Public perceptions are based on media reports; thus, how media portray an organization in crisis is critical. The airline's media relations director further compromised Northwest's critical situation. His antagonistic responses suggested the airline lacked control. This illuminates an important principal of crisis management: Do not alienate the media.

The Issue of Blame

In an effort to minimize the threatening impact of the NTSB's finding, Northwest employed strategies of denial. The legal consequences resulting from human error increased communication and further compromised image. The airline attempted to respond to the incriminating information by identifying evidence to support its position and redirecting the focus of blame. Liability became the major issue during the post-crisis stage, as Northwest ALPA, and McDonnell Douglas each tried to redirect blame onto the other. Northwest used various denial tactics to cast doubt on the prevailing NTSB theory that pilot error was the primary cause of the crash. The flight crew's excellent record left a small window of doubt about human error being the cause of the fatal accident. The crew's spotless record gave Northwest no reason to doubt the crew's actions. In an effort to support its claim, the airline submitted to the NTSB a reanalysis of the CVR recording, but the NTSB did not find the evidence convincing. In other words, Northwest failed to offer reasonable evidence to support its claim. The airline, however, persisted with its efforts. The Safety Board's refusal to listen to the recording again at its public hearing suggests this particular line of defense was weak and perhaps viewed as the airline's attempt to offset liability.

Northwest's efforts to redirect blame resulted in an ongoing battle with McDonnell Douglas. This response further damaged the airline's already negative image. Rather than diverting attention away from Northwest, the strategy of redirecting blame drew attention to the airline. Media reaction suggests that this was a poor choice, assuming the airline was attempting to defend its image. It appears, however, Northwest may have been less concerned with image and more concerned with legal issues. Again, because of its prior negative image Northwest might have been more effective in defending its image after the crash had it emphasized corrective action and downplayed shifting blame.

Northwest Airlines's efforts at communicating to improve its image following the crash of Flight 255 were generally ineffective. The severity of the crisis, assignment of blame, and the airline's prior negative image directly influenced Northwest's attempts to effectively respond immediately after the crisis and to reduce the threat associated with blame.

CONCLUSION

A number of lessons emerge from the case of Northwest Flight 255:

1. Strategic communication choices must be determined in light of the company's performance history and perceived image.
2. Public battles increase media attention.
3. Appropriate strategic communication is best determined from a broad perspective or frame of reference.
4. A highly defensive and antagonistic spokesperson will likely prompt negative media coverage.

When determining strategic communication options to defend corporate image during a crisis, the organization's performance history as well as its perceived image before the crisis must be considered. The effectiveness of strategic communication is influenced to a degree by the company's initial credibility. More specifically, an organization's believability is derived from its credibility. Credibility provides the company with a bank of goodwill on which it can draw.

It is a given that legal issues will influence the process of strategic communication. The influence of positive prior credibility on strategic communication in crisis was observed in the Tylenol crisis. Johnson & Johnson's long-time image as a trustworthy and secure provider of healthcare products provided a reservoir of goodwill among its stakeholders (Fink, 1986). The company's high level of credibility combined with its response to the capsule tampering demonstrated a genuine concern for consumers. Johnson & Johnson's reputation for dealing fairly with consumers and the media was invaluable in helping to restore the product.

Conversely, a company's lack of initial credibility negatively influences its efforts at strategic communication. Northwest's credibility was tainted by the consequences of its merger with Republic Airlines in 1986. The carrier experienced labor disputes, vandalism, service problems, antagonism toward its CEO, and a fatal accident involving a Northwest Airlink flight at Detroit-Metro. In the month prior to the Flight 255 crash, Northwest had the second-highest consumer complaint rate. The airline's chaotic situation subsequent to the merger and prior to the crash created the perception of a company lacking control. This perception transferred over to Northwest's response to the accident. The airline was accused of not taking control and responding inappropriately to victims' families and the media.

Credibility may be negatively affected by a company's initial actions to the crisis. For example, Exxon's inadequate response to the Valdez oil spill in 1989 lessened its credibility and set a negative tone for public reaction to its response (Small, 1991). Despite the positive actions Exxon took in the later stages, media coverage continued to be highly critical.

Stakeholders' efforts to achieve their individual goals sometimes conflict, creating additional effects which can deepen the crisis. Northwest's and McDonnell Douglas's goal to absolve themselves of blame resulted in a public battle. The second lesson illustrated in this case is that publicly battling crisis issues increases media attention. Media feed on the intensity of a battle. When media attention has already focused on an operation, it takes very little to initiate additional attention. Following extreme media scrutiny during the crisis phase, it is unlikely a company will want continued media coverage. When a company's image is already weak, battling issues publicly, particularly those concerning liability, serves to further increase stakeholders' negative perceptions. Aggressive actions tend to strain public credibility. For example, Northwest Airlines's aggressive and persistent efforts to deny blame by providing a reanalysis of the CVR recording appeared desperate. If image is a primary concern, crisis communicators must thoroughly identify all possible approaches and consider how such actions or messages will influence perceptions of the organization.

A third lesson underscores the importance of viewing a crisis from a broad perspective or frame of reference to determine appropriate strategic communication. Frame of reference influences how an organization and its stakeholders will respond to a crisis. Corporate frame of reference may prevent a company from doing what is appropriate or right. Northwest's response to the issue of blame reflected the company's limited frame of reference. The airline's responses appeared to be based on financial and legal considerations. The perception was Northwest seemed more concerned with liability than determining the probable cause of the accident in an effort to prevent a future recurrence. While liability is certainly a critical issue for any business, Northwest's narrow frame of reference and highly defensive position overshadowed any hint of a sincere concern about safety during the NTSB's investigation. A broader view of the situation would possibly have resulted in the airline accepting the blame for the disaster, paying the price, and putting its effort toward preventing a similar incident in the future.

The influence of corporate frame of reference on organizational decision making in crisis was also seen following the Bhopal disaster. On December 3, 1984, a lethal gas leak from Union Carbide's Bhopal India plant killed nearly 3 thousand people and injured another 200 thousand (Shrivastava, 1987). A narrow frame of reference limited Union Carbide's actions following the Bhopal crisis. Carbide based its decision on technical, financial, and legal considerations rather than on a broader social concern. Consequently, the company was perceived as uncaring toward the victims.

A final lesson to be learned from this case is that the presence of an antagonistic or highly defensive spokesperson will result in extremely negative media coverage. The spokesperson represents the entire organization and sets the style for handling the crisis. In Northwest's case, the spokesperson served to further damage the airline's credibility and create the perception that the company was insensitive to the situation. A spokesperson should be credible and knowledgeable, understand the role of media and its processes, and be capable of conveying the message the company intends to communicate. Although it may be difficult for a spokesperson to completely hide his or her personal feelings, it must be understood that how a spokesperson behaves and responds to questions will influence the public's perception of the facts.

REFERENCES

Airline is still refusing to list victims of crash. (1987, August 20). *New York Times*, p. B16.

Airlines safety trend assailed; Public calls for federal action. (1987, November). *The Gallup Report*, No. 166, pp. 28–32.

Amid the wreckage, 4-year-old girl lives. (1987, August 18). *New York Times*, p. B7.

Bohy, R., Martin, R., & Smith, J. (1987, August 21). NTSB: We have a lot more work to do. *Detroit News*, p. 6A.

Bunting, J. B., & Colt, G. H. (1988, April). Anatomy of a plane crash. *Life*, pp. 66–72.

Consumer gripes about air service fell in September. (1987, October 12). *Wall Street Journal*, p. 12.

Cranshaw, A. (1988, January 7). Airlines performance worsens, U.S. reports. *Washington Post*, p. F3.

Delay data: Airlines figures hold surprises—spark controversy. (1987, November 11). *Wall Street Journal*, p. 29.

Diebolt, J. (1987, August 24). Jetliner disaster to cost insurers $200 million. *Detroit News*, p. 8A.

Fink, S. (1986). *Crisis management: Planning for the inevitable*. New York: AMACOM.

Gest, T., & Seamonds, J. D. (1987, August 31). A lawyer's rush for judgments. *U.S. News and World Report*, p. 23.

Gluttons for punishment? Fliers continue using airlines they hate. (1987, November 19). *Wall Street Journal*, p. 33.

Gruley, B., Martin, R., Smith, J., & Warren, H. (1987, November 17). Pilots say flaps, slats set; reports disagree. *Detroit News*, p. 1A.

Hearing opens on airplane crash in Detroit. (1987, November 17). *New York Times*, p. B7.

Houston, P. (1987, September 28). Steve Rothmeier's Northwest looks good on paper. *Business Week*, pp. 58–59.

Houston, P., & Payne, S. (1986, August 18). Northwest and Republic: A wedding but no honeymoon. *Business Week*, pp. 56–57.

Jet rose only 150 feet before plunge. (1987, August 19). *New York Times*, p. A18.

Johnson, D. (1987a, August 18). Among relatives of victims, sorrow, anger, and disbelief. *New York Times*, p. B7.

Johnson, D. (1987b, August 23). Rescuers in Detroit find job doesn't end. *New York Times*, p. D5.

Kerwin, K. (1987a, August 30). Experts say Northwest fumbled crash aftermath. *Detroit News*, p. A1.

Kerwin, K. (1987b, November 17). Some grieved, others studied at the hearing. *Detroit News*, p. A6.

Marbach, W. D., Turque, B., Springen, K., & Cohn, B. (1987, August 31). The riddle of flight 255. *Newsweek*, p. 20.

Market focus. (1987, August 24). *Aviation Week and Space Technology*, p. 15.

Martin, R. (1988, May 11). Report to serve as road map of evidence. *Detroit News*, p. 10.

Martin, R., & Gruley, B. (1988, April 20). Exclusive report: Northwest, pilots, Douglas conflict on 255 crash. *Detroit News*, p. 8.

McGinley, L. (1987, August 28). FAA chief tells pilots public confidence must be restored, training improved. *Wall Street Journal*, p. 2.

National Transportation Safety Board. (1988, May 10). *Aircraft Accident Report: Northwest Airlines, Inc., McDonnell Douglas DC-9-82, N312RC, Detroit Metropolitan Wayne County Airport, Romulus, Michigan, August 16, 1987* (NTSB/AAR-88/05). Washington, DC: National Transportation Safety Board (NTIS No. PB88-910406).

New York GM plant honors 5 aboard jet. (1987, August 19). *New York Times*, p. A18.

Northwest Airlines Corporate Information. (1998, January 19). History [http://www.nwa.com/corpinfo/years/].

Northwest comments, reactions. (1987, August 30). *Detroit News*, p. A10.

NTSB evaluates factors in Detroit MD-82 crash. (1987, August 24). *Aviation Week and Space Technology*, pp. 18–20.

NWA unit tops Continental air in customer gripes. (1987, September 4). *Wall Street Journal*, p. 5.

Peterson, B. (1987, August 27). Northwest courts victims survivors. *Washington Post*, p. A8.

Priest at Detroit crash suspected as impostor. (1987, September 14). *New York Times*, p. B12.

Problems nag airline since merger. (1987, August 17). *New York Times*, p. B5.

Rise in fear of flying linked to Detroit crash. (1987, August 27). *New York Times*, p. 16.

Shrivastava, P. (1987). *Bhopal: Anatomy of a crisis*. Cambridge, MA: Ballinger.

Six who missed ill-fated flight. (1987, August 19). *New York Times*, p. A18.

Small, W. J. (1991). Exxon Valdez: How to spend billions and still get a black eye. *Public Relations Review, 17*, 9–25.

Smith, J. (1987, November 19). Hearing's real issue is liability. *Detroit News*, p. 1.

Smith, J., Martin, R., & Warren, H. (1987, November 20). Crash issues don't settle issue of flaps. *Detroit News*, p. 1A.

Stengel, R. (1987, August 31). Sifting through the wreckage. *Time*, pp. 15–16.

Warren, H., & Smith, J. J. (1987, November). Crew ignored policy, pilots say. *Detroit News*, p. A1.

Wilkerson, I. (1987, August 20). Cockpit data suggest jet flaps were not positioned for takeoff. *New York Times*, p. B16.

Witkin, R. (1987, August 18). Computer warned pilots in crash of stall danger. *New York Times*, p. A1.

Chapter 6 ———————————————————————

American Airlines Flight 191

By the late 1970s, the airline industry was facing numerous challenges from deregulation. An unexpected challenge came in May 1979 following the American Airlines Flight 191 disaster, the deadliest commercial airliner crash in U.S. aviation history. The case of American Airlines Flight 191 reveals how a highly interdependent industry can influence an organization's efforts to defend its image following a crisis. The investigation into the crash uncovered evidence which impacted the entire industry. The NTSB's findings directly implicated not only American, but the aircraft manufacturer, McDonnell Douglas, and the FAA. The FAA's grounding of McDonnell Douglas's DC-10, a consequence of the crash, impacted the manufacturer and other airlines flying the aircraft. Consequently, American's communication efforts after the crash were effected by a high level of stakeholder involvement.

PRE-CRISIS

The first regularly scheduled flight of what was to become American Airlines was made in 1926 by Charles Lindbergh, Robertson Airline Company's chief pilot, in a DH-4 biplane on a mail route from St. Louis to Chicago. In 1929, Robertson and a number of small airline companies consolidated into American Airways, which was reorganized in 1934 as American Airlines (American Airlines, 1989). In 1936, American initiated service of its DC-3 and Douglas Sleeper Transports (DST). The DC-3 proved economical, and by 1938 the airline had achieved its first profitable year. A year later, American moved its headquarters from Chicago to New York City, following the opening of LaGuardia Airport. It was there the airline instituted its first American Admirals Club for VIP travelers. American continued to profit with new and innovative approaches. For example, recognizing the financial success of hot meals on its flights, American formed a subsidiary, Sky Chefs, in the early 1940s to operate its in-flight meal service. During World War II, American Airlines provided transport services for the military. Assisting the war effort enabled American to expand into international markets. Through the years, American Airlines achieved a number of "firsts," including the introduction of the first transcontinental nonstop jet service between New York and Los Angeles, the first computerized reservations system in the airline industry, the introduction of the world's first scheduled DC-10 service, and the introduction of the Super Saver fare program (American Airlines, 1989).

The 1970s were a time of turbulence and growth for the airline industry. Airlines experienced the addition of widebody aircrafts to their fleets and the onset of the energy crisis. The first half of the 1970s saw traffic growth rates decline, but by 1977 the growth rate had increased to record levels. Deregulation increased competition among airlines by allowing them to set rates and pick routes without government direction. Deregulation triggered changing patterns of travel, bargain airfares, increases in traffic, and mergers. In 1979, American Airlines headquarters relocated to Dallas–Fort Worth Airport, Texas. After deregulation, the airline encountered a large domestic expansion. American Airlines was the second largest carrier in the United States in terms of 1978 total revenue passenger miles and served fifty-six cities in twenty-nine states, as well as Montreal, Toronto, Mexico City, Acapulco, Bermuda, Puerto Rico, and other points in the Caribbean (*Standard New York Stock Exchange Reports*, 1979). In January 1979, the company was approved for service on twenty-one new routes, adding nine new cities.

CRISIS

American Airlines Flight 191 was a regularly scheduled passenger flight from Chicago, Illinois, to Los Angeles, California. On May 25, 1979, Flight 191, a McDonnell Douglas DC-10, taxied from the gate at Chicago–O'Hare International Airport, Illinois. The passengers had begun their Memorial Day weekend journey. On movie screens in the jet, passengers could watch a closed-circuit TV picture from the cockpit, while on stereo headsets they could hear the commands of O'Hare's air traffic controllers (Williams, 1979). Weather was clear at the time of departure.

At 3:02 P.M. (CDT), Flight 191 was cleared for takeoff. "American one-ninety one underway," acknowledged the captain (NTSB, 1979). Prior to rotation, sections of the left, or No. 1, engine pylon structure came off the aircraft. About the time Flight 191's nose wheel was lifting off the ground, the entire No. 1 engine (one of three) and pylon separated from the aircraft, went over the top of the wing and fell to the runway. Approximately 6 thousand feet down runway 32R, Flight 191 lifted off, climbed out in a wing-level attitude, and reached an altitude of about 300 feet above the ground with its wings still level. The aircraft soon began to turn and roll to the left, nose pitched down, then descended, continuing to roll left until the wings were past the vertical position. Northwest of the departure end of runway 32R, Flight 191 hit the ground, nose and left wing first, in an abandoned airfield beside the Oasis Mobile Home Park. The aircraft exploded, broke apart, and scattered into the open field and trailer park. Fiery remnants struck some of the mobile homes nearby, severely damaging three of them (Kneeland, 1979).

POST-CRISIS

Search and Recovery

Air traffic controllers at O'Hare were aware Flight 191 was in trouble immediately after takeoff. In the control tower, the watch supervisor pushed the emergency button even before the aircraft hit the ground (Estep, 1979). Almost immediately the crash area was cleared. The supervisor closed the runway Flight 191 had lifted off moments before, as well as all the other runways on the north side of the field. Some runways were reopened later, but departing flights were delayed an hour or more (Feaver & Warden, 1979). O'Hare, packed with holiday weekend travelers, closed briefly. Residents of the mobile home park were ordered out by officials for fear the fire might spread. Fire trucks, ambulances, and police vehicles from the city and surrounding suburbs rushed to the area. Most rescue workers were kept away from the plane by the 150-foot-high flames, only able to mill around the scene keeping onlookers back and out of possible danger. Burning fuel created what some referred to as a "napalm" effect (Williams, 1979). Hours after the crash, smoke still poured from the wreckage.

While area hospitals were placed on alert immediately after the crash, it was soon apparent there were no survivors. On board Flight 191, all 255 passengers and fifteen crew members were killed; on the ground two people were killed and two sustained second and third degree burns (NTSB, 1979). It was nearly 6:00 P.M. before the first bodies were removed to a temporary morgue set up in an American Airlines aircraft hangar. By 11:00 P.M., 250 bodies had been removed from the wreckage (Kneeland, 1979). Medical and dental experts from around the country and a special FBI team assisted in the task of identifying victims (Juneau & Koziol, 1979). Because human remains were so badly burned and dismembered, it was questionable whether victims could be identified.

Investigation

The National Transportation Safety Board was notified immediately after the crash and promptly dispatched its fifteen-member go-team to the crash site (Young, 1979a). The team included one member of the five-member board and experts in structures, electrical and hydraulic systems, powerplants and engines, operations, air traffic control, meteorology, human factors, maintenance, and witnesses (Byrne & Seibel, 1979). At 7:30 the following morning, the NTSB convened a meeting of all agencies involved and formed committees to investigate various aspects of the disaster. Approximately 110 to 115 persons were involved in the investigation, including representatives from the NTSB, the FAA, American Airlines, Douglas Aircraft Company, Allied Pilots Association, Flight Engineers International Association, Association of Professional Flight Attendants, General Electric Company, and the Professional Air Traffic Controller Organization (Galloway, 1979; NTSB, 1979). Investigative groups were established for operations, air traffic control, aircraft structures, aircraft systems, powerplants, human factors, witnesses, cockpit voice recorders, flight data recorder, maintenance records, aircraft performance, metallurgy, and engineering (NTSB, 1979).

The investigators' task was complicated by the fact that the plane had virtually pulverized on impact. The disintegration of the aircraft structure was so extensive that little useful data were obtained from the post-impact examination of the wreckage (NTSB, 1979). The digital flight data recorder and cockpit voice recorder, however, were recovered intact and flown to the NTSB's lab in Washington (Byrne & Seibel, 1979). An accident survey was made by the NTSB and markers were placed where various parts of the plane were found (Galloway, 1979).

NTSB investigators began their day at 6:00 A.M. and ended with nightly debriefing sessions which coordinated their efforts (Gelman, 1979). Each group pursued its designated task. Human factors explored the situation in the control tower and the background information on the entire flight crew. The weather group considered all circumstances related to weather conditions at the time of the crash, such as wind velocity and direction. Maintenance specialists impounded all maintenance records relating to the airplane. Other groups considered the operational history of the crew and aircraft (Byrne & Seibel, 1979). The group assigned to witnesses interviewed those who saw the plane takeoff and crash. Through Chicago television stations and newspapers, the NTSB appealed for anyone having photographs of the plane in flight; they wanted to take a look at the wing structure (Feaver, 1979a).

The powerplants and structures specialists focused on the charred debris of the plane. The powerplant group tagged and marked all the engine fragments, plotted their position on a wreckage distribution chart, and stored them in a nearby American Airline's hangar for further examination (Gelman, 1979). The engine was carefully examined on the runway and later moved to a hangar where it was disassembled (Feaver, 1979a). The plane's three engines were transferred by truck to American Airline's heavy-duty maintenance headquarters in Tulsa, Oklahoma, for a detailed lab inspection by the NTSB. Structures examined the frame of the DC-10 in an effort to determine what caused the engine to disengage from the wing. Other experts examined how the plane behaved after the engine fell off, what the pilot tried to do to bring his plane to a safe landing, and why he failed (Byrne & Seibel, 1979). Many of the investigators returned to Washington after four days at the site of the crash; however, a few remained to continue their tasks.

Preliminary Findings

Questions of sabotage were quickly eliminated by the FBI following its routine post-crash probe (Feaver & Warden, 1979). In the preliminary stages the NTSB explored various factors. Meteorological conditions at the time of the accident were explored, but the weather at the airport was clear (NTSB, 1979). There were no complications with either airport conditions or air traffic control procedures. Personnel information indicated the flight crew and attendants were qualified. A review of the autopsies and toxicological examinations of the flight crew disclosed no evidence of preexisting physiological problems which could have affected their performance (NTSB, 1979). Little information could be obtained from the CVR. The NTSB stated they were able to hear the flight crew complete the pre-flight checklist as they taxied to the runway. Moments after the plane had reached the speed sufficient for flight, the word "damn" was heard on the tape. This was the last word on the recording. A power loss shortly after takeoff wiped out all but a few words (Young, 1979a). Three days after the crash, the NTSB stated at a press briefing that evidence from the DFDR showed the pilot and his crew responded promptly and correctly ("DC-10s face grounding threat," 1979).

The NTSB also addressed questions concerning survival. Early reports from the scene put the death toll as high as 279 people, but American and NTSB officials stated the plane carried 255 passengers, 5 cockpit crew, and 10 flight attendants (Feaver & Warden, 1979). The Safety Board eliminated the possibility of survivors because impact forces exceeded human tolerances. All aboard were believed to have died instantly.

Though the exact sequence of events would not be known for weeks, the NTSB confirmed that the left engine of the aircraft fell off just as the plane was leaving the runway (Young, 1979a). Witnesses assisted in providing accounts of the crash. The air traffic controller who saw the engine fall radioed from the tower, "American 191, do you want to come back? If so, what runway do you want?" There was no answer (Young, 1979a). The trench dug in the field indicated the nose struck first followed by the left wing (Feaver, 1979a). Contributing to the explosion was the fact that the plane was carrying nearly 30 thousand pounds of volatile kerosene fuel (Young, 1979a).

The pylon, which attaches the engine to the wing, soon became the primary focus of the investigation. A DC-10's engine is attached to the wing in three places. At one connection there is a thrust-link, a steel shackle with two bushings or pipes that absorb the engine's 40-thousand-pound thrust (Sheils,

1979). Each bushing is held by a bolt. At first, public attention was drawn to one bolt that attached a link to the main structure of the wing. On the second day of the investigation, investigators stated they were looking for a small, hexagonal bolt that was missing from the mounting assembly of the engine which dropped. This was the first major clue in the investigation (Feaver, 1979a). The following day the bolt was found, cracked and broken in the grass along the left side of the runway. At a press conference the NTSB stated the bolt explained why the engine fell off; however, they stressed that their concerns about the reliability of the engine mounting assembly went beyond the broken bolt (Young, 1979a). The whole technical area of the engine attachment to the wing was under suspicion. Investigators stated the bolt cracked because of fatigue. There was no evidence the engine struck the aircraft.

In making the announcement about the fractured bolt, the NTSB stated it did not explain why the jet crashed (Feaver, 1979b). The three-engine plane should have had enough power to continue taking off even with the loss of one engine. The NTSB Vice Chair stated at a press conference he considered the loss of the engine the first event in a sequence that led up to the crash (Feaver, 1979b). There was no evidence of any pre-impact malfunctions. A few days after the NTSB commented on the fractured bolt they announced that the bolt did not appear to cause the accident, but rather the bolt broke as a result of the accident (Byrne & O'Connor, 1979). Furthermore, other parts of the pylon failed. The Safety Board revealed that an aft flange connecting the engine support pylon to the wing was also broken in half. It was later revealed the collapse of the flange came first, apparently because of metal fatigue, and that the bolt had fractured in an overstress position.

Investigators pursued the possibility that as the engine assembly tore from the left wing it ruptured all three hydraulic lines that independently carry hydraulic power to move flight controls (Witkin, 1979a). Preliminary research indicated that the aircraft lost two of its three hydraulic systems at some point during the thirty-eight-second flight (Feaver & Kiernan, 1979). Experts further explored which hydraulic lines were severed as the engine came off the plane. Evidence indicated that after the pylon damaged the hydraulic system, the aircraft's flaps retracted prematurely, which caused it to fall. The right wing continued to provide the extra lift (Young, 1979b). This appeared to account for the roll of the aircraft.

Probable Cause

A week after the crash, investigators had a clearer understanding of what happened to American Airlines Flight 191. Just as the plane took to the air, a rear strut in the engine pylon cracked as a result of metal fatigue. With the engine at maximum thrust, the thrust link bolt also snapped. At that point the jet engine pivoted upward, wrenching off the last pylon connection at the front of the wing. The top of the pylon apparently knifed through the front edge of the wing. The engine and the pylon then continued up and over the wing before falling to the runway (Nicodemus, 1979). The departure of the engine not only ripped off its own hydraulic connection, but the pylon's slice through the wing apparently severed a line serving the second of the plane's three hydraulic systems. This then cut off the pilot's hydraulic control of the left wing's outboard slats. The slats then retracted after being pushed back into the wing by air pressure.

Evidence indicated that other parts of the pylon failed. This raised questions as to whether the McDonnell Douglas DC-10 had a design problem. At the recommendation of the NTSB, the FAA ordered an inspection of all DC-10 engine mounts and then grounded the fleet temporarily (Gelman, 1979). During inspections, a United Airlines DC-10 engine pylon was discovered seriously damaged. The pylons became the primary focus of the investigation. On June 4, the NTSB stated the crash may have resulted from improper American Airlines maintenance procedures. The NTSB indicated that a forklift truck used during maintenance may have caused cracks in the engine mounting assemblies of some planes (Byrne, 1979a). Other airlines had also used this procedure.

McDonnell Douglas, the DC-10 manufacturer, suggested to airlines that when performing maintenance on the DC-10 pylon they must first remove the engine, then the support pylon. The NTSB's investigation indicated that at the American Airlines maintenance base in Tulsa, Oklahoma, the engine and pylon were being removed and replaced as one unit by a forklift truck, a procedure that saved time ("DC-10s wing crack," 1979). The NTSB suspected that using a forklift in this operation could have caused damage to vital parts. As the giant unit was replaced with a forklift, investigators found it easier to strike the aft pylon bulkhead flange against the wing support, thus inducing a crack. During the Congressional hearings held in response to the crash, the NTSB Chair stated that the Flight 191 aircraft sustained a major crack in the wing mounting during an overhaul in March, but it was not clear if the crack in the bulkhead was a factor in the engine and pylon separating from the wing ("DC-10s wing crack," 1979). This evidence suggested that American's procedures may have damaged the structure.

Public Hearing

Beginning July 30, 1979, a ten-day hearing convened in Rosemont, Illinois. The FAA, American Airlines, Douglas Aircraft Company, Allied Pilots Association, Flight Engineers International Association, Transport Workers Union, and the Air Line Pilots Association were all represented (NTSB, 1979). Those testifying included engineers from McDonnell Douglas and the FAA, and a NASA scientist. Issues discussed during the hearings included maintenance procedures, FAA certification procedures, and the DC-10 design.

Conclusions and Recommendations

From the analysis of evidence gathered during the fact-finding phase, the NTSB determined the probable cause of the crash on December 21, 1979 (NTSB, 1979). The asymmetrical stall and subsequent roll of the aircraft was ultimately linked to the separation of the No. 1 engine and pylon which resulted in the retraction of the left-wing outboard leading-edge slats and the loss of the stall warning and slat disagreement indication systems. The failure of the pylon structure was caused by damage from improper maintenance procedures. Among the factors contributing to the accident were vulnerable designs, such as the pylon attach points and the leading edge slat system; deficiencies in the FAA's surveillance and reporting systems, which failed to detect and prevent the use of improper maintenance procedures; and poor communications among the operators, the manufacturer, and the FAA on the particulars regarding previous maintenance damage incidents.

The Safety Board placed much of the blame on the airline, and attached somewhat less blame to McDonnell Douglas and the FAA. The Board's official ruling of probable cause was highly technical. As a result of the accident and the investigation, the NTSB made eight specific recommendations to the FAA which covered the range of FAA responsibilities from approving the design of an airplane, to establishing appropriate maintenance procedures and piloting techniques, to guaranteeing that problems, once discovered, are made known throughout the industry.

Industry Response

The FAA

The crash of American Flight 191 created a crisis not only for the airline, but for the entire industry, particularly the FAA and McDonnell Douglas. At first, indications were that the FAA, McDonnell Douglas, or both were at fault. American Airlines appeared to be a victim. The harshest criticism was directed at the FAA, including questions about how well the FAA protects public safety. Investigators' findings revealed gaps and compromises in the FAA's design and maintenance safety review systems. For example, following the discovery that improper maintenance procedures appeared to cause the cracks in the pylons of the plane that crashed and in the pylons of other DC-10s owned by American and Continental Airlines, investigators found that airlines had been free to make changes in the manufacturers' approved maintenance procedures without informing the FAA. Further, the FAA had not received complete information on the maintenance and operation of commercial aircraft from the airlines and manufacturer.

Additional evidence presented by the NTSB called into question some of the FAA's judgments about the DC-10 design and its monitoring of day-today operations. Throughout the investigation the FAA received criticism from members of Congress, consumer groups, and members of the aviation industry. Congress, responding to concerns that the FAA's certification procedures for safety and airworthiness were lax, scheduled hearings on air safety. Consumer advocate Ralph Nader attacked both the FAA and the DC-10, denouncing it as "the airline's version of the accident prone Chevrolet Corvair" (Sheils, 1979).

DC-10 Grounding

Early findings by investigators caused the NTSB to recommend the FAA issue an emergency airworthiness directive to inspect all pylon attach points on all DC-10 aircraft (North, 1979). This recommendation by the Safety Board ultimately resulted in a chain of responses by the FAA. The FAA immediately responded to the NTSB's recommendation by issuing the emergency airworthiness directive on May 28. The directive gave a compliance time of 3:00 A.M. (EDT), on May 29 for completion of inspection and added that any aircraft not inspected by that time could not depart on a revenue flight. All operators were directed to report the results of inspections to the FAA. In carrying out the inspections required by the directive, deficiencies in engine mounting assemblies were found on fifteen to twenty McDonnell Douglas DC-10s (Feaver, 1979c). FAA officials issued a grounding order for the DC-10s as of 1:00 P.M. on May 29. Operators were directed to conduct a detailed visual inspection of the pylon. Inspections were to be carried out every 100 hours of flight, or every ten days. The grounding order halted the flights of approximately 135 DC-10s registered in the United States. While the order did not apply to foreign operators of the aircraft, many followed the U.S. procedures.

Following the NTSB's findings concerning a questionable maintenance procedure, an additional inspection was ordered by the FAA. On June 6, after the discovery of more flaws in more planes, the Federal Aviation administrator ordered an immediate indefinite halt to flights of all 138 DC-10 jumbo jets operated by U.S. airlines (Witkin, 1979b). The open-ended grounding would last until tests either pinpointed any basic flaws or proved that the McDonnell Douglas plane met stiff design criteria. The airline industry was in chaos. For American, United, and Northwest Airlines, all of whom had a large number of DC-10s in their fleets, the grounding resulted in major financial losses. It was estimated the grounding cost the airline industry $6 million a day (Byrne, 1979a).

McDonnell Douglas

The crash of American Flight 191 and the subsequent investigation also created a crisis for McDonnell Douglas. The manufacturer was faced with a tarnished reputation as a result of its DC-10 design, costly repairs, and lawsuits that could total more than $100 million ("Why FAA draws fire," 1979). Further, the grounding and suspension of its certificate of airworthiness for the DC-10 heightened uncertainty about the aircraft's sales prospects and the possible damage to the McDonnell Douglas Corporation. McDonnell Douglas took great exception to the FAA's method of dealing with its fleet of DC-10s, calling the suspension of flight extreme and unwarranted (Witkin, 1979b). The company also lashed out at American Airlines and others whose procedures had been contrary to the manufacturer's recommended procedures. On June 15, 1979, Douglas asked the NTSB to revoke the FAA's suspension of the DC-10 operating authority, stating the grounding was not supported by substantial and reliable evidence ("Judge delays action," 1979).

Media Coverage

Following the crash of American Flight 191, media reported on the NTSB's investigation, air safety, and liability. Early reports by the NTSB implied the crash was due to a design problem, focusing attention on McDonnell Douglas. There were reports on the grounding of the DC-10 from a number of perspectives, including the airlines, the manufacturer, and the FAA. Media accused the FAA of reacting too slowly and tentatively and of going too far in indefinitely grounding the DC-10.

CRISIS COMMUNICATION:
AN ANALYSIS OF AMERICAN'S COMMUNICATION

American Airlines implemented its crisis plan following the crash. The airline communicated openly and assigned company representatives to victims' families (Nelson, 1990). In addition to the CEO, appropriate airline executives from various departments were present or in contact. Names of crew members and passengers were not disclosed until families were notified (Lipinski, 1979). Requests for information were filled as quickly as possible. A sales representative was assigned to each victims' family to provide the necessary transportation and lodging and to help with funeral arrangements. Such assistance enabled the airline to demonstrate its human conscience and attempt to offset the negative feelings associated with the crash. The crash was expected to become the most expensive in U.S. aviation history. American, however, indicated it had adequate insurance to cover the claims.

Following the crash, American Airlines communicated as openly as possible with the media. A review of media reports revealed no criticism of the airline for its response immediately after the crash. American Airlines's crisis was complicated by findings from the investigation into the crash of Flight 191. Evidence indicated the airline's maintenance procedures caused the crash. According to the NTSB, American Airlines developed a procedure for removing the engine for reasons of efficiency, safety, and economy. Though the procedure was within its authority, evidence indicated that American's engineering and maintenance personnel implemented the procedure without a thorough evaluation to ensure it would not damage the pylon structure. The NTSB concluded there were deficiencies within the airline's maintenance program which contributed to the accident. The engineering department failed to ascertain the damage-inducing potential from the manufacturer's recommended procedure. The department also failed to adequately evaluate the performance of the forklift to assure its suitability for the task. The assignment of blame required the airline to defend its position and image. American's efforts to defend itself against the assignment of blame are considered in the following analysis.

Responding to the Issue of Blame

The NTSB's finding suggesting that the crash was in some way related to damage done by American Airlines personnel necessitated an immediate response from the airline. American evaded responsibility by pleading ignorance, providing excuses, and scapegoating. The airline pleaded ignorance to avoid responsibility for the crash by contending its maintenance procedures were completely reasonable based on the information available to the airline at that time ("Douglas aircraft denies," 1979). American Airlines argued that McDonnell Douglas failed to adequately warn the airline of maintenance procedure problems. American Airlines officials stated that because a memo questioning its procedures sent by Douglas in November 1978 had not been seen, they could not assess its significance. The airline's vice president of maintenance stated Douglas's concern about the procedure had not been brought to his attention. "I can't tell you what a profound effect Douglas's concern would have had on me. That would have received my immediate attention," he claimed (Feazel, 1979). His statement implied that had the airline been made aware of the potential hazard of the procedure, it never would have been used.

In an effort to justify its actions, American offered the excuse that altering the approved sequence of removal was safer because there were fewer steps than in the Douglas procedure. Furthermore, American explained that Douglas representatives had participated in its procedures for engine and pylon installation and these procedures were used by most airlines flying DC-10s.

The airline attempted to avoid responsibility for the accident by making McDonnell Douglas and the FAA scapegoats. American argued a manufacturing defect in the DC-10 caused the accident. During Congressional hearings, American's senior vice president testified that while maintenance may have caused the crack, it was also possible there might have been a manufacturing error (Feaver, 1979, July 13). Thereafter, a "manufacturing error" became the airline's defense. Testimony by American officials during the NTSB hearing supported this claim. American's vice president of maintenance testified the DC-10 pylon's design was vulnerable to maintenance damage ("Feud over DC-10 maintenance," 1979). Additional blame was directed at the FAA. American's mechanics testified that they had never seen an FAA inspector nor, as far as they knew, had their work been inspected (Feazel, 1979).

American's principal accuser, McDonnell Douglas, criticized the airline for not following the manufacturer's recommended procedures. The airline responded by attacking the manufacturer's process and quality. During the NTSB hearings, American created the impression that McDonnell Douglas's maintenance procedures were not always practical (NTSB, 1979). Further, American's vice president implied negligence on Douglas's part by insisting that two McDonnell Douglas representatives had watched the airline change its very first DC-10 pylon in 1977 and had observed numerous such changes since then and never objected to the one-step method ("Debacle of the DC-10," 1979). American criticized the DC-10 and suggested the inadequate pylon design was a result of poor quality control at Douglas.

In October 1979, American submitted a brief to the NTSB arguing its position. American indicated that it had requested and committed itself to extensive structural and system changes which McDonnell Douglas had agreed to incorporate. The airline attempted to right the wrong and showed its willingness to correct the problem. Following the NTSB's determination of probable cause, American Airlines stated that it did not agree with the emphasis on maintenance-induced damage as part of the probable cause (Feaver, 1979d).

American received criticism for its response during the investigation. Editorials in the *Washington Post* stated American Airlines and McDonnell Douglas were "more interested in passing the buck than solving the problem" ("Checking out the DC-10s," 1979, p. D6) and characterized the NTSB hearing as an argument between American and McDonnell Douglas over responsibility, noting that the "charges and countercharges are doing very little for the reputation of the DC-10 or the airline industry" ("Arguing about the DC-10s," 1979, p. B6).

EVALUATION OF STRATEGIES

Was American Airlines successful in defending its image against allegations of blame for the crash of Flight 191? The severity of the disaster, its accidental nature, and the airline's performance history must be considered when evaluating American Airlines's communication following the crash. First, the crash of Flight 191 became the most fatal air crash in U.S. aviation history. The tragedy claimed 270 persons aboard the aircraft and two persons on the ground. Two more on the ground were injured. The extreme nature of the event presented a clear threat to American's image and required a response. The public needed reassurance that a similar event would not happen. Second, evidence indicated that the crash was caused by a maintenance procedure performed by American Airlines which went against the manufacturer's guidelines. This suggested that the accident was preventable and controllable. Furthermore, American considered the procedure more efficient and economical. Third, American's positive image prior to the crisis provided the company with credibility in defending its position. American Airlines's positive image and performance history likely influenced the airline's effectiveness in responding immediately after the crisis. The company was successful in offsetting some of the negative impressions created by the crisis. These three factors were influential in determining the appropriateness and effectiveness of strategic options.

American primarily employed strategies to reduce responsibility for blame as its line of defense. In light of the highly technical and complicated nature of the accident, this appears to have been an appropriate choice of strategy. Initially, NTSB findings suggested American Airlines was a victim of a flawed aircraft design and FAA negligence. Later evidence implicated the airline's maintenance procedures. The carrier did not deny its maintenance procedure caused the crack in the pylon; rather, it contended that it was unaware of the hazardous nature of the procedure. American argued that it believed the procedure it was using was safer than the manufacturer's prescribed procedure because it involved fewer steps. In other words, there was no intention on the part of the airline to do wrong.

American used the strategy of scapegoating to lessen its responsibility for the accident by placing primary responsibility on McDonnell Douglas, the aircraft manufacturer, and the FAA. According to the airline, the FAA failed in its responsibility to inspect the carrier's maintenance procedure. Had the FAA inspected the airline's maintenance procedure, the company would have realized the danger associated with its process and would have taken immediate corrective action. American's argument against Douglas was twofold. First, the airline argued McDonnell Douglas was aware of the airline's procedure for pylon removal, yet never objected to the process. This implied the airline could only assume it was performing a safe procedure. This argument, along with the fact that other carriers used similar procedures, justified the carrier's actions. Second, American argued that the DC-10 had a manufacturing defect which made it vulnerable to maintenance damage. At times, American was aggressive in its efforts to reduce responsibility. Placing primary responsibility on McDonnell Douglas and using aggressive tactics toward the manufacturer may have diffused blame, but they also created the perception of an airline more concerned over liability than safety. Rather than lessening the credibility of its accuser, American's attack of Douglas was perceived by media as an attempt to "pass the buck." The competitive environment resulting from deregulation served to magnify the conflict between American and the DC-10 manufacturer. The aggressive style used by the airline appeared to backfire, overpowering any positive impact of communication strategies designed to lessen responsibility. Perhaps American would have been more successful in restoring image had it not openly "battled" Douglas.

As in the case of Northwest Airlines, we see that concerns for liability appeared to outweigh concerns for image. American failed to defend its image as an air carrier concerned about safety. At a time when there was great uncertainty about air travel and concerns about the implications of deregulation, it was critical the carrier reassure the public that it valued safety. Strategies of ingratiation and making amends would have been appropriate choices. American did demonstrate its concern by correcting the problem; however, this act occurred after the airline had developed an image of being more concerned with liability than safety.

EPILOGUE

American's 1979 year-end results fell far short of the record performance they had in 1978. Earnings amounted to $87.4 million in 1979 compared with the record $134.4 million in 1978 (American Airlines, 1979). The airline attributed a significant decline in earnings not only to the American Flight 191 accident and DC-10 grounding, but also to the tremendous rise in fuel cost, severe weather conditions in the first quarter in areas served by the airline, and pricing policies initiated by competitors.

CONCLUSION

The case of American Airlines Flight 191 teaches four important lessons:

1. Communicating promptly, openly, and adequately with media lessens the chances of negative media coverage.
2. Because a crisis can threaten the legitimacy of an entire industry, groups that are part of a particular industry should be prepared to handle the consequences associated with an accident.
3. Communication strategies that hedge responsibility are potentially more effective in crises which are extremely complicated and technical and implicate a number of stakeholders.
4. The strategy of aggression or attack can easily backfire and overshadow positive strategies.

A failure to communicate in a timely, open, and sufficient way increases uncertainty about the company in question. In other words, delaying communication and being tight-lipped with media creates the perception that a company has something to hide, and often results in negative media coverage. Prior to the crash of Flight 191, American Airlines was in an enviable position in an increasingly competitive and rapidly changing industry. Following the crash, the company communicated as openly as possible with the media. As a result, American received no criticism for its immediate response to the crash.

A number of organizations have demonstrated through their actions or inactions the negative consequences of delaying disclosures and failing to be open with media. For example, NASA's delayed actions following the explosion of Challenger on January 28, 1986, served to compound an already critical situation. Initially, NASA isolated itself from the general public and press, retreating into what some referred to as a "Fortress NASA." Five hours passed before the agency held its first news conference (Brown, 1990). NASA created the impression that it had something to hide. Consequently, NASA's silence damaged its image, credibility, and support. Exxon's slow reaction in terms of managing and communicating publicly about the worst oil spill in American history created the impression of a company unconcerned about the accident (Benoit, 1995). The company received extreme criticism by the press.

The legitimacy of an entire industry can be threatened by a crisis. Crisis has been described as a complex system of interdependent events involving multiple conflicting stakeholders. In a highly interdependent industry, one organization's crisis can easily result in a crisis for industry stakeholders. Airline crashes, for example, typically result from a number of factors which may implicate various groups. The airline which operates the aircraft that crashes is always a major stakeholder. Other industry groups may be legally liable for damages caused by their products, actions, or services, including aircraft design engineers, airframe and engine manufacturers, government groups (such as the FAA, ATC [Air Traffic Control], or NWS), and external groups such as outside contractors hired by a carrier. The case of American Airlines Flight 191 demonstrates how stakeholders not directly linked to a crisis can be affected. The problems detected in the DC-10s following the crash of American Flight 191 affected not only the entire DC-10 fleet around the world, but the McDonnell Douglas company as a whole, the future of other airplanes, and the entire airline industry worldwide. Because an airline accident can impact the entire industry, the industry's image is at stake whenever a crash occurs.

Other organizational crises have demonstrated this point as well. Bhopal, Chernobyl, and Challenger all influenced the future development of their related industries—chemicals, nuclear energy, and space (Pauchant & Mitroff, 1992), respectively. Each of these crises impacted public perceptions of their respective industries, and, in the case of Union Carbide, raised questions about the role of multinational companies in Third World countries (Shrivastava, 1987). Therefore, the better prepared each industry group is to handle an accident, the easier it is for the entire industry to survive the crisis.

Strategies that offer excuses may be more effective in situations which are extremely complicated and technical and implicate more than one stakeholder. A crisis situation in which the probable cause is clearly identifiable offers little ambiguity. In other words, available facts either support or contradict accusations of blame. But in situations where the probable cause is difficult to determine and other stakeholders are implicated there is more room to hedge responsibility. The strategy of scapegoating, for example, may be more effective in such a situation. Scapegoating diffuses blame and creates the impression that no one organization is solely responsible for an event. McDonnell Douglas and the FAA became scapegoats for American Airlines. The airline argued that the DC-10 had a manufacturing error and that the FAA failed in its role of inspecting maintenance procedures. The highly complex nature of the accident and the fact that McDonnell Douglas and the FAA were implicated in investigative findings made the strategy of scapegoating reasonable. Of course, corporate credibility would enhance strategies to evade responsibility.

Following the Alaskan oil spill, Exxon attempted to make scapegoats out of the captain for causing the disaster and Alaska state officials and the Coast Guard for delaying the cleanup efforts (Benoit, 1995). The facts clearly assigned blame to Exxon. This made scapegoating a difficult strategy for Exxon to successfully execute. Joseph Hazelwood, captain of the Valdez, was easily an identifiable scapegoat (Benoit, 1995). Once the results of his blood tests were announced, Exxon fired Hazelwood. While it appeared Exxon had eliminated the source of the accident in an effort to prevent a recurrence, the fact that the company had been aware of Hazelwood's alcohol problem and still made him responsible for one of its largest tankers suggested Exxon shared the blame. This underscores Benoit's contention that when shifting blame or scapegoating it is important to place it on someone or something clearly disassociated with the one shifting the blame. Attempting to make scapegoats out of Alaskan officials and the Coast Guard was inappropriate due to the fact that Exxon was ultimately responsible for the spill and the subsequent cleanup.

When accusations of blame are made by certain individuals or groups, a company's initial instinct may be to retaliate with verbal sparring in an effort to defend against such charges. In some instances, counterattacks may serve to undermine the credibility of the accuser and restore the image of the accused (Benoit, 1995). Furthermore, attention may be redirected to the accuser. In the case of American Airlines we see how battling blame through the strategy of aggression or attack can create the perception that liability is of greater concern than safety. Moreover, aggression can translate as "desperation." The negative interpretations associated with an attack can also overshadow potentially effective strategies. This suggests that when responding to accusations of blame companies must weigh the potential outcomes of aggressive strategies. As shown in Chapter 5, strategic communication choices must be made in light of a broad frame of reference, taking into account the many variables which could determine the success or failure of such a choice.

REFERENCES

American Airlines. (1979). *Annual report* (SEC File No. 1-2691). D/FW Airport, TX: American Airlines.

American Airlines. (1989, September). Corporate fact sheet. DFW Airport, TX: American Airlines.

Arguing about the DC-10s. (1979, August 12). *Washington Post*, p. B6.

Benoit, W. L. (1995). *Accounts, excuses, and apologies: A theory of image restoration strategies*. Albany: State University of New York Press.

Brown, M. H. (1990). Past and present images of Challenger in NASA's organizational culture. In B. D. Sypher (Ed.), *Case studies in organizational communication* (pp. 111–124). New York: Guilford Press.

Byrne, D. (1979a, June 5). Third DC-10 grounding; hint safety-check damage. *Chicago Sun Times*, pp. C10–11 (NewsBank, 1979, TRA 34).

Byrne, D. (1979b, June 20). DC-10s groundings costing airlines $6 million a day. *Chicago Sun Times*, p. A11 (NewsBank, 1979, TRA 35).

Byrne, D., & O'Connor, P. J. (1979, June 1). Unlikely that broken bolt caused crash; panel finds. *Chicago Sun Times*, p. B14 (NewsBank, 1979, TRA 34).

Byrne, D., & Seibel, T. P. (1979, May 27). How can an engine fall off of a plane? *Chicago Sun Times*, p. B10 (NewsBank, 1979, TRA 34).

Checking out the DC-10s. (1979, June 10). *Washington Post*, p. D6.

DC-10s face grounding threat. (1979, May 29). *Chicago Sun Times*, pp. B2–3 (NewsBank, 1979, TRA 26).

DC-10s wing crack is laid to overhaul. (1979, June 19). *New York Times*, p. A18.

Debacle of the DC-10. (1979, June 18). *Time*, pp. 14–17.

Douglas aircraft denies agreeing to DC-10 pylon modifications. (1979, October 22). *Aviation Week & Space Technology*, p. 14.

Estep, G. (1979, June 3). No panic when tower hits button. *Chicago Tribune*, p. 16.

Feaver, D. B. (1979, July 13). DC-10 builder, airline official trade charges. *Washington Post*, p. A2.

Feaver, D. B. (1979a, May 27). Missing bolt is first clue in probe of jet crash. *Washington Post*, p. A1.

Feaver, D. B. (1979b, May 28). DC-10 grounding eyed; Broken bolt is found. *Washington Post*, p. A1.

Feaver, D. B. (1979c, May 31). Engine mount faults found on 15 DC-10s. *Washington Post*, pp. B7–8.

Feaver, D. B. (1979d, December 22). Crash probe scores FAA and American Airlines. *Washington Post*, p. A2.

Feaver, D. B., & Kiernan, L. A. (1979, May 29). FAA sets DC-10 deadline. *Washington Post*, p. A1.

Feaver, D. B., & Warden, R. (1979, May 26). 270 killed in Chicago jet crash. *Washington Post*, p. A1.

Feazel, M. (1979, August 13). NTSB expected to tighten transport quality control. *Aviation Week & Space Technology*, pp. 25–27.

Feud over DC-10 maintenance. (1979, August 10). *Washington Post*, p. A3.

Galloway, P. (1979, May 27). Officials sift silently through the remnants. *Chicago Sun Times*, pp. B8–9 (NewsBank, 1979, TRA 34).

Gelman, D. (1979, June 11). The super sleuths of the skies. *Time*, p. 37.

Judge delays action on DC-10 pending FAA safety findings. (1979, June 16). *Washington Post*, p. A8.

Juneau, W., & Koziol, R. (1979, May 27). Dozens of U.S. dental experts fly here to aid in identifying victims. *Chicago Tribune*, p. 4.

Kneeland, D. E. (1979, May 26). 272 die as jet crashes on takeoff in Chicago; worst U.S. air disaster. *New York Times*, p. A1.

Lipinski, A. M. (1979, July 29). Behind the news, airline press chief is well-grounded. *Chicago Tribune*, p. L3.

National Transportation Safety Board. (1979, December 21). *Aircraft Accident Report: American Airlines, Inc., DC-10-10, N10AA, Chicago O'Hare International Airport, Chicago, Illinois, May 25, 1979* (NTSB/AAR-79-17). Washington, DC: National Transportation Safety Board. (NTISUB/E/104-017).

Nelson, M. K. (1990, March 21). Personal communication with author.

Nicodemus, C. (1979, June 4). Grounding of DC-10s is refused by judge. *Chicago Sun Times*, pp. C8–9 (NewsBank, 1979, TRA 34).

North, D. M. (1979, June 4). Crash to boost FAA scrutiny. *Aviation Week & Space Technology*, pp. 35–36.

Pauchant, T. C., & Mitroff, I. (1992). *Transforming the crisis-prone organizational: Preventing individual, organizational, and environmental tragedies.* San Francisco: Jossey-Bass.

Sheils, M. (1979, June 11). How safe? *Newsweek*, p. 34.

Shrivastava, P. (1987). *Bhopal: Anatomy of a crisis.* Cambridge, MA: Ballinger.

Standard New York Stock Exchange Reports. (1979, September 25). American Airlines.

Why FAA draws fire after DC-10 crash. (1979, June 11). *U.S. News & World Report*, p. 8.

Williams, D. A. (1979, June 4). It just disintegrated. *Newsweek*, pp. 24–26.

Witkin, R. (1979a, May 28). Split bolt blamed for loss of engine in jetliners crash. *New York Times*, p. A1.

Witkin, R. (1979b, June 6). U.S. judge bids FAA ground DC-10 airlines. *New York Times*, p. A1.

Young, D. (1979a, May 27). Damn, last word from 191s cockpit. *Chicago Tribune*, p. A1.

Young, D. (1979b, May 30). New flaws ground DC-10s. *Chicago Tribune*, pp. B4–6 (NewsBank, 1979, TRA 34).

Part III

Crisis Stage

Chapter 7 ―――――――――――――――――

Disaster Strikes!
Confronting Crisis

Though views on how to manage and communicate during a crisis may differ, most agree on certain basic principles: An organization in crisis must be visible, show concern and compassion, and demonstrate efforts to correct the problem to ensure similar tragedies do not occur. For critics outside the situation, it seems these principles are easily applied; however, the unpredictable nature of crisis suggests otherwise. As TWA's Director of Media Relations, John McDonald, stated following the crash of Flight 800, "You can certainly have a plan in place and you can certainly train and you can certainly gain experience from others who have been through it. But until you have actually done it, you have no concept of what this is about" (Elsasser, 1996, p. 22).

Crises are highly complex events characterized by numerous factors and issues. A plan is a critical tool for managing such an event; however, it cannot take into account the many unique and unexpected aspects which characterize a particular crisis. Effective crisis communication requires management's understanding of different crisis variables to increase their capacity for thinking about crisis and determining strategic actions. This chapter examines the crisis communication stage and relevant issues and factors which influence strategic communication decisions.

THE CRISIS STAGE

Historically, the ideas of decision, turning point, moment of truth, pathology, and opportunity provided a conceptual understanding of crisis (Lagadec, 1993). Ancient Greeks considered *krisis* a critical period where decisions based on interpretation and choices are made. For Greek physicians, crisis was a turning point preceded by a period of suspense. Greek tragedies dramatized crises as moments of truth, when "light is shed upon characters and events" (Lagadec, 1993, p. 29). Eighteenth-century medical thought explained crisis as pathology, suggesting it is a condition subsequent to an initiating event. Chinese explanations included both danger and opportunity. These varying definitions suggest the universal nature of "crisis." Yet some scholars believe the term has been overused to the point where it has lost much of its meaning. Morin (cited in Lagadec, 1993), for example, explains crisis initially meant "the decisive moment in an uncertain process"; however, it has been transformed into an everyday catch phrase that signifies indecision or "the moment when uncertainty exists at the same time as a problem" (p. 25). The point is that not all situations can be considered a true crisis.

From an organizational standpoint, a crisis occurs when "environmental threats pick out organizations and bring them face to face with their weaknesses and mistakes" (Smart, 1985, pp. 10–11). A crisis may be triggered by a single event, but it may also result from a general trend that leads to a breaking point (Lagadec, 1993). Crises involve numerous interacting elements and groups. Shrivastava (1987) has described crisis as a complex system of interdependent events involving multiple conflicting stakeholders.

From a decision-making viewpoint, crisis presents numerous difficulties. Lagadec (1993) explains as follows:

Crisis: A situation in which a range of organizations, struggling with critical problems and subjected to strong external pressure and bitter internal tension, find themselves thrust into the limelight, abruptly and for an extended period; they are also brought into conflict with one another. . . . This occurs in the context of a mass media society, (i.e., 'live'), and the event is sure to make headlines on the radio and television and in the written press for a long time. (p. 36)

In crisis, a world considered familiar and comfortable suddenly becomes unfamiliar and unpleasant. A world once viewed as secure is now jeopardized. Crisis overwhelms an organization with numerous critical problems which cannot be addressed through normal operating procedures. This disruption of standard operating procedures requires a realignment of resources, roles, and functions (Smart & Vertinsky, 1977).

Characteristics of Crisis

Surprise, threat, insufficient information, time pressures, a lack of control, stress and anxiety, and relational changes and tensions among participants characterize crisis (Lagadec, 1993, p. 32). A crisis is a high-stakes situation for the focal organization and its stakeholders. It threatens significant values and goals and is consequential in determining the future. To determine appro-

priate responses to a crisis, relevant information must be se   98   a
simple task. Too much or too little information creates ad
Information overload or information deprivation compli
efforts. Usually, limited information exists as to causal fa
fects. Unnecessary information can overwhelm managers.
observes, a crisis by definition is a "crisis of information   (p. 201). A high
level of uncertainty typically characterizes a crisis. An unknown situation
increases the difficulty of evaluating the situation and recognizing alternative
responses. As the level of uncertainty decreases, decision makers are in a
stronger position to identify fitting responses.

Time is a critical feature of crisis. There is pressure to make quick decisions and act. Decision makers are given little time to reflect or pontificate
about a given decision or response, therefore limiting judgment. Often, responses must be given on the spot. A sense of urgency to respond often increases the level of stress, anxiety, and fatigue among those who must make
decisions. The duration of a crisis can present additional complications, often
creating a snowball effect. In time, a crisis may unearth more problems that
under normal circumstances are kept contained; in some instances, unresolved
crises may resurface. Furthermore, the interaction of particular variables may
increase the severity of the situation. This underscores the significance of
timely actions. As Lagadec (1993) points out, a crisis has time on its side.
Unfortunately, timely responses are challenged by inadequate information
and uncertainty. The amount of control an organization has over events and
their consequences decreases in crisis. Crises involve a number of groups and
authorities. As a result of stress and pressure, conflicts may occur among
both internal and external individuals and groups.

FACTORS INFLUENCING CRISIS

Numerous elements present in a crisis situation function to influence the
direction of the crisis as well as management's efforts in controlling and resolving the situation. Such factors include pre-crisis planning, organizational
perception, stakeholder perception, uncertainty, stress, and involved groups.

Pre-Crisis Planning

Management's ability to handle a crisis situation and the potential of a
crisis to escalate is often determined by the quality and thoroughness of the
company's prior planning (Lagadec, 1993; Pinsdorf, 1987). It is critical the
company have a clear vision as to how it will approach the crisis. Pinsdorf (1987)
notes an organization's "philosophic base and psychological gyroscope" is a better determiner of success than "checklists" (pp. 38–41). A macroview of crisis
tends to be more effective than a microview of the situation. While a plan

sists the organization in systematically responding to a crisis, it will by no means address all issues. A sound philosophy and concrete objectives provide a clear frame of reference on which to base strategic responses.

Organizational Perception

Perception is the process used by individuals to organize and evaluate stimuli. An organization's understanding of the crisis and its strategic responses are influenced by managers' perceptions of the crisis. Organizational perceptions are seldom totally accurate, but a crisis can further distort perceptions. Shrivastava (1987) notes a crisis "creates panic, chaos, highly emotional conflict, and psychological trauma" which impedes decision makers' ability to evaluate options rationally (p. 137). Consequently, perceptual errors may result in an incorrect analysis of the situation and, in turn, inappropriate responses. Furthermore, preconceived notions and established mindsets can flaw the decision-making process.

The level of uncertainty is often determined by the perceptions of the decision maker. In other words, uncertainty is not just a property of the environment, but of the observer faced with a decision. Downey and Slocum (1975) suggest that perceived uncertainty varies with perceived characteristics of the environment, individual differences in cognitive processes, individual behavioral response repertoires, and social expectations for the perception of uncertainty. Accordingly, these variations create different and perhaps inaccurate levels of uncertainty.

Stakeholder Perception

While organizational perceptions influence crisis, so do stakeholder perceptions. Stakeholder perception of an organization's credibility influences the perceived effectiveness of that organization's response in a given situation. Credibility is determined by whether stakeholders perceive the organization as trustworthy, knowledgeable, competent, and sincere. The organization's credibility prior to a crisis certainly weighs heavily on stakeholder perception, but organizational credibility is further influenced by how the organization positions itself in response to the crisis.

Credibility is generally enhanced through the company's openness and honesty with its members, media, and other stakeholders; however, crisis dynamics can make this a difficult approach. Following the assignment of blame, for example, there is a natural tendency for the accused to resort to mudslinging tactics. This will eventually damage the company's credibility. Rogers (1993) notes, "If the news is bad, it won't improve with age, so company management should face up to it, acknowledge the downside realities, and then get on with damage control efforts" (p. 133). From an organizational position, differences among stakeholder perceptions (varying interests, assumptions, values, and interpretations) must be considered in developing an understanding of the situation (Shrivastava, 1987).

Uncertainty

As discussed earlier, uncertainty is a primary characteristic of crisis and an influential factor in determining the direction of the crisis. Uncertainty refers to the absence of needed information. It is a function both of one's knowledge of cause–effect relationships and the probable conditions of the environment in which the outcome takes place (Leblebici & Salancik, 1981). The degree of uncertainty associated with a crisis influences the effectiveness of management and communication. Decision situations are characterized by uncertainty that results from predicting outcomes from the actions taken to achieve them. Very few responses can be determined with certainty. A lack of knowledge of response options and/or an inability to predict the likely consequences of a response choice complicates the decision-making process.

Organizations employ various strategies to reduce uncertainty. Following general rules, using rituals, relying on habitual patterns, or, more self-consciously, setting goals and making plans to meet them are ways organizations contend with uncertainty (Turner, 1976). When an organization is at a loss for what to do because there are no clear objective standards for guidance, it will observe others in similar situations and employ their strategies to reduce uncertainty (Pfeffer, Salancik, & Leblebici, 1978). These methods reduce uncertainty for present actions; however, organizations are never certain if present actions will be adequate in reaching goals. Consequently, organizations adopt simplifying assumptions about the environment to make action possible. Simon (1957) refers to this as a framework for bounded rationality.

Stress

A crisis is a manager's worst nightmare. Lost lives, financial devastation, and fear of damaged credibility and legitimacy increases the level of stress associated with a crisis. In the context of crisis, stress can impact management's ability to effectively manage the crisis and communicate. Extreme stress contributes to numerous problems. Internal and external conflicts, paranoia, the inability to focus, oversimplification, poor judgment, avoidance, and extreme defensiveness are all consequences of stress. Such responses only compound the crisis situation. Lagadec (1993) observes the following:

To face a crisis effectively, the individuals must be in excellent condition, with solid mental stability, and their intellectual ability must be at its height. This is the only way they will be able to reflect, anticipate, rethink the steps they need to take, and find new approaches to situations that seem insoluble. At the same time, a major event severely curtails all these aptitudes. (p. 62)

There is a direct relationship between crisis planning and stress. The level of preparation prior to a crisis tends to influence the amount of stress. A solid, well-tuned plan tends to lessen the amount of stress experienced by managers.

Involved Groups

A crisis has a tendency to resonate beyond the focal organization, affecting numerous others. Consequently, a number of individuals and groups may be directly involved. From an interorganizational perspective, a crisis brings together many organizations to resolve a situation which affects them all to varying degrees. Various parties who are basically unfamiliar with one another must learn to adapt and relate. Different goals, perspectives, interests, and responses makes this a challenge and it is most likely easier said than done. When groups involved act independently and fail to integrate their action plans, conflict is likely to occur.

Prior planning should take into account the difficulties of interorganizational cooperation. In some situations the organization may lose its independence. In an airline crash, for example, the airline must comply with the NTSB, the primary authority overseeing the crash site and investigation. In addition to the airline, a major accident investigation brings together a number of parties, including the NTSB, FAA, aircraft manufacturer, engine manufacturer, airport personnel, airline representatives, local emergency and disaster response groups, and others. Human error and the implications of blame can further complicate crisis management by increasing the involvement of groups. Pilot error, for example, involves the Air Line Pilots Association, the largest union for pilots. Aircraft or engine complications involve manufacturers. These groups generally take a hard line in responding to assignments of blame, often increasing the attention given a crisis. Victims, community, government, and elected officials may also become players in a crisis.

Victims

In the case of an airline crash, those most deeply affected are the victims and their families. The fate of victims can substantially determine the severity of a crisis. Fatalities, for example, will increase media attention. A crisis naturally evokes organizational concern over financial and strategic issues, but when a major loss of life occurs the event becomes one of trauma, pain, and suffering. Managerial concerns go beyond financial issues to the victims' plight. They must now confront and respond to the pain and suffering of anguished victims and their relatives and friends. Companies respond to such ordeals by offering assistance, counseling, gestures of compensation, and expressions of remorse through memorial services honoring the victims. The responsibility and ability to acknowledge the human factor is indeed a significant aspect of managing crisis.

Legal issues concerning victims complicate the crisis situation. The litigious nature of society has influenced how an organization will respond to a crisis and its victims. For example, organizations may feel that any humane demonstration will be interpreted as an acknowledgement of responsibility (Lagadec, 1993). Therefore, the organization may refrain from a sensitive gesture toward victims or families due to risk. Consequently, the lack of such actions tends to create the image of an uncaring organization.

Liability increases the chaotic nature of crisis, and victims' compensation is a primary issue following an airline disaster. The legal aspects of an airline accident can be highly technical and vicious. Airlines and their insurance companies have been accused of ruthless behavior toward air-crash survivors and victims' families when battling in the courts. Though airlines may want to offer full and fair compensation to victims or their families, certain legal standards may prevent this. For example, the 1929 Warsaw Convention specified the limitation of damage awards for international flight accidents (where the airline is not charged with willful misconduct) to $75 thousand per victim. U.S. maritime law further specifies that for "at sea" air crashes, only wives and dependent children may claim damages (Hosenball, 1996). Such laws emphasize the awkwardness of placing a price tag on a human life. Airline crashes make for big-stakes litigation and the legal battles can last for years.

In recent years, airlines have been criticized for the perceived failure to adequately care for passengers' families after a crash. Horror stories abound of family members receiving news of their loved one's death on answering machines, their lack of information concerning the passenger list and recovery and identification of victims, and the medical information obtained in interviews with airlines being used to assist defense attorneys in future claims. Media are quick to report such incidents, often painting a picture of a cruel and cold industry. In response to the families' frustrations with airlines and government, the National Air Disaster Alliance was formed. This group unites families who share a common grief and has advanced crash-related issues to the forefront in an effort to influence and legislate change. The alliance has been a highly vocal and influential force in recent years.

As a consequence of the many difficulties associated with handling families of crash victims, legislation was passed directly affecting the airlines' process in dealing with the issue. Prompted by the TWA Flight 800 disaster and testimony from victims' families from almost every major airline accident between 1986 and 1996, Congress passed the Aviation Disaster Family Assistance Act in 1996. The legislation established the Office for Family Assistance within the National Transportation Safety Board. This office is charged with handling certain areas relating to victims' families. The Family Assistance Plan is discussed in detail in Chapter 10.

While this book focuses on external communication, the importance of internal communication cannot be ignored. A crisis throws an organization and its employees into turmoil. An airline disaster generally includes airline personnel among its victims, creating an additional crisis for the organization. It is critical for organizations to communicate openly with its employees and provide information to reduce uncertainty and offset rumors. Organizations which have a poor communication climate prior to a crisis will likely have difficulty communicating following a crisis.

Government Authorities

Depending on the nature and magnitude of the crisis, an organization will be placed under a series of powerful microscopes by a number of sources, such as government agencies, who function through inquiries or investigations and hearings. In the case of airline accidents, the NTSB and the FAA are the investigating government agencies. Government intervention places a constraint on the organization by virtue of its authority. Whenever an organization is investigated the chance exists that impropriety will be identified, often compounding the situation. Moreover, government involvement may prolong a crisis after organizational efforts have controlled the situation (Rogers, 1993). Conversely, government intervention may serve as a positive influence (Ray, 1997). For example, in its post-crash investigation of an airline crash, the NTSB functions as an advocate for the organization and the industry by helping to address threats and questions concerning the legitimacy of the organization as well as the industry.

Elected Officials and Politicians

These individuals may see the crisis as an opportunity to demonstrate their concern, assert their authority, and possibly win a few votes. While intentions may be good, problems may occur as a consequence of political involvement. Elected officials may be more interested in obtaining information regarding the event than actually assisting with coping efforts (Lagadec, 1993). Some officials may seek media exposure, which can create problems for those attempting to manage the crisis. An official's desire to visit and observe the site may divert attention from more important matters. The elected official may make inaccurate or unwise statements which serve to complicate the situation.

Crisis Management

When disaster strikes, there is no warning. Some crises may have signals, but they often go unrecognized. Whatever the case, an organization's world is instantly turned upside down. The first few hours of a crisis are critical. Experienced crisis experts believe the perception of crisis is determined by the organization's responses in the first twelve to twenty-four hours. Public opinion will be based as much on how the company responds to the crisis as the cause itself (Doughty, 1993). But no matter how quickly a company mobilizes itself, time will have been lost. While a crisis plan eliminates some of the confusion and controls many of the difficulties associated with crisis, it rarely prepares the organization for the constant media assault, the emotional impact of the event, and damaging information and headlines which threaten the organization's survival.

An organization must determine its position from the beginning and remain consistent in its actions. A crisis plan assists in this effort, but it by no means takes into account the numerous factors the organization finds itself battling. For example, in the beginning key members and executives may be absent. The unexpected nature of crisis makes this a likely scenario, and it may take time for the individuals to arrive at the crisis site. If the individual is the CEO, this can present problems, since media and the public expect his or her presence. Those in charge of managing the situation may be overwhelmed by the presence of numerous unfamiliar faces demanding their attention and making conflicting requests. A proactive position enables the company to better control the crisis, whereas a reactive response tends to prolong the situation. Being proactive requires members to anticipate events and their consequences. The requirement of a coordinated response is often complicated by the dynamics of the crisis situation.

How a company responds to a crisis is guided by how it views the crisis. Somehow, order must be made out of chaos. Establishing and maintaining a clear focus is often difficult when others see sensation or catastrophe; nevertheless, focus is critical. Responding to the question, "What is the problem I choose to tackle?" and reflecting on this response throughout the crisis is one way to focus (Lagadec, 1993). In addition, the management team should define a universal course of action, points of intervention, and ways of handling problems. Initially, the problem must be analyzed. Lagadec warns against the tendency to act first, think later. He emphasizes the importance of taking time and critically distancing oneself from the situation to estimate the complexity of the problem. This process enables one to fully grasp the breadth and depth of the problem and ultimately address the root problems, not just obvious symptoms.

Pauchant and Mitroff (1992) describe the crisis stage as one of containment and damage limitation. "Damage limitation mechanisms" must be implemented to prevent damage to untouched areas of the organization (p. 138). Successful containment and resolution requires the crisis management team to immediately act, make decisions, and maintain a sense of perspective and objectivity. Initial actions and decisions are generally the ones stakeholders remember. Furthermore, these initial strategies set the stage for later strategies. General rules for crisis management are to question, anticipate, and take initiatives; avoid radical responses and magic tricks; think about the consequences of your decisions; and seize opportunities presented by crisis (Lagadec, 1993).

Initially, crisis response involves providing fundamental alerts, coordinating actions, implementing emergency procedures, initiating rescue operations, securing information, and communicating with victims, personnel, and media. In light of the rate at which events occur, it is wise to document information received, procedures taken, and choices made throughout the organization (Lagadec, 1993). A crisis logbook must be kept and updated constantly in order for everyone to be aware of who did or said what and which steps have been implemented. This is extremely beneficial, particularly when the crisis is lengthy and individuals or teams change. As Lagadec notes, "Without a logbook, it is very difficult to provide for a smooth transfer from one team to another" (p. 202). The process further assists in mentally focusing individuals.

Decision Making

A principal aspect of crisis management is critical decision making. In regard to crisis and decision making, ten Berge (1990) notes crisis is a situation requiring quick decisions among a limited number of options. A lack of action generally results in negative consequences. Crisis presents critical choices. Denying the severity of the situation, developing a bunker mentality, being overcome by emotion, scapegoating, adopting recently heard opinions, extreme defensiveness, hypervigilance, narrowmindedness, rigid or egocentric reasoning, and arbitrary decisions are all common pitfalls for decision makers in crisis (Lagadec, 1993). Some of the difficulties associated with decision making during crisis can be avoided by laying the appropriate groundwork. Defining responsibilities and lines of authority, for example, will offset some confusion.

Internal problems may complicate the management team's process. While the crisis management team brings a variety of skills and perspectives to the table, Lagadec (1993) notes the general confusion which results when diverse personalities and interests come together. These differences, combined with the pressures, stress, and long hours associated with a crisis often contribute to conflicts. Janis (1982), on the other hand, acknowledged the phenomenon of "groupthink," a condition in which the group becomes closeminded and strives for unanimity. Although not as common, groupthink is potentially more dangerous because it is difficult to recognize and can lead to a flawed decision-making process. In a groupthink situation, members may fail to adequately survey options and objectives, examine risks of preferred choices, reappraise rejected options, and thoroughly secure and process information. Victims are gradually closed off from outside influences, which limits their ability to resolve a crisis. With groupthink there is a tendency to simplify. While this decreases the complexity and ambiguity of a difficult situation, it may result in poor choices.

THE MEDIA CHALLENGE

What media choose to present and the manner in which they convey the information creates a strong impression on organizational stakeholders. Media function as the public's "watchdog," providing information and evaluating, analyzing, and assigning value to contemporary events. The influence of print and electronic media is pervasive and their role in a crisis is fundamental and powerful. Stakeholder perception of an organizational crisis is based, more often than not, on media interpretation of the event. The type of information, the way in which the event and the crisis organization are portrayed, and the amount and intensity of coverage given will generally impact a crisis in some way. For crisis managers, media presence contributes an additional dimension to the situation. Media influence reactions from the public, politicians, and even those directly involved in the crisis. In fact, media may influence the direction of a crisis.

Communication technology offers instantaneous global coverage. We experience events live. Television provides immediacy to a wide audience and its ability to deliver live, up-to-the-minute coverage gives us a sense of "you are there." On January 13, 1982, the nation witnessed the rescue of survivors being pulled from the ice-covered waters of the Potomac River following Air Florida's Flight 90 crash into Washington's 14th Street bridge. The drama of the event created an indelible image for those who watched. Today, management's first view of the event may come from CNN or one of the major news networks. In the last few years, technological advancements have brought us new communication vehicles that "interconnect" the world. Global computer networks, for example, proved their value following the TWA Flight 800 disaster. A record number of users turned to Web sites devoted to the crash (Barboza, 1996). CNN alone reported 3.9 million hits a day in the first few days following the crash.

Instantaneous coverage may be viewed as advantageous; however, in a crisis situation it may be problematic, particularly in the first few hours, because information is often vague, fragmented, and conflicting (Newsom, Turk, & Kruckeberg, 1996). Journalists pressured by time constraints have little opportunity to think through ethical dilemmas and decisions (Deppa, 1994). Furthermore, the instantaneous nature of communication places additional pressures on those directly dealing with a crisis, such as the crisis organization, victims, emergency personnel, and government agencies.

Factors Influencing the Degree of Coverage

The intensity of media coverage during a crisis determines the severity of the crisis and influences the organization's response to the situation. Three factors generally tend to influence the amount and quality of media coverage: the location, the time, and the individuals (Pinsdorf, 1987). A crisis that occurs in a location not easily accessible to reporters or television crews will receive less coverage than a crisis that occurs in close proximity. An airline crash in a metropolitan area, for example, will come under a siege of media, whereas an accident in a remote area difficult to reach will receive less attention. Media today are highly mobile and can access locations considered impossible twenty years ago. The time of year and the time of day also influence coverage. Summer months and Christmas holidays are typically slow news periods and find reporters anxious for a story. When an event occurs close to the evening news hour, the likelihood of coverage increases.

The individuals involved in a crisis are also significant. An airline accident in Detroit that kills a number of U.S. citizens will receive more attention from the American press than a foreign air-carrier accident in China with primarily Chinese citizens, which will likely be buried in the middle of a newspaper's "world" section. TWA's experience following the crash of Flight 800 certainly illustrates how location, time, and individuals influence the amount of media coverage. When the 747 crashed in New York, media capitol of the world, during the slow summer months of 1996, with 230 souls aboard (primarily U.S. citizens), Trans World Airlines was bombarded with nonstop coverage for weeks.

The trend for coverage in the initial stages of a major crisis is established by the national and international media; however, as the event winds down it is usually the local media who continue coverage until the situation is resolved (Newsom, Turk, & Kruckeberg, 1996). In the case of an airline crash, prestige media coverage is at its height during the on-site investigation of the accident. An occasional story will appear if the NTSB or FAA make an announcement regarding the crash. Coverage is generally brief during the public hearing and for the final report. Local media may continue coverage throughout the investigation.

Type of Coverage

The type of coverage has become somewhat predictable. Human interest or sensational stories typically overshadow or replace technical ones. Early stories tend to focus on death and destruction. Ferguson (1994) notes, "Follow-up reports entail a three-step sequence: First come the colorful descriptions of personal heroism, grief, and suffering by individuals. . . . Next come discussions of property damage and cost. . . . Finally, come the discussions of preparedness and competence of response by authorities" (p. 324). Initial media coverage of a major airline crash generally includes causal theories, victim biographies, grieving families, details of the on-site investigation, the airline and its history, the safety of air travel, and factors unique to the particular crash.

Media presence and the type of coverage may serve to compound a crisis. Many journalists present fair and honest coverage; however, there are those whose questionable approaches to the event serve to increase the difficulty and trauma of the situation. In some instances, media coverage may not always represent reality. Though reporters usually try to remain open and objective, facts do not always win out in a crisis situation when a "story" is desired. Lagadec (1993) notes

While officials do everything they can to prove that systems are organized to withstand crises, the press churns out masses of contradictory statements, frightening images, outrage, and declarations that scarcely flatter the person quoted. It digs out old stories and revives discussions that had already created strain, both in-house and with the outside. (p. 130)

Managers find it much easier to deal with journalists who are familiar with the particular industry in question than a reporter who has been cast into an unknown and complex situation.

How media depict the grief and tragedy of an event directly reflects upon an organization's image. Pictures communicate pain and suffering more powerfully than words. In the first few weeks following a crash, photographs and film footage emphasizing grief and tragedy are found in newspapers, newsmagazines, and on television. Pictures of family members grieving and mourning the loss of their loved ones create a strong image in the minds of media consumers, emphasizing the drama of the event. In the emotional aftermath of an airline disaster, such photographs may indirectly reflect upon the airline as the source of families' pain and anguish.

Journalists argue that depictions of grief give meaning to tragedy. "If the reader or viewer gets to know the victim as a real person, what happened doesn't get lost in the statistics of murders or plane crashes" (Germer, 1997, p. 106). Yet what are the limits of newsgathering in a tragedy? To what degree are media entitled to a story? Media are often considered an invasive force in a tragedy. They are seen as intruders on families' private time of shock and grief. Competition and eager editors contribute to what nonjournalists perceive as highly insensitive actions and a callous disrespect of victims and their families. Journalists often give the impression of pouncing on families and friends mercilessly, hoping for an exclusive story or a memorable quotation. As columnist Ellen Goodman (1989) wrote, "The right of the public to know, to see and to be affected is considered more important than the right of the individual to mourn, or even die, in privacy" (p. 292). Deppa (1994) suggests that while media behavior can be harmful, sensitive media attention to the bereaved can be positive and provide a helpful service for those dealing with a tragic event. Though crisis managers may not directly control media practices, it is critical they recognize and understand how such practices impact the total crisis picture. This understanding will determine appropriate communication strategies.

Information Requirement

In the event of a crisis there is often a conflict between the organization and the media: Media require information and the organization has a need to control information. Media influence requires the organization to acknowledge their powerful role and recognize the importance of cooperating, as much as possible, with their requests for information. Areas of media inquiry typically concern who is to blame, when the problem was discovered, and what the organization is doing to correct the problem (Ferguson, 1994). Initially, media want specifics in regard to the fatalities, damage, and other issues involved.

Following an airline crash, answers to these questions and others are generally provided by the NTSB. The NTSB functions to facilitate and control the flow of information through its open and comprehensive process. The Board is responsible for reporting the conditions and circumstances relating to accidents and making accident reports public. Throughout the investigation, information is made available to the media. For example, during the on-site investigation, information released is limited to factual developments and made by a NTSB member present at the accident scene, a representative of the Board's Office of Public Affairs, or the investigator in charge. Following the on-site investigation, information is provided through interim reports. Because of its legitimate authority, the NTSB is perceived as a reliable source of information and media usually look to the Board as their primary source of information. Media coverage of a crash and investigation generally concludes following the NTSB's presentation of its final report. This suggests that the NTSB's final report substantively removes the issue from the media's agenda (Ray, 1991).

COMMUNICATING DURING CRISIS

Though an organization may not be able to control the direction of a crisis, it is in the position to control its own communication. More to the point, an organization has the ability to control stakeholder perception of the situation. Communication is critical to controlling a crisis. An organization's inability to effectively communicate its message during a crisis can prove disastrous. Numerous companies have experienced added crises as a consequence of ineffective communication. Fink (1986) notes, "No matter how good your crisis team is, no matter how complete your crisis management plan, if you cannot communicate your message during a crisis you have failed" (p. 96). Effective crisis managers recognize the value of both internal and external communication. Four immediate and critical communication challenges are presented: communication within the organization, among the actors involved, with the media, and with the concerned public (Lagadec, 1993).

How should a company communicate during a crisis? It is easier said than done. No one crisis is like any other; however, by examining specific forms of crisis we begin to identify consistencies. The dynamics of a crisis situation and the numerous associated variables present a number of constraints and barriers to communication. Not having information to communicate, or having information but not communicating it effectively, are common scenarios. Sometimes the difficulty of communicating a message is a result of the message itself. Such instances may require "reshaping, redirecting, or rethinking" the message (Fink, 1986). Other constraints, particularly legal concerns, may prevent the organization from communicating freely and openly. The inconsistency of information generated during crisis further complicates the ability to provide accurate information to stakeholders.

The organization's established communication climate can also be a constraining factor to communication (Newsom, Turk, & Kruckeberg, 1996). An open communication climate is critical in a crisis. The availability of information to both internal and external stakeholders is less likely to create rumors and increase uncertainty about the organization. Consequently, stakeholders will develop a more accurate perception of the organization.

The goal in any crisis situation is to control and manage the crisis, the message, and the communication (Fink, 1986). Therefore, it is crucial the organization respond as quickly as possible before media gain control. Control involves identifying the basic position of the organization. Will the company be aggressive or more subtle in its approach? What will be its strategy? Crisis experts agree the most effective approach is one which is fact based and straightforward, rather than evasive. Effective crisis communication requires a thorough understanding of the organization's audiences or stakeholders, as well as the various dimensions of the crisis.

Crisis Communication Principles

The previous discussion has emphasized the importance and difficulty of identifying the nature of the message to be communicated to stakeholders. The crisis communication principles discussed in this section are derived from the existing crisis literature. In general, there are eight crisis communication principles managers should consider. Each principle is listed with comment.

An organization in crisis should strive to be perceived as the most reliable source of information.

Three messages should be communicated: The problem has been recognized and the company is in control; much is unknown, but actions are being taken to acquire information and resolve the situation; and information will be given when available (Lagadec, 1993). A lack of information should not discourage the company from communicating with stakeholders. Rather, what it has to say is limited.

Following an airline crash, the initial information which can be communicated is usually limited to the flight number, the type of aircraft, the routing of the plane, the location of the accident, and the number of passengers and crew believed to be aboard. Anything more would be considered speculation. The issue of the passenger manifest following an airline crash is significant. Media and families clamor for information concerning the names and identification of victims, demanding the airline provide them the information on the spot. Airlines are sensitive to releasing such information prior to family notification. Media have been critical of the airlines' time frame in accomplishing this task. While the media's argument of time may be legitimate, the premature releasing of this type of information could be potentially disastrous. Only information that will not change should be communicated. When a company confirms information and it is disputed in later reports, the organization is seen as lacking control. In the case of airline disasters, for example, we often hear conflicting reports of the number of fatalities in the early hours.

In a context of extreme emotions and a lack of information, rumors thrive. Rogers (1993) notes that rumors are produced when the company in crisis fails to provide a high-level, accessible, and knowledgeable spokesperson who is close to the situation. Newsom, Turk, and Kruckeberg (1996) suggest efforts to counter rumors should include a thorough analysis of the seriousness of the rumor prior to taking action, an understanding of the origin and reason for the rumor, reassurance to those affected by the rumor, and the provision of accurate information on the issue without referring to the rumor. The organization should control the situation by issuing a statement as soon as possible, providing confirmed information and indicating additional information will be available as it is verified. This prevents media from seeking secondary and less reliable sources. As Rogers (1993) notes, "The first player frames the debate that follows" (p. 126).

Communicate with one voice.

Statements and actions must be coordinated and contradictions avoided. Conflicting messages create confusion and the image of an organization out of control.

An open and honest response that conveys compassion and concern is the best approach.

Johnson & Johnson's strategies of high visibility, honesty, and caring during the Tylenol crisis proved effective (Fink, 1986). Legal issues greatly influence the content of the message. Concerns about liability tend to create paranoia and suppress communication efforts. Stonewalling raises suspicions and increases uncertainty about the organization, creating the impression the company has something to hide (Fink, 1986). "No comment," carries the same impact and often creates an arrogant impression. Silence communicates—and in the context of crisis may be interpreted as guilty. An open and honest response that conveys compassion and concern is the best approach. If an organization is trying to hide something, most likely the media will find out and the organization's crisis will escalate. Admitting ignorance is less damaging than lying.

Public battles generate more media coverage.

Following the assignment of blame, organizations may go on the defensive. Redirecting blame is a common defensive response. A public battle in which accusations are exchanged among organizations is considered news-worthy. This type of coverage does little for the organization's image. The impression often given is an organization more concerned with liability than safety. When responding to media questions about issues of blame, spokes-persons should be cautious. Negative questions promote defensive or reac-tive responses; therefore, respondents should reframe a negatively worded question into a positive one that communicates the message or point you want to convey (Fink, 1986).

Crisis communication involves more than words.

We cannot not communicate. In other words, we are always communicat-ing, even if we do not intend to communicate. Gestures, underlying attitudes, and physical presence or absence speak volumes. The context of a crisis (a dramatic situation) frames these actions (or inactions), and interpretations will likely differ from normal circumstances.

The medium through which a message is communicated is as important as what is communicated.

Content is important, but so is process. Communication difficulties are experienced in both the sending and receiving of messages. Those in charge of communication should be knowledgeable of the various means of commu-nication and their particular advantages or potential problems and recognize which method is most appropriate for a given stakeholder.

Immediate communication is not always a requirement.

The emphasis in crisis literature is to communicate immediately; however, there are situations in which immediate communication can result in negative consequences (Lagadec, 1993, p. 214). Terrorism is an example. The choice to remain silent in such a situation is strategic in and of itself. Such a decision should be arrived at through careful consideration of the risks involved in communicating or not communicating. Lagadec warns that silence may be perceived as an attempt to cover up; therefore, companies must be prepared to offer convincing and honest responses about choosing the silence option.

Effective communication requires a full and complete understand-ing of the event and its circumstances.

Factors present in the pre-crisis stage directly influence events in the crisis stage. Therefore, managers must recognize these factors when anticipating the direction of the crisis. Understanding the advantages and disadvantages of specific communication strategies is good; however, the potential effec-tiveness of crisis communication depends on the manager's understanding of the breadth and depth of the crisis situation. Specific message strategies complement all other efforts. As Pauchant and Mitroff (1992) point out, a good and effective message does not necessarily resolve a difficult crisis. Strategic communication involves surveying the environment for factors which could impact the company and developing ways to lessen their impact, viewing the organization the way relevant stakeholders do, and developing an appreciation for the media's position (Pinsdorf, 1987).

Responding to Media

When media demand information which is unavailable, managers are placed in a troublesome situation. The inability to answer questions due to a lack of information creates the perception that the organization is uncooperative and not in control. Television cameras present the challenge of communicating to all stakeholders simultaneously. Answering reporters' questions, which are designed for sound bites, follow-ups, and emotional responses can be difficult for even the most skilled spokesperson. Mistakes are reported to the world, potentially compounding the organization's crisis. When responding to media, it is important to predetermine major ideas and communicate these points, consider questions from the public's point of view, provide relevant answers, be positive and brief, explain why you cannot release information, never lie, never speculate on the cause of an event, always verify information before communicating it to media, and do not be afraid to admit ignorance (Martin, 1990; Ferguson, 1994). Where media are concerned, "off the record" is never off the record (Martin, 1990).

Crisis managers should deal with the media by learning their process and understanding their "world." This information can be extremely helpful in the thick of a media blitz. Resources offering advice and lessons on handling media in a crisis should be consulted. It is important for key organizational representatives to develop a rapport with media from the start. Providing information as quickly as possible gives the impression the organization will do its best to cooperate. Contacting key groups who can offer insight on particular reporters is also helpful. For example, NTSB personnel are generally familiar with the press corps present at the accident site and can assist airlines with reporters' questioning patterns. The organization in crisis must closely observe media reports to determine accuracy and be quick to correct any inaccurate information.

CRISIS MANAGEMENT: THE AIRLINE INDUSTRY

The practice of an airline representative quickly overpainting the name of the airline on wreckage following a crash has long since disappeared. Major airline crashes catapult the airline, as well as the industry, to the forefront of the public's attention for an unpredictable period of time. Airlines cannot and do not try to hide their accidents, but generally issue appropriate and candid information as soon as possible. In addition to organizing and acting to protect their own immediate and long-term corporate interests and public image, the airline in crisis is expected to fully cooperate in the NTSB investigation with regard to fact finding, technical assistance, and providing staff support (Hill, 1970).

In the event of an airline accident, Robert Doughty (1993), former manager of external communications for United Airlines, suggests the following: Cooperate with the media by providing them with timely and accurate information, position the company as one that takes safety seriously, avoid speculating on the accident, respond immediately to inaccurate reports or statements, cooperate with investigating government agencies, acknowledge external groups for their assistance, release the passenger manifest (passenger and crew list) to media as quickly as possible following notification of next of kin, and provide information about the investigation to internal groups (Doughty, 1993).

Following an air-carrier accident, airlines experience general concerns, such as enforcement proceedings against individuals, certificate limitations, or revocation proceedings against the company. In addition, there are concerns for safety, humanity, property, public relations, and legal relationships. A concern for safety primarily suggests that the airline needs to find out the cause of an accident to prevent it from happening again. This concern is dealt with through an investigation of the circumstances leading to the accident and identifying appropriate measures to prevent the accident from reoccurring. The airline's concern for humanity and its image prompts immediate action to insure safety, determine the condition and provide maximum comfort to the passengers and the crew, and provide for the relatives and friends of those involved in the crash. The airline is obligated to provide information to the public, other airlines, manufacturers, government agencies, and airline stockholders, officers, employees, and potential customers. Finally, the airline must consider its legal relationships and future legal action resulting from personal injury and property damage.

Though every airline may not adhere to identical procedures and policies during an accident investigation, there are common responses all airlines in crisis are obligated to make. Following a crash, verifiable information includes the flight number and type of equipment, aircraft location, time of accident or its discovery, passengers and crew conditions, and the extent of damage. Initial notification of the accident is then made to the NTSB, the FAA, and the airline. The airlines must fully cooperate with the NTSB and the FAA. The airline designates appropriate personnel to insure proper handling of the accident and in cooperation with the NTSB and the FAA arranges equipment, outside services, and facilities necessary for recovery and holding operations (Hill, 1970).

The first priority of the airline is providing for the needs of passengers, crew, and others involved in the accident and establishing communication between corporate headquarters and the accident site. Intraorganizational communication is usually handled from a field office established at the accident site. The airline's home office is responsible for confirming and verifying passenger lists and cargo. Other responsibilities include notifying next of kin and providing them with information and transportation, handling medical information and records, arranging for identification of remains and a mortuary, safeguarding of personal items, and examination of the uninjured (Hill, 1970).

After the airline has accomplished these immediate tasks, their attention is focused on the investigation. Generally, an airline representative is assigned to the NTSB accident headquarters to coordinate the communication of information between the NTSB and the airline (Hill, 1970). Failure of the airline to stay informed about the details of the investigation puts the company at a disadvantage with regard to strategic communication as well as legal proceedings.

REFERENCES

Barboza, D. (1996, August 5). After the TWA crash, the web proves its worth as headline service and bulletin board. *New York Times Cybertimes* [http://www.nytimes.com/w...ek/ 00806twa-internet.html].

ten Berge, D. (1990). *The first 24 hours*. Cambridge, MA: Basil Blackwell.

Deppa, J. (1994). *The media and disasters: Pan Am 103*. New York: New York University Press.

Doughty, R. A. (1993). United Airlines prepares for the worst. In J. A. Gottschalk (Ed.), *Crisis response: Inside stories on managing image under siege* (pp. 345–364). Detroit: Visible Ink Press.

Downey, H. K., & Slocum, J. W. (1975). Uncertainty: Measures, research, and sources of variation. *Academy of Management Journal, 18*, 562–578.

Elsasser, J. (1996, September). TWA's long, hot summer. *Public Relations Tactics*, pp. 1, 18, 20–22.

Ferguson, S. D. (1994). *Mastering the public opinion challenge*. Burr Ridge, IL: Irwin.

Fink, S. (1986). *Crisis management: Planning for the inevitable*. New York: AMACOM.

Germer, F. (1997). How do you feel? In J. Gorham (Ed.), *Mass media 97/98*. 4th ed. (pp. 106–110). Guilford, CT: Dushkin/McGraw-Hill.

Goodman, E. (1989). Protection from the prying camera. In S. Biagi (Ed.), *Media reader: Perspectives on mass media industries, effects, and issues* (pp. 292–293). Belmont, CA: Wadsworth.

Hill, W. C. (1970). U.S. air carrier accident investigation procedure. *Journal of Air Law and Commerce, 36*, 414–420.

Hosenball, M. (1996, August 12). Why are you doing this? *Newsweek*, pp. 46–47.

Janis, I. L. (1982). *Groupthink: Psychological studies of policy decisions and fiascoes*. Boston: Houghton Mifflin.

Lagadec, P. (1993). *Preventing chaos in a crisis*. London: McGraw-Hill.

Leblebici, H., & Salancik, G. R. (1981). Effects of environmental uncertainty on information and decision processes in banks. *Administrative Science Quarterly, 26*, 578–596.

Martin, D. (1990). *The executive's guide to handling a press interview*. Babylon, NY: Pilot.

Newsom, D., Turk, J., & Kruckeberg, D. (1996). *This is PR: The realities of public relations* (6th ed.). Belmont, CA: Wadsworth.

Pauchant, T., & Mitroff, I. (1992). *Transforming the crisis-prone organization: Preventing individual, organizational, and environmental tragedies*. San Francisco: Jossey-Bass.

Pfeffer, J., Salancik, G. R., & Leblebici, H. (1978). Uncertainty and social influence in organizational decision-making. In M. W. Meyer (Ed.), *Environments and organizations*. San Francisco: Jossey-Bass.

Pinsdorf, M. K. (1987). *Communicating when your company is under siege*. Lexington, MA: Lexington Books.

Ray, S. J. (1991). *Post-crisis investigations: The National Transportation Safety Board and the airline industry*. Unpublished doctoral dissertation. Wayne State University, Detroit, MI.

Ray, S. J. (1997). Investigating commissions as external advocates: The National Transportation Safety Board and the airline industry. In J. D. Hoover (Ed.), *Corporate advocacy: Rhetoric in the information age*. Westport, CT: Quorum.

Rogers, R. (1993). Anatomy of a crisis. In J. A. Gottschalk (Ed.), *Crisis response: Inside stories on managing image under seige* (pp. 123–140). Detroit: Visible Ink Press.

Shrivastava, P. (1987). *Bhopal: Anatomy of a crisis*. Cambridge, MA: Ballinger.

Simon, H. (1957). *Administrative behavior*. New York: Free Press.

Smart, C. F. (1985). Strategic business planning: Predicting susceptibility to crisis. In S. J. Andriole (Ed.), *Corporate crisis management* (pp. 9–21). Princeton, NJ: Petrocelli Books.

Smart, C. F., & Vertinsky, I. (1977). Designs for crisis decision units. *Administrative Science Quarterly, 22*, 640–657.

Turner, B. A. (1976). The organizational and interorganizational development of disasters. *Administrative Science Quarterly, 21*, 378–397.

Chapter 8 ━━━━━━━━━━━━━━━━━━━━━━━━━━━

Delta Airlines Flight 191

Generally, it appears an organization's preexisting image significantly influences stakeholder perception of the organization's crisis communication efforts. As we learned in Chapter 5, Northwest Airlines's poor image prior to the crash of Flight 255 influenced the effectiveness of its crisis communication efforts following the accident. In this chapter, we see how a positive organizational image impacts the perceived effectiveness of crisis communication. Specifically, this chapter examines the crash of Flight 191 and Delta's subsequent response to the assignment of blame. The Delta Flight 191 accident tarnished three of the best safety records in aviation—the airline, the airplane, and the airport were all ranked among the safest in the industry. While the NTSB's findings placed blame on the airline, Delta's position remained as it was prior to the crash. Delta was commended on its response to the disaster, and there was virtually no impact on its operations or profitability.

PRE-CRISIS

Delta Air Lines began as the world's first crop dusting service, Huff-Daland Dusters, in Monroe, Louisiana (Davies, 1990). In 1928, C. E. Woolman and partners bought the service and chartered Delta Air Service, Inc., named for the Mississippi Delta region it served. Woolman was named general manager. The following year, the airline inaugurated passenger service from Dallas to Monroe. It was not until 1934 that Delta received a U.S. Postal Service contract. The carrier obtained the route from Dallas to Charleston, South Carolina. In 1941, Delta moved its headquarters from Monroe to Atlanta.

That year, the airline gained the Atlanta to Cincinnati route. Like other American airlines, Delta assisted in the military effort during World War II. In 1945,
Delta was awarded the prized Chicago to Miami route and changed its name
to Delta Air Lines, Inc. (Davies, 1990).

Following its purchase of Chicago and Southern Airlines in 1952, Delta became the fifth largest U.S. airline. The acquired routes included service to the
Caribbean, making Delta an international carrier. By the early 1960s, Delta was
developing its route system on the West Coast. Delta's purchase of Northeast
Airlines in 1972 expanded its service to New England and Canada. As the airline
grew, it developed the reputation of the best and least criticized carrier. In 1983,
Delta posted its first loss, but by 1985 the airline was once again profitable.

As of June 1985, Delta employed over 39 thousand workers and served
100 domestic cities in thirty-five states, Puerto Rico, and the District of Co-
lumbia. During 1984, the airline carried 39 million passengers and ranked
sixth among U.S. airlines in total revenue passenger miles flown (*Standard
New York Stock Exchange Reports*, 1985). Delta was one of the industry's
most profitable carriers and continuously ranked above others for the quality
of its service (Wayne, 1986). The company's aircraft purchases provided it
with one of the most modern fleets. With the exception of its pilots, Delta was
not unionized and its employee relations were among the best in the industry,
with generous salaries and a no-layoff policy. Delta, which owned or leased
about 230 jets, was the second-largest carrier serving Dallas.

Previous Accidents

Having gone twelve years without a fatal accident, Delta was in an enviable
position. Prior to Flight 191, Delta Airlines's last crash occurred in July 1973,
when eighty-eight people were killed after a McDonnell Douglas DC-9 came in
short of the runway at Boston's Logan Airport (McFadden, 1985). Following its
investigation of the crash, the NTSB placed blame on the Delta flight crew's
failure to monitor altitude and recognize "passage of the aircraft through the approach decision height where the decision would have been made to land vi-
sually or to abort the approach" ("NTSB urges renewed emphasis," 1974).

Declining Confidence in Safety

Nearly two thousand people died around the world in commercial air accidents in 1985. Most of these fatalities occurred in a two-month period beginning with the explosion of an Air India 747 over the Irish Sea on June 23 and
ending August 12 when a Japan Air Lines 747 slammed into a mountain,
killing 520 people in history's largest single-plane accident. In December, a
DC-8 military charter crashed and burst into flames while taking off from
Gander, Newfoundland, killing 248 soldiers and eight crew members. Along
with these accidents was the highly publicized fatal single-engine crashes

with singer Rick Nelson aboard. These accidents resulted in an ongoing decline in public confidence about air safety.

CRISIS

Delta Airlines Flight 191 was a regularly scheduled passenger flight between Fort Lauderdale, Florida, and Los Angeles, California, with an en route stop at the Dallas–Fort Worth International Airport (DFW) (NTSB, 1985). On August 2, 1985, at 3:10 P.M. EDT, Flight 191 departed Fort Lauderdale with 152 passengers and a crew of eleven. The flight was uneventful until passing New Orleans, where a line of weather along the Texas–Louisiana gulf coast had intensified. The flight crew elected to change their route of flight to the more northerly Blue Ridge arrival route to avoid the developing weather. At 5:43 P.M., the Fort Worth Air Route Traffic Control Center (ARTCC) cleared Flight 191 to begin descent. At 5:56 P.M., Flight 191 received an all-aircraft message from Regional Approach Control's Feeder East controller stating the presence of a "little rainshower" north of the airport. At 6:00 P.M., the approach controller asked Flight 191 to reduce its airspeed to 150 knots for sequencing behind a Lear jet. Following clearance to land, the first officer called for the before-landing check. Flight 191 continued its descent along the final approach course.

During its passage through the rain shaft beneath a thunderstorm, Flight 191 entered a microburst which the pilot was unable to traverse successfully. Witnesses on or near State Highway 114 saw the aircraft emerge from the rain about a mile from the end of runway 17L, suddenly plunge belly first to the ground, bounce off the turf and come down again a quarter mile away, grazing one car on Highway 114 and demolishing a second car whose driver was decapitated (Becell, Malone, Noble, Pusey, & Timms, 1985). The plane skipped across a grassy field, ricocheted off a water tower, then burst into flames as it slid across the tarmac into two water tanks. Four million gallons of water poured from the tanks onto the burning remains of the main fuselage (Becell et al., 1985). Portions of the airplane were scattered over hundreds of yards. The tail section, which skidded away from the fire, was the only recognizable part of the wreckage (Magnuson, 1985). Within seconds, the thunderstorm unleashed a torrent over the scattered debris of Flight 191 (Becell et al., 1985). Fourteen minutes after the crash, an airport wind shear alarm—signaling abrupt and dangerous shifts of wind speed and direction—sounded (NTSB, 1985).

POST-CRISIS

Search and Recovery

Following the crash, a full alarm went out to airport police, fire stations, and area police. The DFW Airport's Department of Public Safety Communication Center was notified of the accident and followed its FAA-approved

DFW Airport Emergency Plan. All fire and emergency units were immediately alerted (Pryzant & Hoppe, 1985). Rescue workers, including more than fifty state troopers, DFW's airport police, ambulances from several counties, Red Cross officials, FAA workers, and Dallas and Fort Worth Civil Defense crews rushed to the crash site (Perry, 1985). A group of priests from a local Catholic college were called to the scene to administer last rites (Timms, 1985a).

Most fires were either extinguished or under control within about ten minutes after notification despite heavy rains, high winds, and wind gusts. Firefighters then assisted in rescuing trapped and injured persons. A large crane lifted pieces of wreckage to search for bodies. Rescue workers established a medical screening area at the crash scene to facilitate aid for victims found alive in the burning wreckage. The injured were transported to nearby hospitals. Emergency personnel directed traffic, sealed off the crash site, and helped to locate and carry away bodies. A temporary morgue was established at a Delta hangar (McFadden, 1985). Bodies were later transported by refrigerated trucks to the Dallas County medical examiners office for identification.

Two planes bound for DFW Airport were diverted to Dallas Love Field immediately after the crash (Timms, 1985a). Passengers at the airport were also transported to Dallas Love Field, and later returned. A vast traffic jam developed on State Highway 114, hindering ambulances and rescue crews streaming to the scene (Connelly, 1985). Through the night the death toll mounted and some of the critically injured were not expected to survive. Rescuers continued to work in the rain with floodlights illuminating the scene. On board, 134 passengers and crew members were killed, including all three members of the cockpit crew; twenty-seven passengers on board the plane were injured and two passengers were uninjured (NTSB, 1985). The survivors were seated in the tail section of the plane.

Investigation

The National Transportation Safety Board received notification of the accident at approximately 7:30 P.M. EDT. A few hours after the crash, the twelve-member investigation go-team arrived at the site and began their investigation. The team included one member of the Safety Board and specialists in air traffic control, engine functions, hydraulics, aerodynamic structures, human performance, emergency response, and meteorology (Pusey, 1985a). By the next day at noon, more than 100 NTSB staffers, industry experts, and experienced consultants gathered to assist in the investigation (Pusey, 1985c). Parties to the investigation included the FAA, Delta Airlines, the Air Line Pilots Association, Lockheed California Company, Dallas–Fort Worth Airport, Rolls Royce Ltd., National Weather Service, Federal Bureau of Investigation, and Airport Operators Council International (NTSB, 1985). Investigative groups were formed for operations, air traffic control, witnesses, meteorology, survival factors, structures, power plants, airplane systems, DFDR, maintenance records, CVR, airplane performance, human performance, and airport emergency response (NTSB, 1985, p. 91).

At the site of the crash, investigative groups began their activities early each day and reported their findings at nightly progress meetings (Pusey, 1985c). Teams assessed the wreckage, secured records, reviewed flight and weather data, and interviewed key witnesses. Wreckage pieces were charted and key pieces which evidenced breakage, wear, or metal fatigue were secured. Engines were examined and the positions of gauges or operating parts were recorded. Investigators studied the remains of the wings to see how the plane was configured (Reid, 1985). Structures, systems, and powerplants were also examined at the crash site as well as aircraft records and records obtained from the control tower at the airport and NWS.

While technical specialists attempted to reconstruct the physical condition of the aircraft, weather and air traffic control specialists examined the flight conditions at the time of the crash (Pusey, 1985a). Tests were conducted on airport wind sensors. Investigators interviewed air traffic controllers, witnesses on the ground, surviving passengers and cabin crew, and flight crews landing at or departing DFW at the time of the crash. The tape recording of a conversation between Air Traffic Control (ATC) and the Delta crew during approach was obtained by investigators (Reid, 1985). Officials from the Dallas County Medical Examiner's Office attempted to identify the bodies and determine the cause of death (Timms, 1985a). By determining the cause of death, the medical examiners could identify where and how the fire started. A limited toxicological analysis was also conducted on the flight crew (NTSB, 1985).

Following the accident there was little doubt the crash was weather related. Witnesses described a rapidly developing storm at the time of the accident with treacherous conditions in the vicinity of the landing (Reinhold, 1985b). Some witnesses reported seeing lightning strike the plane; however, NTSB investigators stated this was unlikely since jets are electrically grounded (Reid, 1985). In addition, an experienced flight attendant who survived the crash said she saw no lightning strike (Timms & Pusey, 1985).

After the first full day of investigation, investigators stated that while they could not provide a reason for the disaster, wind shear was a prime suspect because of the aircraft's sudden drop to the ground. Wind shear (a sudden turbulence that can destabilize a plane) was not a new term. Between 1964 and 1985, wind shear had been blamed for twenty-eight accidents. In 1982, a Pan American World Airways jet crashed in a rainstorm near New Orleans, killing all 145 people aboard and eight on the ground (Greer, 1985). While wind shear had long been identified as a flight hazard, particularly dangerous during takeoff and landing operations, wind shear detection systems at most U.S. airports were inadequate. Since 1983, the NTSB had made twenty-two recommendations to the FAA regarding wind shear, but the FAA was slow to implement improved systems and develop a wind shear training program. Existing technology, in the form of Doppler radar equipment, could successfully track microburst movements. However, budgetary politics delayed installation of the system (Sanger, 1985). As a consequence of the present detection system, there was much uncertainty about wind shear and its effect on the safety of air travel.

Preliminary findings from the flight data recorder, indicating several fluctuations in airspeed during the final minutes of the flight, strengthened the likelihood that Flight 191 had encountered wind shear (Klose, 1985). No severe weather bulletins were transmitted from Dallas–Fort Worth's control tower to any planes and no dangerous conditions were detected by the airport's wind shear warning devices, although wind shear alarms sounded several minutes after the crash (Malone, 1985c). Tests conducted on the wind sensors at Dallas–Fort Worth showed them functioning at the time of the accident, but investigators noted that wind shear detectors did not always detect the brief, violent weather phenomenon. Recordings from the plane's CVR indicated the pilots of Flight 191 were not concerned just before the accident. These findings suggested the crew and air traffic controllers were not aware of the severity of the storm (Pusey, 1985b). Investigators continued to probe the possibility of wind shear.

On the second day of the investigation, the NTSB disclosed information about the role of the controller in the events leading to the accident. An air traffic controller had directed the Flight 191 pilot to slow down to 150 knots because he was overtaking a Lear jet. Investigators suggested the order to decrease speed may have been fatal since speed was necessary to control the aircraft during wind shear. When the controller saw Flight 191 come out of the rainstorm, the aircraft appeared to be only 50 to 100 feet from the ground. He frantically ordered "Delta go around!" However, the order for Flight 191 to abort its landing came too late (Reinhold, 1985a). Evidence indicated the flight crew did not hear the controller's order and the plane had already struck the ground by the time the controller warned him (Klose & Reid, 1985). While preliminary findings raised questions about the controller's actions, there was no evidence the controller committed any error (Reinhold, 1985b).

Investigators sought information concerning the flight crew's actions prior to the crash. The flight crew was properly certificated and each crew member had received the training and off-duty time prescribed by FAA regulations. There was no evidence of any preexisting medical or physiological conditions which affected the flight crew's performance (NTSB, 1985). Moments before the crash a cockpit ground proximity alarm had warned the crew of Flight 191 to "Pull up! Pull up!" This occurred before the Dallas–Fort Worth controller spotted the plane emerging dangerously low from the thunderstorm. Evidence had not been gathered to determine whether the crew had responded to the alarm (Klose, 1985). A preliminary examination of the plane's flight data recorder showed an abrupt burst of power applied prior to crashing, indicating the pilot may have sensed the plane was in trouble and was trying to gain altitude (Reinhold, 1985a).

Officials continued to investigate other possible causes. The airplane was certificated, equipped, and maintained in accordance with federal regulations and approved procedures (NTSB, 1985). There was no evidence of any malfunctions of major control or power systems that would have affected its performance (Klose & Reid, 1985). Preliminary tests showed the jet's three Rolls Royce turbofan engines were in working order (Timms & Pusey, 1985). In addition, the plane's flaps and rudders were in the correct position (Reinhold, 1985b).

While aircraft and maintenance difficulties were eliminated, questions arose concerning whether Flight 191 would have disintegrated had it not collided with the two water tanks near the runway at the Dallas–Fort Worth Airport. The NTSB believed the aircraft would most likely have emerged intact had it missed the water tanks; however, the tanks were in an area well away from the runway according to the FAA's prescribed criteria (Pusey & Timms, 1985). Officials noted the two tanks may have prevented an even greater tragedy, since the aircraft was heading for a cargo area where personnel were at work and additional aircraft were parked.

One week after the crash the NTSB had answered many of the questions surrounding Delta Flight 191, though they were still months away from stating the cause. At the end of September, the NTSB released reports which confirmed initial suspicions and dispensed additional information regarding the events surrounding the crash of Flight 191. Technical evidence verified that Flight 191 encountered severe wind shear immediately before crashing and confirmed initial accounts that the crew and air traffic controllers were not aware of the potential dangers of the storm (Golden, 1985a). The CVR contained exchanges which indicated the crew only realized shortly before crashing they were in trouble. At 6:03, the pilot of Flight 191 stated, "Tower, Delta 191 heavy out here in the rain, feels good," but at 6:05 the captain told his copilot, "Watch your speed. You're gonna lose it all of a sudden, there it is." He quickly followed the warning, "Push it up! Push it way up!" The CVR recorded sounds of the engine at high thrust, followed by the captain saying, "That's it . . . Hang onto . . ." The captain called for the copilot to abort the landing attempt and climb away from the airport (Witkin, 1985).

According to the NTSB, weather advisories were inaccurate. The National Weather Service area forecast called for isolated thunderstorms with moderate rain showers for northern and eastern portions of Texas, but no severe weather warnings, local aviation warnings, severe weather watches, or central weather advisories were in effect for the time and area of the accident (NTSB, 1985). NTSB documents indicated the first official weather observation received by the tower came five minutes after the thunderstorm began and one minute after the crash, and described conditions such as thunderstorms, lightning, and rain showers. The NTSB stated that at no time did the thunderstorm over Dallas–Fort Worth meet the NWS severe thunderstorm radar criteria (Ott, 1985).

The NTSB discovered that air traffic controllers received information about the possibility of thunderstorms from the weather service ten minutes before the accident, but did not relay the information to Flight 191. An air traffic controller advised the crew of the plane behind Flight 191 that there was a "little bitty thunderstorm sitting right on the final," but the Delta crew had already tuned into the radio frequency of arrival Radar One which instructed the jet to begin its final descent (Malone, 1985b). Delta was then passed from arrival Radar One to Local Control and entered the cloud bank. The control tower then gave clearance to land. The mention of a thunderstorm was potentially significant because the Delta crew had no indication that the cloud bank they flew into was anything more than a rain shower. The last weather transmission Flight 191 received from the tower did not indicate danger.

The NTSB reports also disclosed that pilots of aircraft nearing the airport at the time of the crash experienced or observed severe weather, but did not report it to the controllers. The crew of a Delta plane detected strong winds and observed a water spout at the end of the runway three minutes before Flight 191 was to use it. The pilot of a private Lear jet preceding Flight 191 to the same runway encountered a sudden loss of airspeed and altitude, a typical sign of microburst wind shear, but did not immediately report it (Feaver, 1985). This evidence further supported weather as the cause and raised questions concerning the responsibility of pilots.

Investigators examined the response of the crew of Flight 191. While the 191 flight crew was aware of storms, investigators suggested it may have looked fairly benign from the cockpit until it was too late to recover (Feaver, 1985). Additional evidence indicated otherwise. One minute before the crash the first officer reported seeing lightning directly ahead of the aircraft (NTSB, 1985). Though Delta training procedures specified that departures or approaches should never be flown through a thunderstorm cell, Flight 191 continued its approach (Timms, 1985b). Prior to the public hearing, the NTSB released a report stating the severe microburst wind shear Flight 191 encountered on approach could have been successfully flown through had the flight crew utilized different techniques. A review of records indicated the crew of Delta Flight 191 had completed annual recurrent training where they received information on how to handle the unpredictable microburst (Ott, 1985). Since the performance of the flight crew was not analyzed, blame could not be assigned (Golden & Nelson, 1985).

Public Hearing

On October 29, 1985, a four-day public hearing convened in Irving, Texas. Those testifying included survivors, ground witnesses, air traffic controllers, meteorologists from the NWS, pilots from aircraft that landed at or approached DFW Airport at the time of the crash, and a NASA engineer. One additional deposition was taken on December 12, 1985 (NTSB, 1985). Parties represented at the hearing were the FAA, Delta Airlines, the ALPA, the Lockheed California Company, the Professional Flight Controllers Association, and the NWS (NTSB, 1985).

The NTSB public hearings explored the technology for detecting wind shear, adequacy of the system for disseminating weather information, and whether the Flight 191 pilots took appropriate actions to avoid crashing. The NWS and air traffic controllers defended their positions. Employees at the NWS stated that the storm cell had not appeared significant enough for them to issue special warnings (Golden, 1985b). Testimony from Dallas–Fort Worth controllers indicated they never received clear information from the NWS or pilots about the weather Flight 191 encountered (Golden, 1985d). The NTSB presented evidence that the controllers were busy performing their primary duties of separating traffic, and that disseminating unofficial weather information was secondary and would have interfered.

The flight crew's lack of pertinent weather information and failure to use prescribed recovery techniques when they encountered the wind shear received further attention in the hearings. Experts from NASA testified that data from the plane's flight recorder showed the pilots did not attempt to raise the airplane's nose and apply full power as it encountered a sudden tail wind, which might have kept the airplane airborne (Golden, 1985c).

Conclusions and Recommendations

The crash of Delta Flight 191 occurred when the aircraft encountered, at low altitude, a microburst-induced severe wind shear from a rapidly developing thunderstorm located on the final approach. The Safety Board was presented with two separate analyses by its technical staff. The unusual submission of two reports reflected significant disagreements over the cause of the crash. The technical staff's two separate analyses did not disagree over the factual portion of the investigation, only over what conclusions should be drawn (Tarrant, 1986). One view proposed the aircraft's unexpected encounter at low altitude with microburst-induced wind shear was the single probable cause. This view suggested the Board's determination should be placed on microburst and inadequate weather forecasts, not pilot complacency. The other view contended the probable cause was the captain's failure to recognize the severity of the storm and his decision to bring the plane down (Ott, 1986). The storm should have been visible to the crew as the plane approached the airport. In other words, the disagreement was over whether to place blame on the weather and the lack of adequate forecasts or on the Delta flight crew.

A compromise about probable cause was reached, bringing together elements of the two analyses. The NTSB formally described its findings and offered recommendations on July 5, 1986. The NTSB ruled the probable cause of the accident as the flight crew's decision to initiate and continue the landing approach into a cumulonimbus cloud which they observed to contain visible lightning; the lack of specific guidelines, procedures, and training for avoiding and escaping from low-altitude wind shear; and the lack of specific, "real time" wind shear hazard information which resulted in the aircraft's encounter at low altitude with a microburst-induced severe wind shear from a rapidly developing thunderstorm located on the final approach course (NTSB, 1985). Based on their findings, the NTSB made recommendations to the FAA, the NWS, the National Oceanic and Atmospheric Administration, the DFW Airport, the American Association of Airport Executives, the Airport Operators Council International, and the National Fire Protection Association. The recommendations concerned such topics as training, staffing, weather information, flight-attendant seats, and disaster response.

Industry Response

Soon after the crash, the NTSB reported that the air traffic controllers, employed by the FAA, did not tell the crew of Flight 191 about a weather forecast indicating the possibility of thunderstorms (Engelberg, 1985). In early October, the NTSB released a report indicating that the pilot of Delta Flight 191 had criticized the air traffic controllers for not being alert ("Controllers defended," 1985). This spurred defensive responses by the FAA and the DFW Airport. An FAA official stated the captain's statements were either incorrect or were reported out of context from transcripts of the CVR. The Dallas–Fort Worth Airport manager stated that controllers felt mistreated and were very concerned about these inaccuracies. During the public hearings on the crash, the air traffic controllers responded by defending their actions in the events leading to the crash (Golden, 1985d).

The crash of Delta Flight 191 reaffirmed wind shear as a major hazard in air travel. Efforts to deal with wind shears were accelerated following the accident. Government and industry responded after the Safety Board announced that the aircraft had encountered wind shear and expressed the need for the development of Doppler radar, which could predict in advance where wind shear might occur. Donald Engen, the Federal Aviation Administrator, stated his agency was spending millions of dollars to develop the radar, but the research was not complete. He called the system a "top priority" (Engelberg, 1985). A group of government and industry experts asserted the accident was probably avoidable with the Doppler radar equipment, but admitted budgetary politics and bad planning had delayed installation of the system (Sanger, 1985). The concern for wind shear technology prompted a U.S. House investigation into both the Delta crash and a federal funding delay stalling the development of the Doppler radar system (Reifenberg, 1985).

A Congressional hearing on wind shear and air safety issues was held in early October, drawing witnesses from government and industry who urged speedy implementation of the sophisticated Doppler radar (Golden, 1985a). During the hearings, NTSB members responded to questions concerning the Delta crash and its circumstances. In November of 1985, the Transportation Department awarded a $1.8-million contract for a training program to help pilots detect and handle sudden wind shifts ("Training aims," 1985). While the FAA Administrator denied the Delta crash was the main cause of the program, it was a contributing factor.

Media Coverage

Immediately following the crash, radio station WNWS in Fort Lauderdale, Florida, Flight 191's origination point, suspended its regular programming to broadcast a live feed from KRLD radio in Dallas, with crash news ("Relatives, friends on both coasts," 1985). Media reports focused on accounts of survivors, reactions from victims' families and the Dallas–Fort Worth communities, and liability (Adams, 1985; Parmley, 1985). Other stories included the Dallas County Medical Examiner's task of identifying bodies, postal workers salvaging crash mail, as well as reported premonitions about the crash (Bedell, 1985; Riner, 1985; Weiss, 1985). Television journalists provided live impressions of the crash and its effects. Several hours after the crash, ABC's "Nightline" devoted its entire program to the crash (Shales, 1985).

Newspapers from around the country carried daily accounts of the go-team's findings and progress. From the beginning, media reports indicated that the crash was weather related.

CRISIS COMMUNICATION:
AN ANALYSIS OF DELTA'S COMMUNICATION

Delta immediately implemented its long-established crisis plan, not used since the airline's 1973 crash at Boston's Logan Airport. Immediately following the crash, Delta's command team, composed of top officials, gathered to implement emergency plans. The airline communicated openly with its employees, families, and media (Fulton & Tarrant, 1985). While Delta communicated openly, the information it provided was limited due to restrictions imposed by the NTSB pending investigation. The air carrier responded immediately to liability concerns by indicating it had adequate insurance to cover any claims (Shapiro & Travella, 1985).

Assistance was provided by more than 90 out-of-state employees and at least 120 other local employees (Tarrant, 1985). Company representatives assigned to each family offered financial help, counseled, accompanied families to the crash site, and assisted in identifying bodies and arranging funerals. Delta paid for the families' transportation to the crash site, accommodations, medical care, and funerals (Nichols, 1985). After releasing the list of fatalities subsequent to family notification, the flag at the main gate of Delta's

Atlanta headquarters was lowered to half-staff (Nichols, 1985). Delta Airlines Flight 191 became the second flight with that number bound for Los Angeles to end in disaster. After the crash, Delta dropped "Flight 191" from its list of flight numbers (Malone, 1985a). Flight 191 became Flight 139.

Delta was commended for its immediate and appropriate response following the crash of Flight 191. The airline received praise by the Chairman of the ALPA, who stated, "Under the circumstances Delta did even better than could be expected" (Fulton & Tarrant, 1985). Delta was further challenged by the Flight 191 crisis after evidence suggested pilot error caused the crash. While the aircraft had clearly encountered wind shear, additional findings suggested the Flight 191 captain failed to recognize the severity of the storm and continued to bring the plane down. Responsibility for the accident could potentially damage the airline's image as a safe and reliable carrier. Delta's defense in response to the assignment of blame is examined in the following analysis.

Responding to the Issue of Blame

Throughout the investigation, Delta denied it was in error. The airline contended that no aircraft could have successfully maneuvered through such violent, rapidly shifting winds (Valente, 1986a). Delta, along with the ALPA, redirected blame by maintaining that a breakdown in communication between government-contract weather forecasters and air traffic controllers accounted for the Delta flight crew flying into the thunderstorm (Howlett & Tarrant, 1986). The airline denied any irregular company operations preceding or following the flight and could only provide general information as to why the crash occurred.

The NTSB's disclosure suggesting the ATC may have played a role in the crash proved useful for Delta in responding to liability. In late August, a lawsuit was filed against the airline by the wife of a passenger killed in the crash. The airline sought to have the FAA share in the liability and named the administration as a third party in the lawsuit. On August 29, Delta filed a petition contending the crash was caused by the negligence of air traffic control personnel employed by the aviation agency. Delta sought contribution from the FAA for any liability issued against it as a result of the lawsuit ("Delta names FAA," 1985). Subsequent to the NTSB's announcement that pilot error may have been the cause, Delta directed blame to the FAA by stating the air traffic controllers, employed by the FAA, failed to inform the Flight 191 crew about the possibility of thunderstorms (Engelberg, 1985).

Delta continued to deny responsibility for the crash after the NTSB's ruling on the probable causes. Following the NTSB's determination of the probable cause, Delta and the ALPA argued that the report primarily and unfairly placed blame on the flight crew. Delta officials admitted disappointment in the decision and in a prepared statement called the finding "incomplete, inaccurate, and most painfully flawed" (Valente, 1986b). Delta's general counsel indicated the airline would likely ask the Board to reconsider its decision after company officials examined the Safety Board's report.

Following the NTSB's final report, Delta attempted to lessen responsibility for the crash by offering excuses and pleading ignorance. In March 1986, Delta Airlines responded to the NTSB in a 110-page report in which the airline explained extenuating circumstances. According to Delta, its pilots did everything possible to save the jet from crashing (Golden, 1986). The microburst's violent curls of wind were the most severe ever documented in an aircraft accident investigation and were impossible to fly through successfully. Delta noted the violence of the microburst had not been considered in the NTSB study. The airline also asserted the crew tried to use recommended wind shear procedures, but were hampered by the violent winds. The unpredictable nature of wind shear indicated the crash was an accident which could not have been controlled.

The airline argued the pilots did not have accurate information on which to base their decision because of the "rigid, slow and inflexible manner" in which the NWS data are collected and disseminated by air traffic controllers (Golden, 1986). This suggested the situation was out of the flight crew's control. Following the NTSB's final ruling, Delta's chief accident investigator remarked the NTSB should have focused more heavily on the FAA's failure to move more quickly on installing better equipment for detecting microburst, as well as the inability of the current system to notify pilots immediately of unexpected changes in weather (Valente, 1986b).

On May 5, 1986, Delta, responding to information gained during the investigation, issued a temporary revision to the Pilots Operating Manual concerning wind shear guidelines. The revision stated Delta's policy concerning wind shear continued to be "avoidance" (NTSB, 1985). By acting on the NTSB's findings, Delta attempted to correct the problem.

EVALUATION OF STRATEGIES

Industry analysts indicated the tragedy of Delta Flight 191 had little impact on Delta's operations or profitability (Booth, 1986). In the weeks immediately following the crash, Delta's passenger bookings rose, and the airline continued to be ranked above all other airlines for service quality (Wayne, 1986). This was attributed to Delta's reputation as a high-quality company with an excellent safety record and to the record number of airline crashes in 1985 which limited travelers concerned with a company's safety record (Booth, 1986). Delta was ranked fourth among the twelve major carriers for 1985 revenue passenger miles ("Airline traffic," 1986). Delta's profits and passenger boardings fluctuated following the crash; however, company officials and industry observers attributed the fluctuations to the wars and restrictions on growth caused by unresolved contract negotiations with Delta's 4 thousand pilots.

The effectiveness of Delta's communication following the Flight 191 crash will be evaluated in the following section according to the severity of the disaster, evidence as to cause, and Delta's performance history. First, as with any major airline crash, the damage was severe. The crash of Delta Flight 191 killed 134 and injured twenty-seven passengers on board the plane. The extreme nature of the crisis presented a threat to Delta's image as a safe and reliable carrier.

Second, evidence as to the probable cause of the crash pointed to wind shear. Additional findings indicated the 191 flight crew was aware of the wind shear situation, yet continued the landing approach. While the NTSB assigned blame to the Delta flight crew, the uncertainty associated with wind shear and questions about inadequate information from the National Weather Service and the air traffic controllers suggested the Delta pilots had little control over the situation. The ambiguity of evidence was reinforced when the NTSB technical staff presented two separate analyses to its board members. The issue, then, was act of nature versus human error. An act of nature is generally considered less controllable, whereas human error is seen as more controllable; thus, stakeholders are less likely to negatively respond to acts of nature than human error.

Third, as a consequence of its excellent performance record, Delta had a high level of credibility prior to the Flight 191 crash. This positive performance history functioned to create a "halo effect," in that Delta was perceived as sincerely concerned following the crash. Further, this halo effect extended to reinforce the notion that the cause of the crash must have been a surprising and unanticipated act of nature, rather than human error on the part of Delta. These three factors were influential to Delta's communication after the accident.

Delta's immediate actions following the crash portrayed the airline as sensitive and concerned. The airline's "coming together" tended to reinforce its "family" image. By communicating openly, the airline avoided raising additional suspicions that they were withholding information. These efforts were enhanced by Delta's preexisting positive image. Victims' families expressed appreciation for Delta's compassion (Thompson & Hess, 1986). Commendations for Delta's response to the crash and the minimal impact of the crash on the company's operations and profitability suggest the airline was successful in managing and communicating in the immediate aftermath of the crash.

When evaluating Delta's defense against the assignment of blame in light of the severity of the disaster, evidence as to cause, and Delta's performance history, it is obvious that the airline's strategies of denying responsibility, hedging responsibility, and righting the wrong were appropriate. Delta's performance history effectively supported the strategies of denial and hedging responsibility. The difficulty in detecting wind shear made denial a reasonable strategy. Clearly, flight crews have low control over natural events such as wind shear. Low external control increases an organization's susceptibility to crisis. Consequently, the industry's vulnerability to crisis is recognized. Airline officials further denied responsibility for the crash by redirecting blame to the NWS and FAA. Investigative findings suggested that this was a likely possibility.

Strategies designed to lessen responsibility were practical, based on the situation. In light of available technology in 1985, every airline was susceptible to the volatility of wind shear. Implying the crash was an accident seemed appropriate. A lack of critical information implied that the flight crew could not be held totally responsible. Moreover, righting the wrong was effective in promoting the company's image by showing Delta's concern about safety and the issue of wind shear.

CONCLUSION

Three important lessons surface in the case of Delta Flight 191:

1. Ambiguity of evidence as to the cause of a crisis event may create dissonance in the minds of stakeholders, strengthening the position of the company in question to effectively execute a line of defense which shapes, changes, or reinforces stakeholders' beliefs in accepting its claim.

2. In developing a line of defense, a company should not lose sight of positioning itself as one that takes safety seriously and is concerned about preventing a future recurrence.

3. A high level of corporate credibility prior to a crisis event can function to create a halo effect for the company in question, making its actions and statements more believable.

A company is better able to develop a line of defense to effectively counter accusations and influence stakeholder's opinions when there is a lack of consensus on the probable cause or source of blame for an event and evidence lends itself to reasoning which supports a company's claim of innocence. Reasoning is the process of drawing a conclusion on the basis of evidence. This by no means implies a company should manipulate the situation or evidence through false or unethical methods. Messages should be sincere, factual, correct, and consistent. The fact that the NTSB was presented with two separate analyses of the accident demonstrated uncertainty as to the cause of the crash. Disagreement existed over whether the weather and the lack of adequate forecasts or the Delta flight crew was responsible for the accident. In other words, evidence supported both views. The NTSB's difficulty in determining a probable cause provided Delta an advantage in arguing its position. Delta consistently denied its pilots erred, arguing ATC had been negligent by not informing the Flight 191 crew about the possibility of thunderstorms. The uncertainty associated with wind shear at the time of the accident further suggested Delta had little control over the situation and could not be held fully responsible.

Delta's experience also teaches a second very important lesson. When defending against accusations of blame, a company must simultaneously convey its sincere concern about safety and the prevention of a future recurrence. While Delta's main line of defense was to deny blame for the crash, it demonstrated its concern for safety and the issue of wind shear by taking appropriate corrective actions.

Delta's success in defending its position can be further attributed to corporate credibility. A high level of corporate credibility prior to a crisis event can function to create a halo effect for the company, making its actions and statements more believable. It has long been recognized that credibility is extremely important in persuasion. Establishing and maintaining credibility during crisis is considered critical to achieving strategic communication goals. Delta's credibility enhanced its defensive strategies. At the time of the accident, Delta was one of the most successful carriers in the industry.

While corporate credibility is clearly an asset in crisis, it may not be sufficient to fully influence stakeholder opinions. In 1986, Gerber responded to what eventually proved to be unsubstantiated claims of broken glass in its jars of baby food. The company relied heavily on the FDA's credibility. Gerber utilized the FDA evidence and spokespersons to communicate the truth about the safety of baby food (Lovejoy, 1993). Though Gerber was considered highly credible, the FDA had a greater base of legitimacy than did a commercial entity.

Whatever the situation, crisis communicators should understand one thing: Companies must have credibility for messages to be heard by stakeholders. The absence of corporate credibility will likely perpetuate the crisis.

REFERENCES

Adams, L. (1985, August 3). Survivor report brings relief, despair to kin. *Dallas Morning News*, p. C4 (NewsBank, 1985, TRA 48).

Airline traffic 1985. (1986, April 7). *Aviation Week & Space Technology*, p. 45.

Becell, D., Malone, D., Noble, A., Pusey, A., & Timms, E. (1985, August 11). Final minutes of flight 191's flight into disaster. *Dallas Morning News*, pp. A3–6 (NewsBank, 1985, TRA 49).

Bedell, D. (1985, August 5). Examiner regarded as tops in the field. *Dallas Morning News*, pp. B7–8 (NewsBank, 1985, TRA 49).

Booth, J. (1986, July 31). Experts: Airline profits endure beyond crashes. *Dallas Times Herald*, pp. B10–12 (NewsBank, 1986, TRA 46).

Connelly, R. (1985, August 4). Airports response to crash hit few snags, officials say. *Dallas Morning News*, pp. F7–10.

Controllers defended in jet crash at Dallas. (1985, October 4). *New York Times*, p. A16.

Davies, R. E. G. (1990). *Delta: An airline and its aircraft*. Miami, FL: Paladwr Press.

Delta names FAA in crash lawsuit. (1985, September 5). *New York Times*, p. B14.

Engelberg, S. (1985, August 12). No storm warning for doomed jet. *New York Times*, p. A1.

Feaver, D. B. (1985, October 1). Doomed jets saw storm ahead. *Washington Post*, p. A7.

Fulton, D., & Tarrant, D. (1985, August 5). Delta executives mobilized quickly after jetliner crash. *Dallas Morning News*, pp. B13–14 (NewsBank, 1985, TRA 48).

Golden, G. (1985a, October 3). Data confirms flight 191 hit wind shear. *Dallas Morning News*, pp. A9–10 (NewsBank, 1985, TRA, 62).

Golden, G. (1985b, October 30). Safety board opens hearings. *Dallas Morning News*, pp. B2–3 (NewsBank, 1985, TRA 66).

Golden, G. (1985c, November 1). Crash hearings focus on pilots actions. *Dallas Morning News*, pp. B8–9 (NewsBank, 1985, TRA 66).

Golden, G. (1985d, November 2). Air controllers defend actions. *Dallas Morning News*, pp. B10–11 (NewsBank, 1985, TRA 66).

Golden, G. (1986, March 5). Pilots did everything to save jet, Delta says. *Dallas Morning News*, pp. B11–12 (NewsBank, 1986, TRA 14).

Golden G., & Nelson, M. (1985, October 25). Delta jet could have survived wind shear, report says. *Dallas Morning News*, pp. A12–14 (NewsBank, 1985, TRA 66).

Greer, W.R. (1985, August 4). Windbursts seen as worst hazard. *New York Times*, p. 24.

Howlett, T., & Tarrant, D. (1986, July 16). Airline, pilots union vow to file protests of findings. *Dallas Morning News*, pp. B5–6 (NewsBank, 1986, TRA 40).

Klose, K. (1985, August 6). Cockpit alarm warned of low altitude. *Washington Post*, p. A1.

Klose, K., & Reid, T. R. (1985, August 5). Speed cut before jet crashed. *Washington Post*, p. A1.

Lovejoy, L. J. (1993). Villains and victims of product tampering. In J. A. Gottschalk (Ed.), *Crisis response: Inside stories on managing image under siege* (pp. 175–184). Detroit, MI: Visible Ink Press.

Magnuson, E. (1985, August 12). Like a wall of napalm. *Time*, pp. 18–19.

Malone, D. (1985a, August 10). Flight 191 to get new number Sept. 1. *Dallas Morning News*, p. C9 (NewsBank, 1985, TRA 49).

Malone, D. (1985b, August 13). Flight 191 barely missed hearing storm message. *Dallas Morning News*, pp. G1–2 (NewsBank, 1985, TRA 48).

Malone, D. (1985c, August 24). Death toll rises to 131. *Dallas Morning News*, pp. C8–9 (NewsBank, 1985, TRA 48).

McFadden, R. D. (1985, August 3). Jetliner with 161 crashes in Texas; at least 122 dead. *New York Times*, p. A1.

National Transportation Safety Board. (1985). *Aircraft Accident Report: Delta Air Lines, Inc., Lockheed 1-1011-385-1, N726DA, Dallas–Fort Worth International Airport, Texas, August 2, 1985* (NTSB/AAR-86/05). Washington, DC: National Transportation Safety Board (NTIS No. PB86-910406).

Nichols, B. (1985, August 4). Delta relies on instinct for toughest job. *Dallas Morning News*, p. B6 (NewsBank, 1985, TRA 48).

NTSB urges renewed emphasis on shortcomings of rvr data. (1974, April 22). *Aviation Week & Space Technology*, p. 26.

Ott, J. (1985, October 7). Recorder reveals lightning preceded Delta L-1011 crash. *Aviation Week & Space Technology*, pp. 26–27.

Ott, J. (1986, July 21). NTSB cites multiple probable causes in Delta Air Lines crash. *Aviation Week & Space Technology*, pp. 32–33.

Parmley, H. (1985, August 5). Solace sought in prayer. *Dallas Morning News*, pp. B7–8 (NewsBank, 1985, TRA 48).

Perry, I. (1985, August 4). Looters among first at scene. *Houston Post*, p. A14.

Pryzant, C., & Hoppe, C. (1985, August 3). Crash aid arrives rapidly. *Dallas Morning News*, pp. E2–3 (NewsBank, 1985, TRA 48).

Pusey, A. (1985a, August 3). Inquiry already under way. *Dallas Morning News*, p. F11 (NewsBank, 1985, TRA 48).

Pusey, A. (1985b, August 4). No wind shear reported before crash, officials say. *Dallas Morning News*, pp. F2–3 (NewsBank, 1985, TRA 48).

Pusey, A. (1985c, August 8). Go-team staff assessing jet crash. *Dallas Morning News*, pp. G3–4 (NewsBank, 1985, TRA 48).

Pusey, A., & Timms, E. (1985, August 7). Water tank may have doomed jet. *Dallas Morning News*, pp. G7–8 (NewsBank, 1985, TRA 48).

Reid, T. R. (1985, August 4). Wind shear suspected in jet crash. *Washington Post*, p. A1.

Reifenberg, A. (1985, August 6). House inquiry into crash sought. *Dallas Morning News*, pp. G11–13 (NewsBank, 1985, TRA 48).

Reinhold, R. (1985a, August 5). Delta pilot told to abort landing apparently after it had crashed. *New York Times*, p. A1.

Reinhold, R. (1985b, August 6). Pilot seen as hobbled by order to slow down to avoid 2nd jet. *New York Times*, p. A10.

Relatives, friends on both coasts keep agonized vigil. (1985, August 3). *Dallas Morning News*, pp. C1–3 (NewsBank, 1985, TRA 48).

Riner, B. (1985, August 6). Officials salvage some crash mail. *Dallas Morning News*, p. B2 (NewsBank, 1985, TRA 48).

Sanger, D. E. (1985, August 8). Trying to spot wind shear. *New York Times*, p. D2.

Shales, T. (1985, August 5). Covering the crash. *Washington Post*, p. B1.

Shapiro, S., & Travella, S. (1985, August 12). Insurers reserve $125 million for Delta liability. *Business Insurance*, p. 1.

Standard New York Stock Exchange Reports. (1985, August 20). Delta Airlines.

Tarrant, D. (1985, August 14). Delta employees gather to offer help to grieving families. *Dallas Morning News*, p. 5 (NewsBank, 1985, TRA 48).

Tarrant, D. (1986, July 13). NTSB at odds over 191 crash. *Dallas Morning News*, p. B11.

Thompson, T., & Hess, J. (1986, November 15). Delta accused of Jekyll–Hyde behavior in wake of crash. *Atlanta Journal*, pp. B6–8 (NewsBank, 1986, TRA 68).

Timms, E. (1985a, August 3). Jet crash at D/FW kills 123. *Dallas Morning News*, pp. D3–8 (NewsBank, 1985, TRA 48).

Timms, E. (1985b, October 1). 2nd Delta jet spotted tornado before crash. *Dallas Morning News*, pp. A6–7 (NewsBank, 1985, TRA 62).

Timms, E., & Pusey, A. (1985, August 5). Delta go round. *Dallas Morning News*, pp. E9–12 (NewsBank, 1985, TRA 48).

Training aims at windshifts. (1985, November 30). *New York Times*, p. 48.

Valente, J. (1986a, June 28). Crew misread weather. *Dallas Times Herald*, pp. B7–8 (NewsBank, 1986, TRA 40).

Valente, J. (1986b, July 16). Delta, crew, weather faulted in crash. *Dallas Times Herald*, pp. C2–4 (NewsBank, 1986, TRA 40).

Wayne, L. (1986, March 28). Delta grapples with change. *New York Times*, p. D1.

Weiss, M. (1985, August 4). Premonition. *Dallas Morning News*, p. C14 (NewsBank, 1985, TRA 48).

Witkin, R. (1985, October 1). Crew in Dallas saw bad weather ahead. *New York Times*, p. A1.

Chapter 9

Trans World Airlines Flight 800

As the world awaited the opening of the Centennial Summer Olympic Games in Atlanta, its attention was redirected to a shocking tragedy which claimed 230 souls. The explosion of Trans World Airlines Flight 800 over the Atlantic ocean on July 17 received front-page coverage during the summer months of 1996. The daunting and delayed recovery of bodies and wreckage from the depths of the ocean generated heart-wrenching photographs and stories. An unknown cause deepened the mystery of the doomed aircraft. Speculation ranging from a terrorist bomb, to a missile, to friendly fire kept the story alive for months after the crash. The TWA Flight 800 disaster was voted 1996's biggest news story in an annual Associated Press poll, overshadowing other significant events of the year, including the reelection of President Clinton, the Olympic bombing in Atlanta, the arrest of a suspect in the Unabomber case, and the crash of ValuJet Flight 592 ("Biggest stories," 1997).

The crash resulted in the most expensive and extensive investigative effort ever in the National Transportation Safety Board's history. Jim Danaher (1997), Chief of the Operational Factors Division, NTSB Office of Aviation Safety, noted, "In my 27-years here, there's never been another accident of the magnitude and impact on the staff than this one." Recovery and investigative efforts proved amazing. All 230 victims and 95 to 98 percent of the 747 aircraft wreckage were recovered from the bottom of the ocean. A full-scale reconstruction of the main section of the fuselage, consisting of over 900 pieces of wreckage, became the largest wide body aircraft ever completed in the world. It was truly an inconceivable accomplishment (Hall, 1997b).

TWA Flight 800 illustrates the complexities of crisis management and communication immediately following a major airline disaster. The airline was faced with distraught families, hordes of reporters, and an emotional public. Complications surrounding the completion and release of the passenger manifest, difficulties with family notification, involvement of eager politicians, rumors about the cause of the crash, as well as intense media scrutiny exemplify the chaos TWA experienced during the first few days of the crisis. The case further illuminates the challenges and complexities of post-crisis investigation.

PRE-CRISIS

Historical Background

From its glory days as the airline of Charles Lindbergh and Howard Hughes and a pioneer of intercontinental air transport to its struggle through most of the deregulation era, the history of Trans World Airlines is remarkable. On October 1, 1930, Western Air Express and Transcontinental Air Transport merged to form America's first coast-to-coast airline, Transcontinental and Western Air (TWA). Soon after the merger, the airline began "coast-to-coast all-air service" with an overnight stop in Kansas City (TWA, 1997). During the 1930s, TWA made significant contributions to the airline industry's technological development (Heppenheimer, 1995). Under Jack Frye's leadership, the airline pioneered radio navigation and high-altitude flying and prompted a new generation of transports (Douglas DC-1 and DC-2, and the Boeing 307 Stratocruiser).

Despite its technological success, TWA generated little profit for its owners. In 1939, aviation enthusiast and multimillionaire Howard Hughes became TWA's principal stockholder. The airline made significant contributions to military air transport during World War II and began forming an Intercontinental Division, flying transoceanic flights under military contract. TWA introduced transatlantic service between New York and Paris in 1946. Its expanding international routes resulted in the airline changing its name to Trans World Airlines four years later. In the 1950s, TWA's domestic and international routes experienced faster and longer-range transports and by the end of the decade TWA began Boeing 707 jet service from San Francisco to New York (TWA, 1997). In 1966, Hughes sold his TWA stock and interest to the public.

TWA achieved some notable "firsts" during the 1960s—the first airline to show in-flight motion pictures, to introduce 747 service in the United States, and to offer nonsmoking sections (TWA, 1997). The 1970s, however, presented difficult economic times for the airline. TWA attempted to stabilize its earnings through acquisitions, including Hilton International and the Canteen Corporation. Already troubled by high labor costs and unproductive routes, the Airline Deregulation Act in 1978 further weakened TWA. TWA became a public company in 1983, but soon fell victim to the leveraged-buyout craze of the 1980s. In 1985, Carl Icahn became CEO of the airline following a takeover battle with another corporate raider, Frank Lorenzo. With hopes of reviving the airline, Icahn purchased Ozark Airlines, TWA's primary competitor in the Midwest, the following year. TWA profited in 1987 and 1988, but the heavily leveraged company lost $298 million in 1989. In January 1992, TWA filed for Chapter 11 bankruptcy. A year later Carl Icahn resigned as Chairman of TWA. By the end of 1993, the airline emerged from bankruptcy, with employees owning 45 percent of the airline and creditors owning the remaining 55 percent (TWA, 1997). In 1994, Jeffrey Erickson was named president and CEO. Under Erickson's leadership, TWA successfully completed a record financial reorganization in 1995, placing the airline in its strongest position in ten years. With a team of experienced airline managers and a loyal and dedicated workforce, the airline made a significant turnaround.

Still, Trans World Airlines was far behind the rest of the industry, with the oldest and smallest fleet of all the major airlines and a shrinking route system, as well as a decreased international network. Despite the airline's aging fleet, no major safety accidents had occurred in several years. The FAA asserted with proper inspection and maintenance the age of an aircraft would not affect safety (Alvarez, 1996a). In the early part of 1996, TWA's CEO announced the airline was investing in new technology to improve analysis of route profitability, crew scheduling and routing, revenue accounting, stock control, and aircraft scheduling (Alvarez, 1996a). This was an important move to ensure the airline stayed competitive.

Previous Accidents and Incidents

While TWA had a reputable safety record, it had not been immune to tragedies during its lengthy history. In June 1956, a TWA Super Constellation collided in flight over the Grand Canyon with a United Airlines DC-7, killing 128 people. At the time, the accident was the deadliest in aviation history (Heppenheimer, 1995). The airline's worst safety streak occurred during the early 1970s, when several major crashes took place. On December 1, 1974, a TWA 727 slammed into a ridge in Virginia's Blue Ridge Mountains on approach to Dulles International Airport, claiming the lives of all ninety-two persons on board ("Overseas pioneer," 1996). The accident led to changes in air traffic control procedures. In the same year another TWA jet, a Boeing 707, crashed at Los Angeles International airport when fog hampered visibility. One year later, another TWA jet crashed in foggy conditions at Milan, Italy (Alvarez, 1996a). The airline's last fatal incident occurred in late 1994, when a TWA Boeing 727 collided with a small private plane taking off from St. Louis Lambert Field. Two people aboard the private plane died; however, those aboard the TWA flight escaped injury ("Overseas pioneer," 1996).

TWA became indelibly linked with terrorism following two tragic incidents in the 1980s. The first terroristic act occurred in 1985, when Middle Eastern hijackers held a gun to the head of Captain John Testrake. During the incident, which lasted several days, U.S. Navy diver Robert Stethem was shot and his body dumped onto the runway. Soon after, the takeover ended peacefully ("Overseas pioneer," 1996). The second incident occurred in 1986, when a bomb blew a hole in the bottom of a TWA Boeing 727 over Athens, Greece, and three passengers were sucked out to their deaths. Those remaining aboard the crowded flight from Rome to Greece survived.

A New Beginning

On Wednesday, July 17, 1996, Jeffrey Erickson, along with Mark Abels, TWA's public-relations executive, were in London on a trade mission with officials from Missouri. Earlier in the day Erickson spoke before Parliament on behalf of U.S. airlines's need for more access to Heathrow Airport. Later, in a telephone press conference, he announced to reporters that the St. Louis-based airline recently earned a fourfold increase: "Our fundamentals are strong. They continue to be strong and they project to be strong" ("Crash is latest blow," 1996). The airline was finally maneuvering its way out of the economic distress which had forced it into bankruptcy a few years before. And, despite its aging fleet, TWA's safety record was one of the best among major U.S. airlines.

CRISIS

The 212 passengers, four-member flight deck crew, and fourteen flight attendants aboard TWA Flight 800, a Boeing 747, awaited departure at New York's JFK International Airport. Flight 800, regularly scheduled from New York to Paris's Charles De Gaulle Airport, arrived late that Wednesday afternoon in July from Athens, Greece, following a smooth flight. Scheduled to depart at 7:00 P.M., TWA 800 was delayed twice, first when baggage was pulled for a passenger who showed up late, then when the baggage belt loader broke (Maraniss, 1996). At 8:02, the flight finally left the gate. It lifted off at 8:19 P.M. Both the Captain and the First Officer had been with TWA for thirty years (Dickinson, 1997). At 8:30, Flight 800 acknowledged clearance to 15 thousand feet. One minute later, the aircraft disappeared from radar (Dickinson, 1997). TWA 800 had crashed into the Atlantic Ocean, roughly ten miles offshore to the south of East Moriches on the eastern end of Long Island—sixty miles east of New York City. Initial witness reports indicated an explosion and then flaming debris descending to the ocean (D. Phillips, 1996).

Immediately following the crash, the Long Island, New York, beach resort town of East Moriches swarmed with rescue workers, police, and journalists. The area bordering the crash site was secured by a team from the NTSB's New Jersey office. Wreckage and fuel burned on the water for hours as Coast Guard and Navy planes, along with a small fleet of rescue boats, scoured the dark, choppy waters for signs of life. Scores of volunteers (mariners, fishermen, vacationing boaters) assisted in rescue efforts, pulling human remains from the waters. As darkness fell, parachute flares and floodlights illuminated the waters. On the beaches fronting the Moriches Inlet, a makeshift morgue was set up. As the night wore on it became evident there were no survivors.

POST-CRISIS

Search and Recovery

The enormous rescue effort which began the previous night continued throughout the following day. A massive underwater search and recovery effort was required before the NTSB could begin its investigation. Hundreds of workers and dozens of boats scoured the waters of the 240-square-mile crash site. Coast Guard personnel performed the surface search for bodies and wreckage while the U.S. Navy conducted the underwater search. They were assisted by Oceaneering, Underwater Search and Survey, the National Oceanic and Atmospheric Administration, and dive teams from Suffolk County, New York City, and State Police, Suffolk and New York City Fire Departments, and the FBI (Dickinson, 1997).

The National Transportation Safety Board go-team arrived early and began its investigation. Accompanying the go-team were the Board's vice chairman and members of its Office of Government, Public, and Family Affairs. Parties assisting in the investigation included Trans World Airlines, the Boeing Commercial Airplane Group, Pratt & Whitney, the International Association of Machinist and Aerospace Workers, the FAA, the Independent Federation of Flight Attendants (who have since been absorbed by IAM [International Association of Machinists]), the Air Line Pilots Association, the National Air Traffic Controllers Association, Honeywell, the Crane Company, Hydro-Aire, an FBI terrorist team, and the U.S. Bureau of Alcohol, Tobacco, and Firearms (Dickinson, 1997). In time, over eighteen groups would participate, the most to take part in any NTSB investigation.

The recovery of bodies and wreckage ten to twelve miles offshore and 120 feet underwater was a daunting process. On the second and third days of the investigation recovery efforts were curtailed by fog, rain, choppy seas, and high waves, preventing divers from retrieving bodies and wreckage and even identifying where the wreckage was located. The investigation continued to move ahead, however, as investigators examined pieces of recovered wreckage. With the exceptionally slow progress of victim recovery and identification by the county medical examiner's office, the anguish of victims' relatives grew. In response, New York Governor George Pataki assigned five pathologists and twenty technicians to assist the county medical examiner's office. To further ease families' turmoil, officials flew a small group of relatives over the crash site and briefed them on the recovery effort. A videotape of the rescue scene revealed to other relatives the extent and difficulty of the search (Purdy, 1996).

As time passed the ocean currents spread debris, forcing rescue workers to expand their search area. There were concerns that the extended submersion in salt water would effect the chemical traces of a bomb. The difficulty of recovering wreckage from the ocean necessitated special electronic equipment. Sonar was utilized to identify debris on the ocean floor and special acoustical equipment from the Navy was used in an attempt to locate the flight data recorder and cockpit voice recorder (black boxes). The flight recorders were recovered on July 23.

After two weeks, only 20 percent of the aircraft had been recovered. Investigators encountered the laborious task of untangling mangled masses of metal while Navy ships continued to discover more bodies and salvage aircraft wreckage. Wreckage was transported to a former airplane hangar in Calverton, New York, where it was documented and engineers attempted to piece portions of the aircraft back together. The FBI thoroughly examined the wreckage for traces of chemical residue. Thousands of people were interviewed, ranging from JFK Airport employees, to residents of eastern Long Island, to people who came in contact with the aircraft in Athens, Greece, where the flight originated prior to landing at JFK.

Back-to-back hurricanes in late August and early September delayed recovery operations. Approximately 70 percent of the aircraft had been salvaged and 211 victims recovered. In November, the NTSB employed contract trawlers to drag the ocean floor. Approximately forty square miles of ocean floor were covered by diving and trawling operations throughout the winter and spring, resulting in the retrieval of thousands of items. By April 1997, more than 95 percent of the aircraft was recovered.

With one of the largest task forces in U.S. history, TWA Flight 800 quickly became the nation's most expensive aircraft accident investigation. A month after the accident, Federal and local officials indicated expenses were rapidly approaching $10 million. The NTSB estimated the investigation was costing the agency more than $100 thousand a day (Meier, 1996).

Two Investigations

There was no immediate indication of what caused the crash; however, early on in the investigation the theory that TWA Flight 800 was destroyed by a terrorist bomb or missile became a likely scenario. The explosion appeared very similar to the bomb explosion which downed Pan Am Flight 103 in 1988. Furthermore, the explosion seemed too violent for a mechanical malfunction. Two parallel investigations emerged, one which focused on accidental and mechanical causes and another which considered possible criminal activity. The NTSB investigated possible mechanical failures of the aircraft while the FBI explored evidence supporting criminal activity. The NTSB was the lead agency in the investigation; however, if the accident proved a terrorist event, the FBI would assume responsibility. On the evening following the crash, Federal investigators stated an attack was the most likely explanation; however, the NTSB emphasized that while a criminal act was a possibility, there was presently no evidence to support such a theory and the focus remained on treating the crash as an accident.

Within a few days, officials indicated the explosion and subsequent crash was most likely caused either by a bomb on the aircraft, by something that hit the aircraft (a missile), or by a serious plane malfunction. Examination of pieces of wreckage found along the initial flight path soon revealed that the explosion occurred in the center fuel tank. The Pentagon discounted the missile theory as improbable, though many eyewitnesses reported seeing a light streaking toward the plane moments before the explosion. A week after the crash both of the black boxes were discovered; however, analysis failed to provide investigators with conclusive evidence as to what caused the aircraft to break apart (E. H. Phillips, 1996a). Data revealed the flight was routine until 8:31 P.M., when both the cockpit voice recorder and the digital flight data recorder stopped functioning (Dickinson, 1997).

The similarity of Flight 800's explosion to Pan Am Flight 103, its occurrence prior to the opening of the 1996 Summer Olympics in Atlanta, and the recent terrorist attack which killed nineteen Americans in Saudi Arabia renewed fears about aviation security and terrorism. The fact that the flight originated in Athens, an airport with a questionable security record and a well-known launching point for previous terrorist attacks, increased concerns. A preliminary examination by U.S. intelligence officials of passengers' names aboard the flight from Athens to New York, however, did not reveal anyone suspicious.

With the possibility of sabotage, the disaster site became viewed as a crime scene. Though FBI involvement is common in an NTSB investigation, the magnitude of the agency's role in the Flight 800 crash was unusual. The FBI approached the investigation aggressively. A command center was established at the East Moriches Coast Guard base and the FBI's Terrorism Task Force was activated. Hundreds of agents interviewed witnesses and airport employees. A toll-free number and an e-mail address were provided for witnesses who might have information regarding the crash. The FBI's effort to determine whether the crash was an act of international terrorism involved working with foreign intelligence agencies, the CIA, and the State Department (Kovaleski, 1996).

In the days following the crash, a bomb became a plausible theory. An unexplained noise detected on the CVR, combined with the absence of evidence pointing to mechanical failure and the Olympic bombing in Atlanta, bolstered the likelihood of sabotage. At the end of August, PETN and RDX (two chemicals used in explosive devices) were found on the debris, suggesting that explosives were involved in the crash. But by mid-September the FBI had been unable to link the disaster to any international terrorist group. Nevertheless, they persisted in their investigation.

While the FBI searched for signs of a bomb, the NTSB explored possible mechanical malfunctions. Analysis of the Flight 800 DFDR and the CVR failed to provide any data as to whether the crash was an accident or sabotage, though the noise at the end of the CVR seemed consistent with a low-energy fuel explosion (Phillips & Thomas, 1996). After weeks of tests, computer simulations, and partial reconstruction of the aircraft, investigators determined the center fuel tank exploded, but were unable to determine why. In October, NTSB officials stated for the first time they believed a mechanical failure probably caused the TWA Flight 800 crash. Two months later, the NTSB announced evidence suggesting the explosion was accidental. Investigators suspected the ignition of fuel vapors in the center fuel tank may have led to the explosion of Flight 800, though they did not know what ignition source triggered the blast. The Board issued four safety recommendations, urgently recommending that the FAA require both short-term and long-term safety changes in all 747 aircraft (E. H. Phillips, 1996b). To better understand what occurred aboard the Boeing 747, flight tests, explosion tests, and laboratory examinations were conducted at airfields in the United States and in England. While it appeared the NTSB had identified the explosion was an accident, the FBI continued to pursue the bomb theory. In November 1997, almost a year and a half after the disaster, the FBI announced it would suspend its criminal investigation. The NTSB investigation, however, would continue.

While the NTSB had not issued a probable cause of the accident, investigators had determined what happened to the aircraft. A fuel/air explosion occurred in the nearly empty center wing tank. It was not yet known what ignited the explosive fuel/air vapors. The NTSB convened a week-long investigative public hearing into the crash of TWA Flight 800 on December 8, 1997, in Baltimore. At the hearing the board released mounds of progress reports on the investigation. Almost fifty witnesses testified on the following issues: examination of CVR and DFDR data and the sequencing of the breakup of the aircraft; fuel tank design philosophy and certification standards; flammability of Jet-A fuel; ignition sources; potential flammability reduction techniques and procedures; and aging aircraft (Hall, 1997c). The hearings demonstrated the great effort put forth in finding the cause of the disaster.

Emerging Issues

The critical issues of family rights and aviation security emerged during the Flight 800 crisis. The slow process of victim recovery compounded families' anguish and frustration over the situation. Recovery of Flight 800 victims ultimately became an emotional and politically charged issue. Victims' families vocalized concerns that retrieval of the wreckage, rather than the victims, had become the priority. Forty-five of those on board Flight 800 were French citizens. Though the French government was represented in the investigation, victims' families in France had received little news of the investigation. The situation served to emphasize a complicated dimension of aviation accidents: how governments and airlines should respond to victims' families.

TWA employees assigned to assist family members were praised for their efforts. Nevertheless, the issue of a company which could be responsible for the tragedy functioning as the primary agency to assist victims' families emerged (Alvarez, 1996b). Following his visit with the families of Flight 800 victims, President Clinton proposed the establishment of a specific Federal government office to assist families in the wake of an aviation tragedy. A few months later, Congress passed legislation requiring the NTSB to provide family assistance to the victims of major airline accidents.

The crash of TWA Flight 800 occurred during a period of increased anxiety over both airline safety and terrorist attacks. Airline safety had become a public concern in 1996. In April, an Air Force plane carrying Secretary of Commerce Ron Brown and others crashed, killing all on board. The following month, a ValuJet commercial aircraft crashed in the Florida Everglades, killing 110 passengers. The TWA tragedy occurred approximately two months later. TWA Flight 800 significantly impacted airport security in the United States. A week after the crash, President Clinton ordered increased security measures at U.S. airports and named Vice President Gore to head a commission to investigate security and safety. The security measures were predicted to create long lines and detailed searches and interrogations for passengers. The industry would likely incur additional labor costs and delays. Travel experts predicted the added costs of security measures would be passed along to customers (Cushman, 1996).

Media Coverage

The fact that the crash occurred near New York City, media capitol of the world, elevated media coverage. Media reports of the Flight 800 disaster provided nonstop and in-depth coverage of the crash and investigation throughout the weeks of the on-site investigation. Daily stories centered around search and recovery efforts and the NTSB's and FBI's progress. Moving and heartfelt stories of victims aboard the 747, including the students and chaperons of the Montoursville, Pennsylvania, High School French Club, and their survivors captured the tragedy of the event.

Pre-coverage of the 1996 Summer Olympics in Atlanta was replaced with TWA Flight 800 updates. The media depicted the initial investigative response as "chaotic," with hordes of agents, aviators, and engineers. The possibility of sabotage made it an atypical investigation. FBI involvement created several sources of information where usually there is only one, the NTSB. As the investigation progressed, rumors of tension between the FBI and the NTSB were reported. Later articles considered unusual theories as to why the 747 exploded over the Atlantic ocean. As a consequence of the extreme interest generated by the Flight 800 crash, the NTSB issued more than 500 press credentials at its public hearing in December 1997 (Hall, 1997c).

Public Response

There was an overwhelming public response to the tragedy of TWA Flight 800. The *New York Times* reported a record number of computer users sought the World Wide Web in their pursuit of information about the crash (Barboza, 1996). In addition to the information posted on the Web by numerous news organizations, the NTSB, and the FBI, there were individual sites created as memorials to some of the victims.

In the weeks following the investigation, the NTSB and the FBI could not say for certain what caused the explosion aboard TWA Flight 800. In response to the absence of information, rumors and theories thrived. The notion of "friendly fire" appeared on the internet. Some believed the aircraft was downed by a surface-to-air missile which was mistakenly fired by an American warship (Hosenball, 1996). The story moved into the mainstream press when former White House Press Secretary Pierre Salinger came forth, announcing that there was evidence supporting the friendly fire theory. According to Salinger, a French intelligence agent had provided him with a secret document revealing a massive coverup by the U.S. Navy. Salinger argued TWA Flight 800 was accidentally destroyed by a missile test fired from a U.S. naval vessel (Lacayo, 1996). Both the FBI and NTSB discounted the theory. Salinger later admitted he may have been wrong.

The bizarre theory of a government coverup resurfaced once again in the fall of 1997 when James Sanders's book, *The Downing of TWA Flight 800*, created controversy. The book promoted the theory that a U.S. Navy missile shot down the passenger jet and the government was covering it up. Sanders claimed that a reddish residue found on the aircraft's seats was rocket fuel. As it turned out, the residue was adhesive used in the initial construction of the seats in the aircraft. In December 1997, Sanders, his TWA-flight-attendant wife, and a TWA pilot working on the investigation were charged with stealing documents and seat material from the wreckage.

For a 747 to just explode was incomprehensible to many. After all, it was considered one of the safest aircraft; however, it was not indestructible. In addition to Salinger and Sanders, the mystery of Flight 800 prompted others to express their ideas. The NTSB received thousands of letters from university professors to aviation enthusiasts, offering suggestions ranging from a lit cigarette in the jet's lavatory igniting fuel vapors to the plane being too heavy (Hall, 1997c). It was clear the crash had indeed generated an immense public interest.

Political Involvement

The disaster provided a stage for elected officials to display their concern for victims' families, reassure the public, and assist investigators. To many, their presence was seen as grandstanding. Officials managed to find their ways to the microphones and cameras, commenting on the crash, terrorism, and TWA's response. A day after the crash, a local Congressman falsely announced the discovery of the black boxes. New York's governor, in an effort to console grieving families, inaccurately stated dozens of bodies had been discovered by divers. The President's Chief of Staff and a New York Senator speculated to media about terrorist involvement (Firestone, 1996, July 20). These instances served to compound an already chaotic situation. Perhaps the most visible and vocal official was New York City's Mayor, Rudolph Giuliani, who waged an attack on TWA's management over what he considered an inadequate response to the situation. For TWA, Mayor Giuliani's unrelenting criticism in the days following the disaster created an additional crisis.

CRISIS COMMUNICATION:
AN ANALYSIS OF TWA'S COMMUNICATION

Though TWA had developed a trauma response team, the sudden and surprising nature of the crash found airline executives and members scattered across the country. Jeffrey Erickson was asleep in a London hotel when he received the tragic news. Though Erickson had been in the industry twenty years, he had never been in charge at the time of a major air crash. Mark Abels, TWA's public-relations executive, had accompanied Erickson to London. Johanna O'Flaherty, the human resources executive in charge of the Trauma Response Team, was vacationing in California. At TWA's home base in St. Louis, executives were attending a going-away party for the airline's senior vice president. With Erickson in London, Johanna O'Flaherty in California, and the recent resignations of two top executives, few managers were available to respond. Until Erickson arrived from London, there would be a void of TWA executives in New York. The challenge of assembling the whole team in New York would take hours. But in a time of crisis distraught families and politicians had little patience or understanding for TWA's difficult position. The day after the crash, TWA was dealing with two crises simultaneously—the crash of Flight 800 and the onslaught of criticism waged by New York City's Mayor, Rudolph Giuliani, and Flight 800's victims' families. This analysis considers TWA's immediate response to the Flight 800 crisis and its reaction to the highly public criticism of its handling of victims' families.

Immediate Response

Despite its members being geographically dispersed, TWA managed to activate its trauma response team and incident coordination center. Responsibilities included notifying next of kin and providing them with information and transportation. Throughout the evening, victims' relatives hurried to the TWA terminal at JFK Airport in a hysterical quest for information. Learning of the tragedy, New York Mayor Rudolph Giuliani arrived to assist family members. In an effort to protect and shield grieving families, the airline gathered victims' families at the Ramada Inn near JFK Airport, providing free lodging, food, and trauma counseling ("Daylight brings," 1996). TWA family escorts and employees assisted families by making travel arrangements and accommodations, working with government agencies and private relief groups to provide briefings and assistance, and arranging memorial services, as well as responding to other requests (Erickson, 1996). Every few hours government officials briefed relatives on the progress of the search.

TWA provided factual information to the public concerning the accident through press conferences and the Internet. Moments after the accident, major television networks began live coverage of events. In a news conference at JFK Airport, Mike Kelly (1996), TWA Staff Vice President of Airport Operations, issued an official statement relating known facts and steps the airline was taking to respond to the situation:

I don't think I need to tell you how concerned and upset we at TWA are about this. This is the worst possible thing that can happen, and we will attend to it in the best way possible. We have quite a bit of our staff on site this evening, and we will work through the night and for the next period of time to attend to the family and survivors the best we can.

Responding to a reporter's question, Kelly stated the airline had established a gathering place for family members at one of the terminals.

TWA issued a statement on its corporate site on the World Wide Web. The message contained two special 800 numbers for relative inquiries. The airline further stated its concern over the event: "TWA is deeply concerned for the safety of its passengers and crew and is working closely with federal and local officials. TWA will not make further comment until information can be verified" ("Statement regarding," 1996).

The day after the crash rumors of a bomb surfaced. Erickson and Abels, who arrived at JFK Airport on Thursday afternoon, addressed rumors concerning a bomb at a New York press conference. Abels indicated there was no suggestion of a threat to the aircraft. He commented, "It is our understanding from the various traffic control centers and centers that were in radio contact with the flight, that there were no non-routine transmissions from the flight whatsoever, and no indication of any problem until the flight disappeared and went silent" (TWA 800 crash, 1996).

Initially, there was confusion as to the number of passengers on board. According to Abels, the flight carried 228 people, citing 210 passengers and eighteen crew members. Earlier reports of 229 had been incorrect (the actual count was 230). At that time, 140 bodies had been recovered. Abels indicated thirty-five passengers were TWA flight personnel on their way to assignment in Europe. The airline's early confusion about the number and identity of the passengers raised questions as to whether TWA violated aviation security.

The Flight 800 explosion was very similar to the explosion which occurred on Pan Am Flight 103 over Lockerbie, Scotland in 1988. In that case, Pan Am had been lax in its security at a time when terrorism was at an all-time high. Law enforcement officials expressed concern that perhaps TWA's system of matching bags to passengers was flawed.

Battling Criticism

Throughout Thursday, TWA battled another crisis, as New York Mayor Rudolph Giuliani, who arrived at JFK soon after the incident, and victims' relatives blasted the airline for its slow response. Specifically, Giuliani criticized TWA for its failure to promptly complete a formal passenger list and notify relatives. One family member stated, "I think there are two tragedies here—the tragedy that of course, occurred last night, but an even greater tragedy is the way we, the families, have been treated by TWA. . . . It is now fifteen or sixteen hours after the crash, and to the best of my knowledge, TWA still has not contacted the parents of that child in France" (TWA 800 crash, 1996).

Mayor Giuliani publicly criticized TWA's upper management for its inadequate response. Criticism concerned the absence of high-ranking TWA officials and the airline's delay in confirming the passenger list. The airline's response that the NTSB was the source for delay was vehemently denied by the NTSB. The evening of July 18, on "Larry King Live," guests included the mayor and New York's Governor Pataki. Both continued their attack on the airline. Giuliani argued TWA failed to notify families in a timely way. Confirmation of passengers aboard the flight took eighteen to twenty hours, which, according to the mayor, was unacceptable. Further, the person in charge left at 2:00 in the morning. The mayor continued:

Families are going through enough heartbreak and enough fear and worry; we can't remove that for them, but we can make things easier for them, not harder for them. And in this particular instance, TWA, at the upper management level was making things harder for them. There were a lot of very good people from TWA working with the families, working with the people that were concerned, but at the upper management level they were nonexistent at Kennedy Airport.

Agreeing with the mayor, Governor Pataki added, "A lot has been straightened out since but certainly there was a lot more that I believe could have been done sooner on behalf of the families."

Mayor Giuliani kept up his criticism of TWA the following day, reporting to CNN he had been lied to by the airline. Giuliani stated he was told directly by Erickson that the NTSB prohibited the airline from handing out the passenger list, which the NTSB denied. He further noted the airline lied about when all the families had been notified. These revelations implied the airline could not be trusted (Giuliani, 1996). When asked by a reporter whether he was too hard on the airline, the mayor replied, "No, I think I was too easy on them."

TWA Responds

Three accusations against TWA were made by Giuliani and some of the Flight 800 family members. First, TWA was insensitive to families' anguish and responded irresponsibly. Second, TWA's upper management responded inadequately. Third, the airline's management lied about when all the families were notified; therefore, TWA could not be trusted. TWA responded to these accusations by utilizing strategies of aggression, hedging responsibility, ingratiation, and righting the wrong. In response to the criticism, the airline refuted evidence that implied it had been irresponsible in responding to families. TWA officials contended that they had acted responsibly. According to the airline, to avoid mistakes they had painstakingly compared passenger lists with boarding passes (Finder, 1996). Both Abels and Erickson positively acknowledged New York's mayor. Abels responded to the mayor's disappointment, agreeing the process should be quicker, but emphasized the need for accuracy. Erickson expressed his appreciation to the mayor and his trauma response team which extended the airline's efforts. When asked about the mayor's criticism, Erickson stated, "I'm very appreciative of the mayor and his trauma response team. Obviously, they're all in New York City. Our trauma response team is from all over our system, and came in. So, the mayor and his people really supplemented our own efforts, which are now full scale" (Finder, 1996). Erickson provided the excuse of "geographic complications" for the slow assembly of TWA's crisis team. Though it was some twenty-four hours after the crash before TWA's crisis team was in place, Erickson stated the airline's trauma response team's efforts were now full scale. Such an acknowledgement revealed the airline's appreciation while simultaneously reemphasizing the difficulty of assembling a response team spread throughout the country. He indicated the airline was now in control of the situation.

The airline's loss of its own coworkers and family members created identification between the organization and other victims' families. Erickson stated, "Our task now is to honor the memory of our lost colleagues by caring for the families and each other" (TWA 800 crash, 1996). This statement reinforced the fact that because TWA lost fifty-three employees, it was also a victim of the tragedy.

On Friday evening, TWA's director of media relations, John McDonald, defended the airline's actions following the crash by offering excuses in a CNN interview ("TWA spokesman defends," 1996). McDonald stated that notifying families in the "right" way was not as easy and quick as critics would like to think. Accuracy required a painstaking process. Though perceptions were the airline was slow in responding, this statement implied the company was handling the situation in a professional manner. When asked about the mayor's relentless criticism of the airline, McDonald argued that the airline had been responsible toward families and had done everything it could to quickly notify families. He said, "I can't comment on why the Mayor is doing what he's doing, and it's not my intent. My intent is to let people know that TWA has spared no expense and has spared no effort on personnel and time to make sure that this list was compiled as quickly as possible." He further stated, "TWA lost more than 50 of its own family on that airplane, and it is very unfair, I think to say somehow that TWA was not in anyway interested in making sure that these people were told as quickly as possible." By reiterating the fact that TWA was also a victim, he created identification between the airline and victims' families.

During his interview McDonald hinted at corrective action. In response to whether TWA would reconsider its policies for handling these crises, McDonald explained the airline's crisis response process involved reviewing its policies and procedures after an incident when the investigation was well under way, in an effort to improve ("TWA spokesman defends," 1996).

The following day, TWA employees held a news conference to defend the company. TWA's Flight Attendants Union president stated that fifty-three TWA employees had been killed on Flight 800, reminding the public that TWA was also in mourning. In response to Giuliani's criticism, she used the strategy of aggression:

I would like to make a personal statement to Mayor Giuliani. Now is not the time to make this tragedy a personal agenda or a political career. It serves absolutely no useful purpose; it does more harm than good. We at TWA will welcome a full review of our performance in this incident. A 30-second sound bite is not the appropriate forum for that review. The families of the victims, including our own families, deserve better than that. (Finder, 1996)

TWA workers stood by her side applauding. Such a response made against a backdrop of grieving employees emphasized a positive aspect of the company, its "family" image. It further suggested the mayor was taking advantage of the situation for political purposes.

EVALUATION OF STRATEGIES

The surprising nature of crisis can itself create problems for crisis managers, as observed in the case of TWA Flight 800. When a company in crisis is caught by surprise and then encounters an extremely vocal politician in a highly emotional context and in the media capitol of the world, the crisis may likely escalate. The case further underscores two critical principals of crisis management. First, upper management must absolutely be visibly present as soon as possible. The absence of such officials suggests that the company's leaders are insensitive to the situation. Second, efforts should be made to quickly notify victims' families. In a crisis, time is a critical factor. The complications which arose over family notification following the TWA Flight 800 crash prompted the passage of the Family Assistance Act, which assigned responsibility for family notification after airline disasters to the NTSB.

TWA's immediate response to the crisis received mixed reviews. Some analysts were quick to criticize the airline for the unavailability of airline executives and the inexperience of the airline's CEO in handling a crash. Mayor Giuliani's involvement compounded the crisis for the airline and created a public perception that TWA was disorganized and lacked compassion. It appears that those TWA officials and employees who publicly addressed criticism did so as a single voice. TWA's general approaches of hedging responsibility, ingratiation, aggression, and righting the wrong were appropriate choices to deal with the barrage of criticism directed toward its response to victims' families.

In light of the fact that the accusations appeared true, TWA was wise to avoid making false denials in order to disassociate itself from responsibility for prolonging and increasing families' grief. TWA directly addressed its critics' accusations by explaining extenuating circumstances. Because of geographic complications, team members had difficulty assembling in a timely manner. This excuse also seemed to apply to TWA's upper management. The airline explained that in order to avoid mistakes which could increase families' anguish, it had performed a more tedious yet reliable method of compiling an accurate passenger manifest. This emphasized the professional nature of the company and the fact that, in actuality, the process protected families from any unnecessary grief. TWA admitted the family notification process was slow, but refuted the fact that its response was inadequate.

Ingratiation strategies were critical to counter the developing hostility toward the airline. Giuliani's scathing attack on TWA at a time when emotions were running high could have easily triggered an all-out war between the mayor and the airline. Rather, TWA executives were gracious and positively acknowledged Giuliani, expressing their appreciation to the mayor and his city. Identification was needed to create a connection between the airline and families. TWA was a victim, having lost many employees, and shared in the anguish and grief.

Aggression on the part of TWA's Flight Attendants Union toward the mayor was a clever strategy. The union's president flanked by grieving employees created a powerful image. To publicly accuse the mayor of grandstanding clearly revealed the backbone of TWA's flight attendants: There was no doubt, they had had enough! Aggression would not likely have had such an impact had it been used by management. After all, the airline's employees were commended for their sensitivity and compassion. Upper-level management was the source of controversy. The employees' press conference was useful in creating a united front—employees at various levels had come together in support of their company.

Because TWA admitted it was slow in responding to families, efforts to right the wrong were necessary. That the airline would review its policies and procedures after the fact suggested corrective action would be considered. This strategy would have been more effective if the company publicly specified needed changes. However, a review process in the heat of crisis is an unlikely scenario. The airline could have been more forceful in stating its intentions to revise policies and procedures. For example, a spokesperson might have said, "We recognize that our process can be improved and following a review we will identify ways to improve." The airline would have directly stated its intentions for improvement without committing to specifics. In the transcripts and articles reviewed for this analysis, there was no indication that the airline publicly extended an apology to victims' families. While this may have been done behind closed doors, it was important for the public to hear TWA's regret over the situation. It is possible, since TWA was also a victim, the company viewed an apology as unnecessary.

This analysis suggests TWA was generally effective in its efforts to address criticism concerning its response to victims' families after the crash of Flight 800. The airline did not appear to suffer any long-term damage. Though TWA stock dropped ten points the day after the crash, there was little adverse economic impact on the airline ("Stocks surge," 1996). August proved to be a strong month in terms of the average seat occupancy (load factor) and the number of miles flown by paying passengers (McDowell, 1996). International traffic also increased. TWA indicated there was not a decrease among business travelers after the crash. This was partially attributed to the airline's strong safety and maintenance record (McDowell, 1996).

This case further illuminates the complexity of post-crisis investigation following a major airline crash. The process of the post-crisis investigation will be discussed in detail in the next chapter. As of September 23, 1998, the National Transportation Safety Board continues to investigate the tragedy of TWA Flight 800.

CONCLUSION

Perhaps the most important lesson to be learned from TWA's experience following the Flight 800 disaster concerns the critical nature of crisis planning and communication. While most crisis managers agree planning and communication are fundamental to crisis management, this case provides some very specific lessons which impact the effectiveness of these extremely important aspects:

1. Crisis managers must anticipate the challenges of applying a rational plan to an irrational situation.
2. An organization in crisis must communicate from the beginning that it is in control and concerned about the situation.

3. Promptly and accurately notifying victims' next of kin and releasing names of victims is critical to effective crisis management.

4. In the aftermath of a major disaster, a company may be expected to work with a variety of agencies who may have conflicting agendas; therefore, when planning for crisis companies are wise to develop a strategy which unifies the groups likely to be involved in a recovery effort.

5. A company that finds itself in a hostile and emotional situation may be able to defuse the situation through the communication strategies of ingratiation and corrective action.

6. In the absence of concrete information, rumors and theories thrive.

The best-laid plans sometimes go awry in a highly emotional situation. Crisis managers should anticipate the challenges of applying a rational plan to an irrational situation. Crisis planning is intended to eliminate the confusion associated with a crisis and prepare a company for handling the many challenges and difficulties associated with crisis management, but it cannot fully prepare a company for the surprise, intensity, and emotions which generally accompany a crisis. When a crisis strikes, a company is immediately tossed into a lion's den. How a company responds to the situation will influence public opinion as much as the cause of the crisis itself.

In a crisis, time is a critical factor, especially in the first few hours. A management team must be ready to quickly mobilize and take action. Responding instantly to upset families, a disturbed public, an anxious press, and zealous politicians, along with the pressure of finding out the cause of the disaster, requires forethought. Contingency planning, however, cannot fully counter the surprise of a triggering event. The surprise of a crisis can create problems for crisis managers and catch a crisis response team off guard and out of pocket. Despite the fact that TWA had a crisis plan in place, the sudden and surprising nature of the crash created difficulty for the airline in assembling its crisis response team in New York. The company failed to effectively factor geographic circumstances into its plan. Of course, the human element brings to the situation an extreme level of stress and anxiety. When the complications surrounding the slow gathering of the crisis team interacted with the extreme emotional element, severe criticism by victims' families and local politicians occurred.

A company is naïve to assume that everything needed to deal with a crisis situation is contained in its crisis plan. Crisis managers should expect the unexpected. Crisis planning must take into account unforeseen circumstances which could potentially hinder a crisis response. Planning for unanticipated events requires a clear vision for handling the crisis, since an organization's crisis response is influenced by how it views the situation. As Pinsdorf (1987) noted, concrete objectives based on a company's philosophic and psychological perspective are more effective than checklists when determining strategic responses. For example, Johnson & Johnson's long-standing credo regarding the company's responsibility to consumers, employees, communities, and stockholders provided a sound guideline for making decisions during the Tylenol crisis (Fink, 1986).

An organization in crisis must communicate from the very beginning that it is in control and concerned about the situation. Controlling the crisis requires special consideration of executive management's symbolic role, the message, and the media. There is the expectation that a high-ranking official will be visibly present or in contact early on in a crisis to address questions regarding the situation and provide direction. The presence of high-ranking officials symbolizes the caring nature and concern of a company. Executive management's absence suggests that the company's leaders lack concern and are insensitive to the situation. The absence of high-ranking officials in the early hours after the Flight 800 crash was a primary source of criticism. Exxon received similar criticism during the Valdez crisis. Exxon Chairman Lawrence Rawl was extremely criticized for delaying his visit to the Valdez disaster site until almost a month after the incident occurred (Benoit, 1995). The extended delay created the impression he never did go and therefore did not care.

While most believe upper management must absolutely be visibly present as soon as possible, there are instances when this is not the best approach. Before any decision is made, crisis managers must gather information about the situation.

Union Carbide's chairman Warren Anderson and other Union Carbide India Ltd. top management were immediately arrested when they arrived in Bhopal soon after the accident (Shrivastava, 1987). Had they collected and considered critical information beforehand, they would have recognized an immediate visit was not a good idea.

How a company responds or fails to respond in a crisis communicates a clear message. From the beginning, a company in crisis must immediately reassure the public by showing compassion and demonstrating something is being done in response to the catastrophe. Moreover, a company in crisis must clearly communicate its genuine and sincere concern and compassion through actions and words. Stakeholders must perceive the company as one who cares. Reality is one thing—perception is another. The perceived failure of TWA to notify victims' families in a timely way soon after the crash was interpreted as uncaring and incompetent. TWA contended the airline acted responsibly.

Promptly and accurately notifying next of kin and releasing names of victims is critical to effective crisis management. The delay of coordinating the passenger manifest increased the anguish of victims' families and was a primary source of criticism from both families and politicians. The problem of releasing a passenger list in a timely way is common following major air-carrier accidents. Publicly explaining the intricacies and difficulties of formulating a passenger list will do little to calm anxieties. Because of the sensitive nature of this issue, a company is wise to develop strategies which will expedite the compilation of victims' names in the event of an accident.

In the aftermath of a major disaster a company may be expected to work with a variety of agencies who will likely have conflicting agendas. The involvement of a number of agencies and groups can result in a company losing control over the execution of its plans. Moreover, conflict may occur if these groups fail to integrate their action plans. A number of agencies and organizations may involve themselves with victims and media, creating the potential for inconsistency, inaccuracy, and contradictions. In some situations, conflicting information may present a very confused picture of the situation. The National Transportation Safety Board functions to coordinate and unify these many agencies following a major air-carrier crash. The NTSB controls press briefings, coordinates family support services, and holds daily press briefings during the on-site investigation. TWA Flight 800 highlighted the challenges of dealing with victims' families. In an effort to effectively respond to victims' families following a major crash, the Office for Family Assistance was established within the NTSB. Airlines are generally aware of the procedures following an accident and their subordinate role to the NTSB. This understanding is factored into their crisis plans.

Companies in other industries who are responsible for controlling and coordinating a crisis response must understand the challenges and difficulties associated with this responsibility. When planning for crisis, companies should develop a strategy which unifies the officials and agencies likely to be involved in a recovery effort. Such planning may require contacting these individuals and groups prior to a crisis event. The TWA case also illustrates how political involvement can complicate efforts at crisis management and even escalate a crisis. Avoiding such problems may involve contacting local politicians early on and encouraging them to work with the company, not against it.

TWA teaches crisis communicators a valuable lesson about responding to criticism. A company that finds itself in a hostile and emotional situation may be able to defuse the situation through strategies of ingratiation and corrective action. For TWA, an aggressive line of defense would have aggravated an already extreme situation. Had TWA openly battled the mayor over his accusations of an inadequate response, the company would have appeared more concerned with its own position than that of victims' families and the overall situation. Credibility must be maintained in such a situation. Ingratiation and corrective strategies serve to calm stakeholders, gain approval, and hopefully leave a positive impression on others. Counterattacks will likely damage the company's credibility.

This case demonstrates the challenges instant media coverage presents to those directly dealing with the crisis. In a crisis, a company's primary goal is to immediately control and manage the crisis, the message, and the communication before media take control. TWA's failure to achieve this goal in the early stages of the crisis combined with the fact that the crash occurred near the world's media capitol resulted in media taking control of the situation. The media attention received by the Flight 800 disaster was unprecedented.

Despite officials' efforts to communicate, accurate and up-to-date information does not always suppress rumors and theories when a cause has not been fully determined. In other words, in the absence of concrete information, rumors thrive. Despite the direct efforts of government officials to provide current and accurate information, numerous rumors and theories as to why Flight 800 crashed continued to flourish among the public. The difficulty of immediately determining the accident's probable cause perpetuated public suspicions concerning the mysterious circumstances of Flight 800. Undoubtedly, skepticism about the government in general lessened the credibility of the information which agencies provided. Credibility influences believability. Though the NTSB claimed the accident occurred as a result of a fuel/air explosion, the theory of a government coverup is still very real to some.

REFERENCES

Alvarez, L. (1996a, July 18). Rising hopes turn hollow for company on rebound. *New York Times*, p. 1.

Alvarez, L. (1996b, August 6). Relatives of victims become force in change of methods. *New York Times*, p. A14.

Barboza, D. (1996, August 5). After the TWA crash, the web proves its worth as headline service and bulletin board. *New York Times CyberTimes* [http://www.nytimes.com/w...ek/0806twa-internet.html].

Benoit, W. L. (1995). *Accounts, excuses, and apologies: A theory of image restoration strategies*. Albany: State University of New York.

Biggest stories of 1996. (1997, January 4). *Editor & Publisher*, p. 27.

Crash is latest blow to TWA. (1996, July 18). *CNN Website* [http://cnnfn.com/hotstor...es/9607/18/twa_business/].

Cushman, J. H. (1996, July 26). Delays for travelers and higher costs for airlines. *New York Times*, p. A12.

Danaher, J. (1997, October 15). Personal e-mail to author.

Daylight brings no trace of survivors of TWA crash. (1996, July 18). *CNN Interactive* [http://www.cnn.com/us/9607/18/twa.7a/index.html].

Dickinson, A. (1997, December 8). *IIC opening statement*. TWA Flight 800 Public Hearing, Baltimore, MD.

Erickson, J. H. (1996, August 4). Facing up to the worst at TWA. *New York Times*, p. F8.

Finder, A. (1996, July 21). Could TWA have notified families more quickly? *New York Times Online* [http://www.nytimes.com/y...nt/twa-crash-notify.html].

Fink, S. (1986). *Crisis management: Planning for the inevitable*. New York: AMACOM.

Firestone, D. (1996, July 20). Politicians provide comfort and criticism after crash. *New York Times*, p. A1.

Giuliani, R. (1996, July 19). Flight 800 briefing—Part 1. *CNN Specials*, Transcript #849.

Hall, J. (1997a, July 10). Testimony before the subcommittee on aviation, Committee on Transportation and Infrastructure regarding accident involving TWA Flight 800 [http://www.ntsb.gov/Speeches/jh970710.htm].

Hall, J. (1997b, September 23). Remarks before the Aero Club of Washington, Washington, DC [http://www.ntsb.gov/Speeches/jh970923.htm].

Hall, J. (1997c, December 8). Statement at the opening of the NTSB investigative hearing into the crash of TWA Flight 800, Baltimore, MD.

Heppenheimer, T. A. (1995). *Turbulent skies: The history of commercial aviation.* New York: John Wiley & Sons.

Hosenball, M. (1996, September 23). The anatomy of a rumor. *Newsweek*, p. 43.

Kelly, M. (1996, July 17). Press Conference on Flight 800. *CNN Breaking News*, vol. BN199607, p. 1.

Kovaleski, S. F. (1996, August 6). A massive probe, a grinding pace. *Washingtonpost. com* [http://wp1.washingtonpost.com/cgi-bin/dis...arch?WPlate+18614+%28 twa%29%3Adescription].

Lacayo, R. (1996, November 25). Shot in the dark? *Time*, p. 44.

Maraniss, D. (1996, July 19). Crash probe considers sabotage. *Washingtonpost.com* [http://wp1.washingtonpost.com/cgi-bin/dis...arch?WPlate+15874+%28twa% 29%3Adescription].

McDowell, E. (1996, September 11). Gains for TWA. *New York Times*, p. C4.

Meier, B. (1996, August 27). Cost of inquiry into crash of Flight 800 sets record. *New York Times Online*, p. A16.

Overseas pioneer TWA has good safety record. (1996, July 19). *USA Today Online.* [http://www.usatoday.com/...index/crash/ncrash07.htm].

Phillips, D. (1996, July 18). 747 explodes with 229 aboard shortly after takeoff from New York. *Washingtonpost.com* [http://washingtonpost.com/cgi-bin/ dis...arch?WPlate+15669+%28twa29%3Adescription].

Phillips, D., & Thomas, P. (1996, August 21). TWA voice recorder offers probers nothing definitive. *Washingtonpost.com* [http://wp1.washingtonpost.com/cgi-bin/dis...arch?WPlate+211278+%28twa%29%3Adescription].

Phillips, E. H. (1996a, July 29). TWA probe advances, but no cause found. *Aviation Week & Space Technology*, pp. 26–28.

Phillips, E. H. (1996b, December 23). NTSB's 747 proposals focus on fuel volatility. *Avation Week & Space Technology*, p. 87.

Pinsdorf, M. K. (1987). *Communicating when your company is under siege: Surviving public crisis.* Lexington, MA: D. C. Heath and Co.

Purdy, M. (1996, July 20). Searching for clues on countless fronts. *New York Times*, p. 23.

Sanders, J. (1997). *The downing of TWA flight 800: The shocking truth behind the worst airplane disaster in U.S. history.* New York: Kensington Publishing.

Shrivastava, P. (1987). *Bhopal: Anatomy of a crisis.* Cambridge, MA: Ballinger.

Statement regarding Trans World Airlines Flight 800. (1996, July 18). *Trans World Airlines.* [http://www.twa.com/].

Stocks surge on comments by Greenspan. (1996, July 19). *New York Times*, p. D8.

TWA 800 crash—Victims being comforted. (1996, July 18). *CNN Specials*, Transcript #848.

TWA Spokesman Defends Airline's Actions Since Crash. (1996, July 19). Early Prime. *CNN*, Transcript #1291, Segment 1.

TWA. (1997, October 12). Significant dates in TWA history. TWA Website [http:// www.twa.com/html/contact/sigdates.html].

Part IV

Post-Crisis Stage

Post-Crisis Investigation: The National Transportation Safety Board

Following the initial impact of a crisis, organizations undergo post-crisis inspections, ranging from formal investigations to the more informal media reviews. Depending on the nature and magnitude of a crisis, an organization will be closely examined by a number of sources, such as investigative reporters, government agencies, consumer groups, and the courts, who function through inquiries or investigations, hearings, and/or lawsuits. Major airline crashes typically generate intense scrutiny from many groups.

From the public's view, the most visible aspect of a major aviation accident is the investigation by the National Transportation Safety Board's go-team. Sometimes referred to as the "crash detectives" or "tin kickers," these investigators function to determine the probable causes of aviation accidents and formulate safety recommendations to improve transportation safety. While the National Transportation Safety Board investigates a wide range of commercial transportation accidents, it is most visible when it deals with airline disasters. Through a credible process, the NTSB helps to bring about crisis resolution in the wake of an airline disaster. This chapter considers post-crisis investigation and the National Transportation Safety Board's role in major airline accidents.

POST-CRISIS

Post-crisis may be thought of as the "clean-up" phase which follows the initial impact of the crisis. Bolz (1988) suggests that during this phase an organization may begin to "embark on a more leisurely and less superficial assessment of the situation" (p. 8). Post-crisis may be of indeterminate length, and in some instances appears endless, depending on the nature of the crisis.

It is a period of recovery and self-assessment and a time when unique opportunities may be created or additional negative effects occur. It is the time for investigations, audits, interviews and explanations, revelations by the media, criticism, and blame. Fink (1986) described this stage as the point where the "carcasses get picked clean" (p. 23). This is the stage at which questions of why, how, and who to blame are systematically addressed.

Uncertainty, surprise, stress, threat, and limited response time continue to characterize the post-crisis phase. Organizations experience uncertainty with regard to cause, blame, response, public perception, resolution, and other consequences. Surprise suggests the unexpected or unanticipated nature of events or information. Information arising from post-crisis communication may include surprising revelations concerning organizational members and procedures. Such disclosures complicate a company's ability to manage the crisis. Stress affects those members of the organization working toward crisis resolution and may reduce their ability to perform (Hall & Mansfield, 1971). An organization's response to a crisis is dependent in part on how individuals respond to the stress from the crisis.

During post-crisis, high-priority values are threatened by questioning, suspension of operations, and severe criticism. Threat may compromise an organization's legitimacy. Therefore, a crisis situation requires an organization to "offer justifications and explanations for the violation of normative routines" (Seeger, 1987, p. 5). These justifications are offered in the post-crisis phase. Organizations may also be restricted to a limited amount of time to provide a response. To move past a crisis, the associated surprise, stress, and limited response time must be controlled, uncertainty reduced, and legitimacy reestablished.

Post-crisis is a time for recovery, self-analysis, self-doubt, and healing. Crisis does not always mean disaster. In effective crisis management, the post-crisis phase may also be a time of accolades and praise. As Fink (1986) explains, the post-crisis phase should be viewed as a period of "self-assessment, modification, fine-tuning, and even mid-course correction at all levels" (p. 24). Organizations are given the opportunity to examine their systems and procedures so as to provide insight into its functioning. Post-crisis assessment provides for full cultural readjustment of beliefs and precautionary norms "to the organization's new understanding of the world" (Turner, 1976, p. 381). Readjustment suggests that perceptual problems and resistance to change and inhibiting factors due to uncertainty are overcome. This provides a foundation for forming preventive and coping actions for future crisis. Meyer (1982) argues that crises provide a chance for organizational learning, administrative drama, and an introduction of unrelated changes. Because of the transitional nature of a crisis, the post-crisis stage is an appropriate time for taking advantage of these opportunities.

Conversely, a crisis may be compounded during the post-crisis phase. The organization may experience financial upheaval, management shake-ups, hostile takeover attempts, or bankruptcy. Meyers (1986) suggests that during a poorly managed post-crisis period, shock, uncertainty, and radical change occur: "People are immobilized, hope is lost, and only the hardiest—or fool-hardy—stay around to pick over the bones" (p. 37). Extreme change will occur in the post-crisis stage. Attacks on the other corporate entities or subsidiaries and comparisons with subsequent crises are inevitable.

Post-crisis provides the opportunity for an organization to recover from the initial impact of a crisis and assess its situation. During this period, organizations attempt to resolve the crisis in an atmosphere of uncertainty, surprise, stress, threat, and limited response time. This phase may be a turning point for the organization, in that the organization may change in positive or negative ways. Several factors in the post-crisis phase may influence an organization's fate. One such factor is the investigation by a board.

Investigating Boards

Historically, investigating boards, commissions, and committees have been utilized by almost every level of government for a variety of tasks. Post-crisis investigations are generally concerned with public safety and well-being. Some, however, may be considered "headline grabbing witch hunts" that simply seek scapegoats (Fink, 1986, p. 10). Whenever an organization is investigated, the chance exists that impropriety will be identified, often damaging or embarrassing the organization. An investigation, however, may prove advantageous to the organization. For an organization to move past crisis, it is necessary to publicly demonstrate and dramatize the organization's efforts to deal with crisis in such ways as determining the "likely cause(s) of the crisis, assigning guilt, and identifying steps to insure that similar situations do not re-occur" (Seeger, 1987, p. 2). The investigating board in many instances is the mechanism of choice for this process.

Formal investigating boards usually bring together distinguished persons to study an issue of national importance and act as an instrument of the government. They show concern about a problem, educate the public, provide recommendations, and mobilize support for programs (Popper, 1970). Boards provide a response to an obvious failure or a disaster for which the public demands a complete explanation. Commissions appointed in response to national crises have included the Warren Commission on the assassination of President John F. Kennedy, the Kerner Commission on civil disorders, the Tower Commission on the Watergate scandal, and the Rogers Commission on the Challenger explosion. As a means of resolving a crisis, a public investigation functions to collect, synthesize, summarize, and disseminate information; identify causes and associated factors; suggest ways in which future crisis may be avoided; assign blame and responsibility; and serve as a symbol that something is being done.

Boards function in both an informative and inquisitorial capacity; that is, it is a board's purpose to collect information and investigate questionable situations. Investigating boards contribute to the process of policy formation in a democracy by obtaining the facts; making the facts available to the public; and discussing, debating, and interpreting the facts (Marcy, 1945). By collecting facts and opinions and summarizing this information in a coherent and accessible form, boards educate the public. Information is disseminated through hearings, interim reports, and the release of a final report. The function of collection and analysis of information enables the board to identify the causes and associated factors of a situation and reduce uncertainty. This becomes significant for the resolution of the crisis.

Once causes and associated factors have been identified, a board suggests ways in which future crises may be avoided or a situation improved. According to Popper (1970), boards may not provide new ideas, but serve to publicize existing ones and give them legitimacy. A board may make previous actions more respectable, plausible, and thinkable or mobilize support regarding a specific issue. Constituent representation may increase the meaningfulness of the board for specific constituencies and enhance information-processing characteristics of the board. By identifying facts and involving constituent groups, a board often creates consensus in support of its findings.

A board usually does not seek out individuals on whom to place blame; rather, it is searching for more general facts or trends leading to a crisis (Popper, 1970). During the process of an investigation, however, blame and responsibility may be assigned to individuals. Boards have the potential to uncover surprising information or assign blame in a way that is damaging. When confronted with unexpected reports and revelations of information, the organization must provide an immediate response. Media coverage may serve to enhance the damage to an organization's reputation.

Boards symbolize to the public that a problem is being addressed. Popper (1970) argues that the board is a means of drawing public attention to a problem while at the same time indicating the problem is receiving attention. Because investigating boards represent the general public, their authority and presence legitimizes the investigation. Investigating boards which are credible, open, and comprehensive help to manage threats and questions concerning the organization's legitimacy (Seeger, 1987).

The goal of post-crisis is resolution, which may occur when uncertainty is reduced, the organization's legitimacy is established, and the company publicly demonstrates and dramatizes its efforts to deal with the crisis. The investigating board serves as a mechanism to move past crisis. By virtue of its informative and inquisitorial nature, the investigating board facilitates the communication of information to reduce uncertainty, address questions of legitimacy, and identify organizational efforts in dealing with the crisis. Conversely, the findings and conclusions which arise from an investigation may negatively influence these factors.

EARLY AVIATION ACCIDENT INVESTIGATIONS: THE CUTTING CRASH

On May 6, 1935, Transcontinental and Western Air Flight No. 6, eastbound from Los Angeles to New York, crashed in a dense fog near a small Missouri town (Komons, 1984). On board, two crew members and three passengers were killed, three passengers sustained serious injuries, and five escaped with minor injuries. Inaccurate weather advisories, pilot miscalculations, and maintenance oversight were among the probable causes of the accident. This was not an unusual event and would have gone unrecognized had a U.S. Senator, Bronson Cutting of New Mexico, not been aboard. The accident triggered a response which ultimately placed a Federal bureau under scrutiny.

During this period in aviation history, the Bureau of Air Commerce was responsible for investigating accidents and determining probable cause. The Senate, however, responding to overwhelming grief and resentment over Senator Cutting's death, empowered a five-member subcommittee (the Copeland Committee) to conduct a full and thorough investigation of the accident, which had resulted in the death of "an honored member" of the Senate (Komons, 1984, p. 28). This response was highly unusual, since the facts concerning the accident had not been collected. It implied concern by the Senate and others of problems within the Bureau of Air Commerce (Komons, 1984). Could an agency responsible for establishing and maintaining Federal airways be objective in its function of investigating and determining probable causes of aircraft accidents?

Following its investigation, the Bureau of Air Commerce Accident Board assigned primary responsibility for the accident to TWA and its personnel. According to Bureau findings, TWA violated a number of air-commerce regulations. The Bureau found no evidence that the Department of Commerce was responsible for the accident. Findings by the Senate subcommittee, however, indicated otherwise, reflecting negatively on the Bureau. The publicity generated by these conflicting findings concerned airline officials, who feared that the controversy which followed the Cutting crash would discourage the public from flying (Komons, 1984).

TWA denied its responsibility for the crash. Jack Frye, TWA's President, testified before the Senate subcommittee, explaining the airline's successful safety record and denying it had committed the alleged violations since the regulations involved were not in force when the accident occurred. Frye's testimony raised concerns about the chaotic way in which regulations were established. In addition to Frye, a former Bureau member attributed the cause of the accident to the Department of Commerce, citing their failure to ensure the proper functioning of aids to air navigation. Challenging the Bureau of Air Commerce's findings was significant because it insinuated something was improper at the Bureau. Additional testimony suggested unsafe airways, the Bureau's ability to cover up its own flaws, and the need for new leadership within the Bureau (Komons, 1984). It seemed the Bureau of Air Commerce was more concerned with clearing itself of fault and responsibility than with improving aviation safety.

Eventually, TWA was cleared of its responsibility for the accident. According to the committee report, "We are constrained to believe that an attempt was made to throw the blame on the company by raising the issue of so-called violations" (Komons, 1984, p. 77). The report further criticized the way the government handled the investigation, how the Bureau of Air Commerce was managed, and those responsible for managing it. As a consequence of the Cutting crash, legislation was expedited and the Bureau of Air Commerce was dissolved. In June 1938, the Civil Aeronautics Act placed all Federal aviation activities in a single, independent agency, the Civil Aeronautics Authority. Contained within was an independent Air Safety Board which was completely divorced from other functions of the Authority. The Air Safety Board was authorized to investigate accidents, determine probable cause, and make recommendations independently of the Authority and the Administrator (Komons, 1984).

The Cutting crash exemplifies the awkwardness of early aviation accident investigations and underscores the necessity of an independent and objective agency in maintaining the integrity of an accident investigation. The agency must be able to conduct in-depth objective investigations, draw conclusions from its findings, and make recommendations to improve safety, without bias or influence from industry or other government agencies.

Government investigations of general and commercial air-carrier crashes, however, have improved greatly since the 1930s. Today, major accident investigations are the responsibility of the independent National Transportation Safety Board. The NTSB controls the investigation and determines the probable cause of the accident. The NTSB (1997) functions to "vigorously investigate" aviation accidents with the purpose of providing recommendations to prevent future accidents. This involves continuous review, appraisal, and assessment of the operating practices.

With improved technology, the nature of accident investigations has also changed. Prior to the 1970s, investigations were primarily carried out by hardware specialists who examined the wreckage, determined how the aircraft struck the ground, and worked backward piecing together information based on physical evidence from the wreckage. Drawings of the wreckage were sketched and then analyzed. In the 1970s, requirements for expanded flight data recorders provided substantial information for investigators. As aviation technology has progressed, laboratory equipment and analysis capabilities used in accident investigations have advanced. The NTSB and the process of present day aviation accident investigations are considered in the following discussion.

NATIONAL TRANSPORTATION SAFETY BOARD

The National Transportation Safety Board is an independent federal accident-investigation agency established to promote transportation safety in the areas of civil aviation, highway, railroad, marine, pipeline, and hazardous materials. Recognized for its impartiality, insightfulness, and thoroughness, the NTSB is the most experienced government accident-investigation body in the world. It is the Federal government's transportation investigator and "watchdog" of transportation safety. As a result of its independent role, it is not unusual for the NTSB to address safety issues that are controversial and critical of government or industry standards or operations.

The NTSB's primary role is to determine the probable causes of transportation accidents and formulate safety recommendations regarding preventive actions, based on its investigations and studies, to federal, state, and local government agencies and the transportation industry. The NTSB's responsibilities also include evaluating the effectiveness of other government agencies' transportation safety programs, coordinating Federal assistance to families of victims of catastrophic transportation accidents, and reviewing appeals from airmen and merchant seamen whose certificates have been revoked or suspended. The NTSB is not authorized to regulate the transportation industry.

Aviation specialists comprise the largest portion of the Board's investigative staff. The Board investigates hundreds of accidents annually, including all air-carrier accidents, all in-flight collisions, fatal general aviation accidents, and all air-taxi and commuter accidents. The NTSB may authorize the FAA to investigate accidents not otherwise delegated to it. The Board is responsible for reporting the conditions and circumstances relating to accidents and making accident reports public. In order to carry out these functions, the NTSB has been granted broad statutory powers, which include, but are not limited to, examining and testing of the entire aircraft and component systems, having sole access to the remains of aircraft accidents, holding of hearings on accidents and other topics, and the issuance of subpoenas (Pezold, 1976).

The NTSB is notified immediately of an aircraft accident, an overdue aircraft believed to be involved in an accident, or incidents such as flight control system malfunction, inability of any required flight crew member to perform normal flight duties as a result of injury or illness, and failure of structural components. The NTSB is in charge of the investigation; independent investigations by any other group are prohibited. In the case of a terrorist act, the accident site is considered a crime scene and the FBI is given responsibility for the investigation. The NTSB provides assistance upon request (Goglia, 1996). Furthermore, the Board is the only U.S. accredited representative at foreign accident investigations under the provisions of the International Civil Aviation Organization (ICAO). International aviation accident investigations will be addressed in the latter portion of this chapter.

History

The roots of the NTSB may be traced to the Air Commerce Act of 1926, which authorized the Commerce Department to determine the cause of aviation accidents (NTSB, 1984). The Aeronautics Branch, a small unit within the Commerce Department, carried out this function. In 1938, the Civil Aeronautics Act repealed large portions of the Air Commerce Act and consolidated all aviation functions into an agency called the Civil Aeronautics Authority (CAA). Three separate organizations administered its power: the CAA, a five-member board, established policy; an Administrator of Aviation was responsible for carrying out safety policies; and the Air Safety Board was to investigate accidents and make determinations of probable cause, release its findings to the public, recommend measures to prevent accidents, and make the rules necessary to fulfill all of these functions (Miller, 1981). Members were presidential appointees, with one member required to be an active airline pilot at the time of appointment. The Air Safety Board was empowered to investigate accidents, but could not institute remedial measures. It could only make recommendations to the five-member CAA. Dissatisfaction with this subordinate nature prompted the Reorganization Plan of 1940, which transferred the investigative, economic regulatory, and rule-making function to the newly created Civil Aeronautics Board (CAB) (Pezold, 1976).

With the passage of the Federal Aviation Act in 1958, the Federal Aviation Administration was created. The FAA assumed several CAB responsibilities; however, the CAB maintained its role in the investigation and determination of the probable cause of all accidents, and offered recommendations to the FAA to prevent similar accidents in the future. The CAB was also authorized to direct investigations when civil and military aircraft were both involved (Miller, 1981). In 1966, the Department of Transportation Act (DOT) shifted the CAB's Bureau of Safety (BOS) to the Bureau of Aviation Safety (BAS) under the newly formed National Transportation Safety Board. The DOT Act loosely attached the NTSB to the DOT. However, problems existing between the FAA, DOT, and NTSB prompted passage of the 1974 Independent Safety Board Act, making the NTSB an independent agency, increasing its authority in accident investigation, and severing ties with the Department of Transportation (Miller, 1981). The NTSB's independence from the Department of Transportation, which has authority over the Federal Aviation Administration, is critical to conducting objective investigations and reporting on those investigations without influence or bias from any individuals or organizations (Feith, 1997).

Board Structure and Composition

The NTSB, headquartered in Washington, D.C., maintains regional offices in Chicago, Fort Worth, Los Angeles, Miami, New York City, and Seattle. Smaller satellite offices are also located in Atlanta, Anchorage, and Denver. As one of the Federal government's smallest agencies, the NTSB employs 380 persons nationwide in the areas of aviation, marine, highway, railroad, and pipeline. The Board is composed of five members, appointed by the president and confirmed by the Senate. The full term of each member is five years. Two of the members are additionally designated by the president for two-year terms to serve concurrently as chairman and vice chairman (NTSB, 1984).

The NTSB's staff consists of nine principal organizational elements. The Office of Managing Director assists the chairman in executing his functions and directs the overall operations of the Board. Information concerning the Board's work, programs, and objectives, which is provided for interest groups, is handled by the Office of Government and Public Affairs. Legal advice is received through the Office of General Counsel. The Office of Administrative Law Judges conducts formal proceedings which involve suspension or revocation of certificates, as well as appeals.

Aviation accident investigations are conducted by the Office of Aviation Safety through its Washington headquarters staff and regional offices. The Offices of Railroad Safety, Highway Safety, Marine Safety, and Pipeline/ Hazardous Materials Safety manage the investigations of surface transportation accidents. These offices are staffed by employees located both in the Board's headquarters and its regional offices. The Office of Research and Engineering provides laboratory and technical support to the Board's accident investigations in all transportation modes, and conducts safety studies that examine safety issues in all modes of transportation. The Office is also responsible for maintaining the Board's aviation and surface transportation accident databases. The Office of Safety Recommendations follows up on Board safety recommendations, and maintains a database of all past Board recommendations and their status with regard to remedial or preventive action by the addressees. Finally, the Bureau of Administration provides administrative support.

Office of Aviation Safety

The Office of Aviation Safety has the responsibility of managing the investigation of major aviation accidents, developing proposed probable causes of accidents, formulating recommendations, and preparing reports for other government agencies, Congress, the transportation industry, and the general public (NTSB, 1997). Six divisions comprise the Office of Aviation Safety: Major Investigations, Regional Operations and General Aviation, Operational Factors, Aviation Engineering, Human Performance, and Survival Factors. Members from these divisions compose the NTSB's go-team, which investigates major accidents and selected incidents. Major Investigations provides the Investigator-In-Charge (IIC), coordinates the preparation of safety reports, manages the public hearings, and provides an accredited representative for the investigation of international and civil aviation accidents.

Investigators from the Regional Operations and General Aviation Division are located in the Board's Washington headquarters and regional and field offices. The division's personnel not only provide support to major investigations but also manage the investigation of smaller-scale accidents. The Operational Factors Division examines air traffic control, weather, and flight operations of the carrier and airport, and the flight training and experience of the flight crew. The Aviation Engineering Division includes powerplants (aircraft engines), structures (aircraft structures and flight controls), systems (aircraft flight controls and electrical, hydraulic, and avionic systems), and maintenance records (aircraft systems, structures, and powerplants). The Human Performance Division examines the performance of persons who may have caused or contributed to an accident. Finally, the Survival Factors Division considers factors which influenced the survival of persons involved in accidents.

Accident Notification

Following an aviation accident, local authorities (the police, fire department, paramedics, and the coroner) respond immediately to secure the accident site and prevent the disturbance of wreckage, provide medical care and assistance, and identify and remove those who have perished. Federal agencies which have jurisdiction in this area are immediately notified of the accident, including the Department of Transportation, the FAA, Federal Emergency Management Agency (FEMA), and the NTSB. The FBI may be notified in some instances (Goglia, 1996). Once initial notification of a major accident is received, the NTSB Regional Director immediately notifies the Office of Aviation Safety or the Chief of Major Investigations. The NTSB's Washington office is directly responsible for all major catastrophic air-carrier accidents, accidents with national significance, and most general aviation accidents and incidents occurring outside the continental limits of the United States. The Chief of the Major Investigations Division, once notified of an accident, contacts the Director of the Office of Aviation Safety concerning the decision to dispatch the go-team and then notifies and briefs the Board Chairman on the situation, who will then determine whether a Board Member should attend. The Chief is also responsible for notifying the Managing Director, the Office of Public Affairs, Board Members, and the Office of Congressional and Intergovernmental Affairs. The regional office nearest to the accident site is then notified of the plans and the Chief directs their initial efforts.

Upon initial notification of the accident, a preliminary assessment of the magnitude of the tasks and likely scope of the investigation is made and the needed size and expertise of an investigation team is determined. Usually, there is a direct relationship between the size of the aircraft (number of injuries and fatalities) and the size of the team. Approximately two to three hours after accident notification, an NTSB go-team is dispatched from Washington to the accident site. Prior to the go-team launch, there is significant interaction among NTSB staff, the FAA, and other aviation industry officials. The NTSB go-team is led by an Investigator-In-Charge, a senior air-safety investigator, supported by several NTSB Group Chairmen. These chairmen specialize in powerplants, systems, structures, operations, air traffic control, weather, survival factors, aircraft performance, human performance, cockpit voice recorder, FDR, witnesses, and maintenance records.

Party System

The NTSB's investigation process involves a party system, allowing participation by various interested parties. Party status to an investigation is not a "right," but is considered a privilege. Only organizations or agencies whose employees, functions, activities, or products were involved in the accident and who possess specific factual information or skills which would otherwise be unavailable are approved to actively assist in the field investigation. This typically includes the airline, airframe manufacturer, engine manufacturer, and pilots' union. Parties are selected by the NTSB's IIC on the basis of need. Representatives of claimants or insurers are not allowed. Although information from the investigation may be used in litigation, participation is not for the purpose of preparing for litigation. Those whose interests conflict with the basic safety objectives of the investigation, such as attorneys, are not allowed to participate and if inadvertently included as part of the team are immediately removed from the investigation by the NTSB. By law, the Federal Aviation Administration is always a party to the investigation. The FAA provides technical expertise and institutional knowledge (NTSB, 1994). FAA representatives are assigned to actively participate in every major accident investigation and every full field investigation. Parties to the investigation do not participate in the analysis and probable-cause findings, but the NTSB does accept and consider written submissions by the parties that address their respective views regarding findings and probable cause of the accident.

The purpose of the party system is twofold. First, the various parties involved offer specialized technical expertise which the Board may lack. The limited staffing of the NTSB requires additional staffing for the investigation. Available NTSB investigators may not be knowledgeable in every phase of the accident investigation. Participants may be asked to describe their qualifications. Second, the "party" concept allows organizations immediate access to information concerning the accident which enables them to quickly initiate preventive or corrective action (NTSB, 1994). It is not always wise to wait for NTSB recommendations when a problem can be immediately remedied. For this reason, the FAA, which can mandate immediate fixes, is always a party to the investigation. In addition, the party system results in a more thorough investigation of the facts and issues. In March 1997, Barry Strauch, Chief of the Human Performance Division of the NTSB's Office of Aviation Safety, explained as follows:

What invariably happens is that one of the parties will raise issues with us, often times for the purpose of basically trying to shift responsibilities for the accident away from them to somebody else. Our job then becomes one of following up on that issue so we're satisfied that we've either put it to rest or that it is a legitimate issue which needs to be examined. Parties with competing interests in the investigation keep each other honest, and force us to follow up on an issue we might otherwise overlook. By the time the investigation concludes, those involved are satisfied that everything was thoroughly addressed.

Most parties to an investigation are familiar with NTSB procedures. Each party to the investigation is managed by an organization or company party coordinator who has the authority to make decisions on behalf of the company during the on-site investigation. This person is the NTSB's direct and official contact for the company, and the single representative and spokesperson at the nightly progress meetings. Party participants are assigned to working groups led by NTSB group chairmen for the duration of the on-site investigation.

The airline in crisis is expected to comply with the authority of the NTSB. The NTSB requests the airline provide technical expertise to the investigation. These airline personnel contribute background information concerning flight procedures, pilot training, and maintenance. In addition, the Board requests that the airline provide documentation concerning the flight crew, airframe, engines, and airplane components.

Accident Investigation Process

The accident investigation process consists of three phases: the investigative phase, the public hearing phase, and the analysis phase. The investigative phase is a fact-finding or information-collection phase conducted by the go-team at the site of the crash and at the Board's laboratory. This phase is an effort to document and develop as comprehensive a record as possible of what remains and what was seen and heard. Depending on various factors concerning the crash, a public hearing may be held. Additional information is collected from witnesses and the issues involved in the accident are made public. The final phase is the analysis of factual findings and the presentation of the final report. The final report provides safety recommendations which designate the expected actions to be taken. The entire investigation process of information collection and identification of the cause normally takes several months (NTSB, 1984). A particularly complex case may take longer. An investigation, however, is never closed. The following section is a detailed discussion of the three phases of an aviation accident investigation.

Investigative Phase

The go-team, which consists of a member of the Board, the IIC, technical specialists, NTSB accident investigators, a public-affairs officer, and family assistance representatives, is immediately sent to the scene of the accident. The go-team concept is the more publicly visible aspect of a major NTSB accident investigation. Each Monday, a go-team listing, identifying the names and numbers of all Board personnel on duty, is published by the Office of

Aviation Safety. These individuals remain on stand-by duty for immediate assignment to a major accident investigation. A Board member serves as the senior representative on the scene, and along with the Board's Public and Governmental Affairs representative and family assistance representatives handles all media contacts.

Major accident investigations may involve over 100 technical specialists from a dozen parties and multiple Federal and local government agencies (NTSB, 1994). This group possesses a wide range of accident-investigation skills. The NTSB regional field office is responsible for the initial stakedown of the accident scene and wreckage. Prior to the arrival of the go-team, the aircraft wreckage may not be disturbed unless to remove an injured or trapped person, protect the wreckage from further damage, or protect the public from injury (NTSB, 1984). The IIC exercises full control over the on-site investigation. His first concern is to secure all relevant evidence.

The NTSB's emphasis on teamwork demonstrates the significance of this concept in the context of crisis. Teamwork is considered essential throughout major investigations "to ensure proper utilization of the expertise of the parties and international officials and experts" (Feith, 1997). Upon arrival at the accident site, the IIC convenes an organizational meeting at the NTSB command post to provide preliminary accident information, introduce participants, organize participants into investigative groups, and establish investigation rules. Parties to the investigation designate a coordinator who reports and responds to the IIC. These coordinators ensure their personnel comply with NTSB rules and procedures (Feith, 1997).

Coordinators also function to transmit information to the parent organizations involved. Investigation committees and parties are designated by the IIC. Factors affecting team size include size of the aircraft, accident type, aircraft type, aircraft damage and loss, ground damage and loss, likelihood of a major narrative report, aircraft injuries and fatalities, ground injuries and fatalities, public interest, and the likelihood of a formal Board hearing (Miller & Halnon, 1970). The degree of public interest is perhaps the most complex factor to evaluate. Media interest is gauged by identifying factors associated with the event which could arouse public interest. Those authorized to be present and observe during the investigation include newsmen, local government officials, and others who have a need to observe the wreckage in a more comprehensive manner than the general public.

Numerous teams perform the largest part of the investigative work. Each team consists of a NTSB specialist as chairman, and representatives of interested parties. The group chairman delegates specific assignments (Miller & Halnon, 1970, p. 408). Teams function to determine "the facts, conditions and circumstances" which relate to their respective area of investigation and may have a bearing on the probable cause of the accident. Established teams debrief witnesses, examine flight data and cockpit voice recorders, and study air traffic control, meteorological records, human factors, operations, maintenance, structures, systems, and powerplants (Pezold, 1976).

A team's task often requires off-site engineering studies or laboratory tests which may extend the fact-finding stage. The NTSB operates its own technical laboratory with the capability to "readout" aircraft cockpit voice recorders and decipher flight data recorders. Board metallurgists perform post-accident analysis of wreckage parts ranging from aircraft components to railroad tracks. The laboratory is capable of determining whether failures resulted from inadequate design strength, excessive loading, or deterioration in static strength through fatigue or corrosion (NTSB, 1984). Occasionally, outside laboratories and testing facilities are used, but in all cases the appropriate investigative group observes all such activities to ensure unbiased analysis and conclusive evidence.

Generally, the on-site investigation lasts from seven to ten days. Progress meetings are held at the conclusion of each day's activities. At these meetings each team chairman summarizes the team's factual findings of the day and formulates an agenda for the following day. These meetings further provide information to the Board member for dissemination to the media. With continuing assistance from his or her group, each group chairman compiles a set of factual field notes. Then, at the end of the on-scene phase of the investigation and before the group is released, the notes are agreed to by group members and submitted to the IIC. These notes are later used to prepare each group chairman's written factual report. These factual reports become a permanent part of the Board's public record of the investigation and, if there is a Board public hearing, they are used as hearing exhibits.

After completing his or her portion of the investigation, each group chairman prepares a written analysis of the facts compiled by his or her group. These analysis reports are NTSB internal documents that are considered by the staff in preparing the proposed final Board report of the accident. They are not released to group members, party coordinators, or the public.

Public Hearing Phase

Following the on-site investigation, the Board may decide to hold a public hearing to collect additional information and to make public the issues involved in an accident. The decision to hold a public hearing is made by the Chairman of the Safety Board. The chairman's decision is based on such factors as the degree of public interest in the accident, the seriousness of possible deficiencies in the aircraft or related equipment, the type of operation involved, and the potential benefits for accident prevention. Generally, hearings are held for major disasters. Evidence is exhibited (factual reports covering areas of investigation, photographs, diagrams, charts, witness statements, transcripts, and reports of tests or examinations) and a list of witnesses is compiled and set forth in a hearing outline. Key issues and witnesses are identified prior to the hearing. Parties designated to participate in the hearing generally include government agencies and companies or associations whose employees, functions, activities, or products were involved in the accident and whose specialized skills and knowledge can contribute to the development of evidence.

The hearing, which is open to the public, is held before a Board of Inquiry which consists of the chairman, the presiding officer, the director of the Office of Aviation Safety, a hearing officer, and general counsel. The Board is responsible for forming a public record of all known facts pertaining to the accident. A technical panel, primarily responsible for the questioning of witnesses, is generally composed of NTSB technical personnel who served as team chairmen during the field investigation. The length of the hearing is dependent on the conclusiveness of the field investigation. For example, if the safety issues identified during the investigation are fairly straightforward, the hearing is likely to be short. If evidence is conflicting and issues are complex and controversial, the hearing may be prolonged and highly technical. At the completion of the hearing and within a specified time, any person may submit recommendations as to the proper conclusion to be drawn from the hearing. A complete transcript and exhibits are also made available following the hearing.

The inquiry is not held for the purpose of determining the rights or liabilities of private parties, but is a fact-finding procedure intended to assist the Safety Board in determining the cause and identifying prevention measures to avert similar accidents. There are no formal pleadings or adverse parties, although it may serve as a forum to plead innocence and place blame. In other words, testimony may have a self-serving theme. During the course of a hearing, diverse points of view are presented. A hearing may not provide new revelations, but it helps to substantiate material and establish the Board's thoroughness, independence, and impartiality.

The public hearing is the media's first opportunity to access written factual information on the accident. Therefore, it is in their best interests that various parties prepare for media inquiry. For example, reporters are often drawn to flight-crew transcripts and may take comments out of context. Though the NTSB is prepared to field questions, it does not prohibit parties from disclosing factual information at this phase of the investigation. Thus, if a party feels it must respond to reporters, the NTSB will not object.

Analysis Phase

With the completion of the fact-finding stage, analysis of the findings is conducted at the Washington headquarters. Based on a consideration of all the information available, the analysis results in what the Board terms the "probable cause" of the accident. The Board's staff drafts a final report which is circulated within the Office of Aviation Safety for comments and sent to the director for review. The accident report is then presented to the full five-member Board for discussion and approval at a public meeting in Washington. Safety recommendations are among the Board's most important end products. Each recommendation issued by the Board designates the person or the party expected to take action, describes the action the Board expects, and clearly states the safety need to be satisfied.

The composition of the final report is entirely at the discretion of the Board. The report includes the facts, conditions, and circumstances which led to the accident and bear on the determination of the probable cause of the accident, and recommendations for future changes. The major share of the Board's air-safety recommendations are directed to the Federal Aviation Administration. The recommendations have resulted in a wide range of safety improvements in areas such as pilot training, aircraft maintenance and design, air traffic control, procedures, and survival equipment requirements. An accident investigation is never closed but is kept open for the submission of new and pertinent information as it may become available. Once the Board has adopted the report, recommendations, and probable cause, interested parties or persons can formally petition the NTSB to reconsider all or part of the analysis, conclusions, or probable cause.

Communicating with Stakeholders

The NTSB's guiding informational policy is as follows:

The Board is a Public Agency engaged in the public's business and supported by public funds. The work we do in the business of safety is open for public review; the Act under which we operate makes this mandatory. Today, the Safety Board believes that briefing news personnel factually during the on-site investigation of an aircraft accident should be a normal operational part of that investigation. (NTSB, 1994)

The Independent Safety Board Act requires the results of any NTSB investigation be made available to the public, and the NTSB readily complies with this responsibility. When a probable cause of a major accident is not immediately apparent, the press and public are inclined to speculate as to what happened. The Board's process of providing factual information at regular press briefings during the investigation is intended to limit speculation. Information must be communicated in a way that does not confuse or mislead the public or damage innocent parties. Briefing media on the facts during the on-site investigation is a common NTSB procedure.

In the aftermath of an airline crash, the NTSB is on the scene, prepared to deal with the media. All inquiries are directed to the Board. Congressional members, government officials, news media, and others seeking accident information refer their queries to Board officials. Once parties to an investigation assemble, they are told explicitly by the IIC that the Safety Board will speak for the investigation to assure consistency and accuracy in what is released. The NTSB is the focal point to which all questions and concerns are directed. Logistical problems associated with the onslaught of reporters are handled by a member of the NTSB's public affairs staff.

An NTSB Board member, the IIC, or the public affairs representative serves as spokesperson during an investigation. If the Board member is unavailable, the IIC or public affairs officer is responsible for handling the press. The IIC, along with the public affairs officer, generally assists the Board member in preparing for the briefing. The IIC reviews the high points of the progress meeting and identifies information which is unconfirmed or unsubstantiated so as to advise the Board member regarding information which should or should not be released (NTSB, 1994). These individuals anticipate press questions which would likely follow the release of particular information and the cause of the accident in general. The IIC attends the press briefing, and if called on by the Board member provides assistance. Participants must refrain from giving information or discussing the accident with the public or press. Violation of this request is considered a major infraction of Board rules and may lead to dismissal from the investigation.

Media are restricted from the investigation command post and daily progress meetings. Two basic forms of press contact are used by the NTSB. First, press briefings are conducted daily. Briefings on the progress of the investigation usually follow the investigative team's daily meeting. These briefings provide reporters with the latest factual information. Second, press contact occurs through a steady stream of phone calls and visits by reporters and camera crews. Photo opportunities are supervised by a press officer so as to minimize disruption of investigative work.

The NTSB keeps the public informed as to the progress of an investigation and assures the determination of the probable cause of the accident and remedial action to avert a recurrence. Interim disclosures given by the Board are factual and clarified to prevent misunderstandings. Documented information is provided to deter the press from inventing investigative findings or relying on less-reliable sources. The Board does not speculate on the cause of the accident and discourages speculation on the part of the press. Facts are released as they are documented. Information is limited to the facts obtained during the day; however, that which might complicate the NTSB's gathering of additional factual information is not released.

In some instances, information obtained during the investigation has the potential to adversely affect one or more parties. Prior to releasing information to the media, the NTSB briefs the parties on the inevitable disclosure of the facts. The Safety Board's rules and procedures regarding release of information gathered during an investigation are intended to prevent parties with vested interests from "leaking" or releasing information that would adversely reflect on other parties. In other words, parties with something to gain are prevented from making unauthorized releases (NTSB, 1994).

Because of its independent and objective nature, the NTSB is viewed by media as a credible and reliable source of information. The NTSB's philosophy regarding communication with the media demonstrates its clear understanding of the media's value and critical role. When communicating with media, the NTSB assumes a tolerant and helpful posture. More often than not, reporters' errors result from misunderstandings. The NTSB assists the media with understanding and "getting the facts right." Immediately following an air-carrier accident, the NTSB's initial contact with local media is limited to general facts concerning the securing of the wreckage site and the arrival of the Washington go-team.

The NTSB maintains strict control over information dissemination during the on-site investigation. Information flow is controlled to a great degree through the identification of a single spokesperson who maintains contact with the press. However, no individual or team is to withhold information from the IIC. Violation of this policy may result in dismissal from the investigation. Team members are to provide information to their respective Safety Board team chairmen. Team chairmen forward this information to the IIC. The IIC will provide factual information and developments to each of the party coordinators, who then relay this information to their respective organizations. This information is not for public release; rather, it is for purposes of accident prevention, remedial action, or other similar reasons. The party coordinators are expected to clarify how the information will be put to use (NTSB, 1994).

Family Support Services

On October 9, 1996, the Aviation Disaster Family Assistance Act was passed by Congress and signed by President Clinton. This Act gave the NTSB additional responsibility for helping families of victims of domestic aircraft accidents. In response to this charge, the NTSB developed the Federal Family Assistance Plan for Aviation Disasters, which delegates responsibilities and describes the airline and Federal response to major aviation crashes. The plan is developed according to three possible crash scales, based on the number of injuries or fatalities, which influence the supporting organizations' process. The Federal Family Assistance Plan applies to all domestic or foreign aviation crashes which occur within the United States, its territories and possessions, and territorial seas. In the event of a crime-related accident, the Board would still function in this role.

The NTSB's Family Support Services (FSS) functions to coordinate Federal government resources and other groups to support the local and state government and airline in responding to families of victims of major catastrophic aviation disasters. The FSS is responsible for notifying Federal agencies to mobilize an appropriate response with the airline. Federal agencies who may be notified include the American Red Cross, Department of State, Department of Health and Human Services, FBI Operations Center, FEMA, Department of Defense, and Department of Justice. The plan identifies seven Victim Support Tasks which participating organizations may support. These include NTSB Tasks, Airline Tasks, Family Care and Mental Health, Victim Identification, Forensic and Medical Services, Assisting Families of Foreign Victims, Communications, and Assisting Victims of Crime (NTSB, 1997, April 9).

Specifically, the NTSB is responsible for coordinating the participating groups and serving as liaison between the airline and family members. Following a major airline crash in which there are numerous fatalities, the director of family support services (an NTSB employee) joins the NTSB go-team. As soon as possible, the director is required to establish a toll-free number to provide information to families. This number is considered an alternative source of information when families are unable to connect with the airline's 800 number. The passenger manifest is requested from the airline by the Office for Family Assistance after a reasonable period of time has elapsed and most notifications have been made. If it is apparent the airline is failing to make prompt notifications, then the NTSB will supplement the airline's response.

The Board maintains communication with the airline regarding the status of next-of-kin notification, conducts daily coordination and review meetings with the airline and support groups, provides family briefings, discusses the process of DNA testing with the medical examiner, arranges for families to visit the crash site, briefs media on information related to the family support area, and maintains contact with family members to keep them informed about the investigative efforts (NTSB, 1997, April 9). In addition, the Board is responsible for facilitating the recovery and identification of victims. The NTSB supervises the work performed by the Department of Health and Human Services and their National Disaster Medical Service (NDMS) mortuary teams, which support local response. In some cases, the NDMS mobile mortuary may be transported to the accident site. Its trained staff has the ability to identify hundreds of victims in a brief time period.

The airline continues to have the central responsibility for families; however, under the Family Assistance Act the airline is in a collaborative position with the families, NTSB, and supporting organizations. The airline's responsibilities include providing timely notification to victims' families; providing the NTSB with a current copy of the passenger manifest; securing facilities at departure, arrival, and connecting airports to shield family members from media and solicitors; providing continuous information regarding the passenger manifest and additional information on the crash; providing logistical support (transportation, lodging, meals, security, communications, and incidentals) for family members who travel to the incident site; securing (at an appropriate time) dental records of victims; arranging for a joint family support operations center and private area for medical examiner personnel to collect information from families at the site; supplying information to Department of State liaisons regarding foreign passengers; providing the public with notification updates; arranging to meet families when they arrive and continuing to assist families once they return to their residences; maintaining daily contact with families who do not travel to the site; arranging for the return of personal effects; and consulting with family members regarding airline-sponsored monuments, including any inscriptions (NTSB, 1997, April 9).

While the legislation allows airlines to continue their primary responsibilities, communication between the airlines and family members concerning information to assist in victim identification is conducted by officials appointed by the NTSB. The law further specifies that airlines, along with their insurance companies and any plaintiff lawyers, be restricted from discussing settlement issues or lawsuits with family members for thirty days following an accident. The legislation requires that airlines submit disaster response plans for review by a task force comprised of representatives from the Department of Transportation, NTSB, FEMA, Red Cross, airlines, and family victims groups. The task force is expected to provide recommendations on handling attorney and media intrusion, ensuring equal treatment for foreign families, and utilizing military assets for identification purposes.

INTERNATIONAL AVIATION ACCIDENT INVESTIGATIONS

A foreign airline crashes in the United States. A U.S. airline crashes overseas. A U.S. airline operating a foreign-built airplane crashes overseas. These accidents involve a number of international interests: the U.S. airline, the foreign manufacturer, and the country in which the accident takes place. The expanding globalization of the aviation industry poses challenges for international accident investigations. An increasingly competitive environment has forced airlines to establish international partnerships and aircraft manufacturers to adopt multinational production arrangements. Today, an aircraft could have components or parts manufactured in three or four countries, be assembled in another country, registered in still another country, and so on. With expanding world trade, economic growth in foreign countries, and increased interest in international travel the international market continues to grow. The U.S. airline industry has a significant stake in this global transportation system because of its leading role in the technological progress of aviation. Consequently, worldwide public reaction to a major international air disaster will likely have a negative effect on U.S. airlines.

International Civil Aviation Organization

The rights of each country, given their role in the operation of the airplane and the accident, are established by the International Civil Aviation Organization (ICAO). The principles and arrangements which guide participants in the international civil aviation industry go back to the Convention on International Civil Aviation (the Chicago Convention), held in November 1944, which brought together the likely postwar civil aviation powers, fifty-two nations in all, for the purpose of crafting a multilateral agreement governing international civil aviation to control economic and technical problems while allowing for the future growth and regulation of the industry (Canetti, 1995). This meeting resulted in the establishment of ICAO.

ICAO establishes international standardization in the technical, economic, and legal areas of civil aviation. It is the organizational medium through which necessary international understanding and agreement are reached. In other words, it functions to achieve international cooperation in aviation matters. Headquartered in Montreal, ICAO is one of the specialized agencies of the United Nations family and is comprised of more than 180 sovereign states. International rules governing all areas of aviation are developed by ICAO, including rules governing navigation, safety, security, the environment, training, and facilitation. The establishment of international standards, recommended practices, and procedures covering the technical fields of aviation is one of its primary responsibilities. Among the areas standardized by the organization is that of aircraft accident investigation.

Contracting states of ICAO are expected to carry out investigations in accordance with Annex 13 to the Chicago Convention on International Civil Aviation. Investigations are the responsibility of the country in which the accident occurs. In principle, the rules governing an investigation are subject to national legislation; however, ICAO contracting states endeavor to comply with the specifications contained in the Annex. States are further expected to inform ICAO of any differences which may exist between their national legislation and the Annex. These differences are also published by ICAO. (As a contracting state of ICAO, U.S. regulations have few differences with the standards in Annex 13.) Depending on their different capabilities and the setup of their investigation authorities, the actual procedures may vary from country to country. Small countries, for example, may not even have such an authority and would carry out major investigations through experts recruited on an ad hoc basis. Others have made arrangements with larger states to obtain assistance.

Cooperation between the different states involved in any given investigation is stressed in the Annex (R. Menzel, personal communication, September 28, 1997). Each contracting state has reference to an Aircraft Investigation Manual (AIM) which identifies methods for organizing and investigating. The guidelines set forth by ICAO are used by all contracting states, and even by some nonsignatories. For example, because ICAO is part of the United Nations effort, Taiwan has not joined the group because of their domestic politics. Nevertheless, when an accident occurs in Taiwan, the Taiwanese adhere to ICAO investigation requirements. Regarding the subject of continuing reliability (airworthiness) of aircraft, the provisions of Annex 8 specify the obligation of the state of design and manufacture to notify all operators about aircraft airworthiness problems that have been reported back to the manufacturer. This provision ensures the worldwide reliability of the fleet.

International investigations often present difficulties resulting from legal and cultural differences. In countries which have the Napoleonic Code as their basis for law, such as France, the local judge is responsible for the wreckage. The judge may have no expertise, knowledge, or experience in accident investigation; however, he may feel it is his responsibility to oversee or control the investigation because the deaths occurred within his jurisdiction. Japan is similar. Unlike the United States, the multilayered Japanese bureaucracy, including law enforcement, injects itself into aviation investigations and restricts the air-safety investigations from functioning with total freedom.

Additional problems may occur in more isolated areas of a country. Robert MacIntosh, NTSB IIC and U.S. Accredited Representative, explains as follows:

Frequently in a remote area there are a lot of "have nots" who would prefer we adhere to a code that once something is destroyed or deceased, it's no longer of use to anyone other than those who come upon it. Therefore, we may find bodies stripped of their clothes and jewelry, aircraft parts sitting on someone's front porch, or the seats of an aircraft occupying the shady spot under the tree, rather than being left at the wreckage site. It gets more clandestine when people assume that somebody is going to be looking for those parts so they'll just put them away and wait until the bounty is ready to be paid.

Following a crash, the respective government accident investigation authority of which the air carrier is registered, operated, or designed and manufactured is notified and invited to appoint an Accredited Representative and advisors from the airline, the design and manufacturer, and regulatory authority to participate in the investigation. For international investigations, it is the responsibility of the NTSB to appoint a U.S. Accredited Representative who will oversee the advisors from the U.S. aviation industry and the FAA. In the case of an accident which involves a U.S. registered and/or operated aircraft, the NTSB may assist in the following ways: directly support the on-scene investigation; contribute advisors and technical assistance to the state in charge of the investigation; provide laboratories for readout and analyses of flight recorders and/or metallurgical tests; upon request, serve to manage the investigation; furnish technical reports of the investigative activities conducted by the U.S. team; and render draft report-writing services to the state conducting the investigation.

An increasingly international environment has clear implications for aircraft accident investigations—investigation agencies must become more interconnected to work effectively. As Hinton (1995) observes, "The day may come when an independent, multinational investigation agency will exist, but it will not be soon. In the meantime, accident investigation authorities can increase their effectiveness by increasing communication and interaction with each other" (p. 8).

Cultural and legal differences, as well as government investigating agencies' varying approaches to accident investigation further challenge post-crisis management and communication. It is critical for crisis managers to recognize and understand how these variables can influence a crisis and plan accordingly.

CONCLUSION

In post-crisis, organizations seek resolution in an environment of surprise, uncertainty, threat, stress, and limited response time. Opportunities or additional negative effects may occur during post-crisis. This stage provides a chance for organizational assessment and increased understanding of the system's overall functioning. It is a time to correct problems, develop and implement preventive actions, and introduce needed change.

Post-crisis is also a point where the crisis organization undergoes intense scrutiny from various sources. For an airline experiencing a major air-carrier accident, one form of scrutiny is a formal investigation. This chapter examined the U.S. NTSB and its role in major aviation accident investigations. The NTSB is a credible body designed to promote transportation safety. When investigating accidents, the NTSB collects information, examines questionable situations, determines probable causes, and provides recommendations.

Following an airline crash, the NTSB provides an immediate response in a situation where the public demands an explanation. While a crisis tends to disrupt and suppress communication, the NTSB facilitates communication by focusing the crisis into a public and rational forum to promote dialogue and consensus. This is necessary to eliminate confusion and crisis and bring about resolution. By providing a rational, systematic, and orderly response to the crisis, the NTSB assists the airline in managing the crisis. The NTSB functions to eliminate the fundamental causes of the accident, enabling the airline to focus on the immediate effects of the crisis.

The NTSB's investigation process will likely influence the airline's and industry stakeholders' communication efforts following a crash. Investigative findings may serve to enhance or further damage the image of an organization. The assignment of blame or evidence which publicizes mistakes, for example, presents a threat and motivates a defensive response. Investigative findings may also assist the airline in determining appropriate responses, particularly strategies which are corrective in nature.

The NTSB and its process provide a number of advantages to the airlines as well as the industry. From the public's perspective, the NTSB contributes a "corporate ethos" to the airline industry by virtue of its knowledge, authority, and independent and objective nature. The NTSB functions as an advocate for the industry by creating a favorable, reasonable, and informed public opinion.

REFERENCES

Bolz, B. J. (1988). *Implications for a three phase model of crisis communication.* Unpublished master's thesis, Wayne State University, Detroit, MI.

Canetti, C. (1995). Fifty years after the Chicago conference: A proposal for dispute settlement under the auspices of the International Civil Aviation Organization. *Law & Policy in International Business, 26,* 497–522.

Feith, G. (1997, March 17). Interview with author.

Fink, S. (1986) *Crisis management: Planning for the inevitable.* New York: AMACOM.

Goelz, P. (1997, March 17). Interview with author.

Goglia, J. (1996, June 28). *Overview of responsibilities of National Transportation Safety Board.* Presentation before the American Bar Association Seminar on Aviation Litigation, Washington, DC.

Hall, D. T., & Mansfield, R. (1971). Organizational and individual response to external stress. *Administrative Science Quarterly, 16,* 533–547.

Hinton, T. (1995, September). Close ties between accident investigation authorities in different countries is more important than ever. *ICAO Journal, 50,* 6–8.

Komons, N. A. (1984). *The Cutting air crash: A case study in early federal aviation policy.* Washington, DC: U.S. Department of Transportation, Federal Aviation Administration.

MacIntosh, R. (1997, March 17). Interview with author.

Marcy, C. (1945). *Presidential commissions.* Morningside Heights, NY: Kings Crown.

Meyer, A. D. (1982). Adapting to environmental jolts. *Administrative Science Quarterly, 27,* 515–547.

Meyers, G. C. (1986). *When it hits the fan: Managing the nine crises of business.* New York: Mentor.

Miller, C. O. (1981). Aviation accident investigation: Functional and legal perspectives. *Journal of Air Law and Commerce, 46,* 237–293.

Miller, C. O., & Halnon, W. L. (1970). Procedure and conduct during on-site investigation of aviation accidents. *Journal of Air Law & Commerce, 36,* 394–420.

National Transportation Safety Board. (1984). Pamphlet documenting NTSB. Washington, DC: NTSB.

National Transportation Safety Board. (1994). *Investigator's Manual.* Washington, DC: NTSB.

National Transportation Safety Board. (1997). Pamphlet documenting NTSB. Washington, DC: NTSB.

National Transportation Safety Board. (1997, April 9). *Federal family assistance plan for aviation disasters.* Washington, DC: NTSB.

Pezold, R. K. (1976). National Transportation Safety Board: A critical review of information availability. *Journal of Air Law and Commerce, 42,* 363–384.

Popper, F. (1970). *The Presidents commissions.* New York: Twentieth Century Fund.

Seeger, M. W. (1987, November). *Investigating commissions and the maintenance of legitimacy.* Paper presented at the Annual Meeting of the Speech Communication Association, Boston, MA.

Strauch, B. (1997, March 17). Interview with author.

Turner, B. A. (1976). The organizational and interorganizational development of disasters. *Administrative Science Quarterly, 21,* 378–397.

Pan American World Airways Flight 103

In December 1988, the world witnessed the horrific consequences of international politics. The downing of Pan Am Flight 103 by a terrorist bomb over Lockerbie, Scotland, killed 270 innocent victims and ultimately contributed to the demise of a legendary airline. It became the worst civil air disaster in the United Kingdom.

The case of Pan Am Flight 103 illuminates the complexities associated with managing an international airline crash. The disaster became a global media event. Because of its international status, numerous countries were involved. Once it was realized the disaster was an intentional act, more nations were implicated. Outrage from a bombing, fear of terrorism, distraught and angry families, controversies over an unreported bomb threat, and intense media coverage combined to create a complex crisis for Pan American World Airways.

PRE-CRISIS

In the early days of aviation, airlines relied primarily on Post Office Air Mail contracts, rather than passenger revenue, to continue operating. The government chose the recipients of foreign airmail contracts; thus, opportunities awaited ambitious entrepreneurs who procured them. One such entrepreneur was Juan Trippe, and the airline empire he established became Pan American Airways. It was 1927 when three groups of businessmen formed Pan American Airways and secured the coveted U.S. airmail contract for the route from Key West, Florida to Havana, Cuba. Trippe was named president of the airline. Under his leadership and driving force, Pan Am became the government's "chosen instrument" for international aviation operations (Heppenheimer, 1995).

In the period of a few years, Pan Am extended its route system between Florida and Cuba, Mexico, Central America, the Panama Canal, the Dominican Republic, Haiti, and Puerto Rico. There were many challenges associated with establishing foreign routes. For one thing, acquiring landing rights in countries such as Mexico, Venezuela, and Colombia was often a laborious process. Furthermore, countries which negatively viewed the United States promoted their own native airlines. Pan Am countered these problems by persuading former U.S. diplomats and powerful Latin American insiders to secure privileges (Heppenheimer, 1995). By 1929, Pan Am controlled all the mail routes linking the United States to Mexico, Central America, and the Caribbean. In 1930, Trippe bought out New York, Rio, and Buenos Aires Line (NYRBA), making Pan Am the largest airline in the world.

Pan Am pioneered new routes in the early 1930s (Heppenheimer, 1995). Charles and Anne Lindbergh flew two survey flights for Pan American. The first was to navigate the "Great Circle Route" to the Orient and the second was to explore the most northern and southern routes to Europe. As the "chosen instrument," the airline constructed air facilities on Guam, Wake, and Midway for the U.S. Navy. This eventually enabled Pan American to provide service across the Pacific in 1935. During World War II, the airline constructed a network of military bases and served the Air Transport Command, the Army Air Force branch which controlled overseas air services. In 1945, Trippe took the lead in establishing the International Air Transport Association, an organization of airlines which set fares (Heppenheimer, 1995)

Pan Am failed to win a domestic route after World War II, but continued to retain the largest portion of overseas routes. The airline encountered financial struggles because of rival airlines in the late 1940s, but with the steady increase of international travel in the 1950s and 1960s, Pan Am once again improved its finances. In the 1950s the airline began to diversify. Pan Am contracted to create a missile-tracking range in the South Atlantic, operated a nuclear-engine testing laboratory in Nevada, marketed a corporate jet (the Falcon), constructed the largest office building in New York, and operated a worldwide chain of hotels (Heppenheimer, 1995). The 1960s saw Pan Am's passenger loads increase and profits strengthen.

In its early years, Pan Am's "fleet" included a mix of land planes, but Trippe's vision to "conquer the oceans" required seaplanes. Following the NYRBA acquisition, Pan Am operated amphibians and flying boats in the Gulf–Caribbean region and South American waters (Heppenheimer, 1995). Trippe's vision of serving faraway international routes encouraged aircraft manufacturers and technological developments, ultimately advancing commercial air transports and changing the worldwide airline industry. As air traffic grew in the 1960s, Trippe recognized the need for larger aircraft. Jets such as the Boeing 707 and the Douglas DC-8, and DC-9 appeared in the early 1960s. Trippe's influence ultimately resulted in the Boeing 747 (O'Lone, 1991). With the Boeing 747, Trippe committed Pan American to a major program of expansion.

In 1968, Juan Trippe retired, leaving the airline with a debt from the purchase of 747s and standing on the threshold of a deregulated industry. During the next two decades the airline would experience a series of leadership successions. Following Trippe was Harold Gray, who assumed the chairmanship, and Najeeb Halaby, who took over as chief operating officer (Heppenheimer, 1995). The following year the airline experienced the first in what would be a series of financial losses due to a decrease of air travelers, the cost of the Boeing 747s, and the beginning of the Arab oil embargo. Pan Am also received criticism from consumers for its poor service. Halaby replaced Gray in 1969, but resigned in 1972. He was succeeded by William Seawell, who began the process of "overhauling" the airline, cutting personnel and relinquishing unprofitable routes. Under Seawell's aggressive leadership, the airline's situation improved briefly. Because Trippe had focused solely on dominating the overseas market, Pan Am had no domestic routes. With its competitors now operating both domestic and international routes, the airline faced a real problem. In hopes of gaining domestic routes, Pan Am took over National Airlines in 1980, but the airline again encountered financial losses. Seawell sold the lease on the Pan Am building and gave up the hotel chain and the corporate jet division.

C. Edward Acker replaced Seawell in 1981. In an effort to return Pan Am to profitability, Acker sold 23 percent of Pan American's routes, including all the Pacific routes, to United Airlines and began a Pan Am shuttle service between Washington, New York, and Boston. Though the airline experienced some short-term success, by 1987 it had suffered a net operating loss of $170.3 million. Acker resigned in January 1988 and was succeeded by Thomas Plaskett. Plaskett's goal was to stabilize Pan Am; revitalize its service, facilities, and aircraft; and create a route system through a merger or acquisition ("Plaskett's persistence," 1991). Under Plaskett's leadership, the airline reduced its losses in 1988.

Despite Pan American's financial difficulties, its reputation for service problems, and a shrinking international route system, it was still the largest American carrier in Europe. Pan Am's memorable blue and white logo was well known on both sides of the Atlantic. As 1988 came to a close, the airline was optimistic about its prospects for the coming year.

Previous Accidents

In the late 1970s and early 1980s, Pan Am experienced two tragic accidents. The world's worst airline tragedy to date occurred in 1977, when a KLM 747 collided with a Pan American 747 on a foggy runway at Tenerife, in the Canary Islands, killing 583 (Denham, 1996). Seventy-seven people survived aboard the Pan Am aircraft. In 1982, a Pan Am Boeing 727 crashed following takeoff from New Orleans International Airport during a thunderstorm. The accident claimed all 145 lives on board the aircraft and eight on the ground, and demolished a number of homes. The probable cause of the crash was wind shear. Human error, mechanical failures, and severe weather conditions have consistently contributed to airline disasters, but in the 1970s and 1980s another factor created the potential for disaster: terrorism in the air.

International Terrorism

Hijackings by heavily armed terrorists occurred throughout the 1970s and 1980s. As a result of its international status, Pan American World Airways had fallen prey to such incidents. In September 1970, the Popular Front for the Liberation of Palestine coordinated a series of hijackings. A Pan Am 747 was seized by two Palestinians and taken to Cairo, where they set it on fire with explosives. The passengers were evacuated only moments before. In 1973, PLO terrorists bombed a Pan Am airplane at Rome's airport, killing thirty people. Airplane passengers being held hostage by a hijacker demanding to be flown to a certain destination prompted airlines to develop strict security measures. X-ray machines functioned to screen passengers and their luggage for concealed weapons.

Because of the difficulties in smuggling weapons aboard airplanes, terrorists soon turned to more sophisticated approaches. By the 1980s, a new kind of plastic explosive was developed which could not be detected by conventional X-ray devices or vapor-sniffing machines. In 1985, an Air India 747, en route from Montreal to London, exploded over the North Atlantic, killing 329 people on board. The crash was determined to have been caused by a bomb in the forward luggage hold. More terrorist attempts occurred in 1986. In April, a bomb exploded aboard a TWA plane on the ground in Athens, Greece, killing four people. Two weeks later, terrorists attempted and failed to place a bomb aboard an Israeli El-Al jet in London. In June, a bomb exploded at a terminal in Madrid (Horton, 1991). As the number of incidents increased, the international airline industry felt its effects. Though FAA inspectors routinely reviewed airport security (by attempting to smuggle phony weapons aboard commercial aircraft) and monitored airport personnel, it was physically impossible to completely control the situation.

In an effort to convince the flying public its airline was secure, Pan American in 1986 hired an Israeli consulting firm to review its security system. The firm's findings revealed the airline was highly vulnerable to a terrorist attack. Pan Am relied too heavily on X-ray machines, failed to identify suspicious passengers, and did not regularly test its own procedures. It was imperative the airline restructure its entire security system. Pan Am responded by establishing its own security system, Alert Management Systems, Inc. (Horton,

1991). The system did little to improve security. Critics argued the airline was more concerned about its image as a "safe" airline than about truly ensuring passenger safety. Implementation of security measures often delayed departure times, which increased concerns about losing business. For financial reasons, Pan Am chose to keep security at a minimum at a time when terrorist groups were a major presence in Europe (Horton, 1991). Following a routine check during the fall of 1988, the FAA discovered flaws in Pan Am's security at the Frankfurt Airport. The airline's security system failed to track suspicious passengers and x-ray interline baggage (Horton, 1991). In early December 1988, the FAA announced it would fine twenty-nine airlines for 236 detection failures. Pan Am was fined for nineteen of the infractions (Watson, 1989).

On December 5, 1988, the American Embassy in Helsinki, Finland, received a phone call from an unidentified source who stated that sometime within the next two weeks there would be a bombing attempt against a Pan American aircraft flying from Frankfurt to the United States. Though the call was viewed as a hoax, advisories were still sent to U.S. Embassies and other installations on December 7. In Moscow, a memo was posted for all employees at the U.S. Embassy notifying them of the threat. Informed of the warning by Washington, Pan Am said it would increase its security (Horton, 1991).

CRISIS

On December 21, 1988, Pan American World Airways Flight 103 arrived at London Heathrow from Frankfurt, West Germany. This was the first leg of a long journey that would continue to John F. Kennedy International Airport in New York, and then on to its final destination, Detroit Metropolitan Airport. In London, passengers from Flight 103 were transferred from the Boeing 727 on which they had flown from Frankfurt to a Boeing 747, "Clipper–Maid of the Seas," which arrived from San Francisco that afternoon. Additional passengers also boarded Flight 103 at Heathrow (U.K. Aviation, 1990). Altogether there were 243 passengers and a sixteen-member flight crew. The passengers, primarily American citizens, included a group of thirty-five Syracuse University students returning home from studying abroad, businesspeople, and military persons from U.S. bases in West Germany. Most were going home for the holidays.

Flight 103 departed London Heathrow at 6:25 P.M., twenty-five minutes past its scheduled departure time. At 6:56 P.M., the aircraft leveled off at 31 thousand feet, 175 miles north of London. A few minutes later Flight 103 exploded over Lockerbie, Scotland. At the Shanwick Oceanic Control, radar returns fanned out downwind for a considerable distance. There had been no mayday call or radio message from Flight 103.

Below, a storm of debris and bodies pummeled the small village of Lockerbie, located in the Annandale Valley of southern Scotland. Residents reported hearing a rumbling noise shortly after 7:00, which gradually increased to deafening proportions (U.K. Aviation, 1990). Shredded aircraft, flaming jet fuel, luggage, cargo, and bodies were strewn everywhere. The 747's massive engines and wings landed in Sherwood Crescent, the area of town most impacted by the disaster, pulverizing homes and producing a deep crater in the earth. Seismic monitoring stations nearby measured the impact at 1.6 on the Richter scale (U.K. Aviation, 1990). Fires of enormous proportions were ignited throughout the village. Other large parts landed in the countryside east of Lockerbie, including the cockpit and the forward fuselage section. Wreckage scattered far and wide, carrying debris as far as the North Sea (U.K. Aviation, 1990).

POST-CRISIS

Search and Recovery

In a single moment, the tiny, peaceful farming community of Lockerbie had become total chaos. Roads going in and out of the town were blocked. Telephones were down. At the town's south end a row of houses were burning. Police patrol in Lockerbie immediately transmitted a radio message reporting the aircraft crash to the Dumfries and Galloway Constabulary. All available fire trucks, ambulances, and police cars rushed to the accident site. In the next few hours, a major emergency operation took place according to the guidelines established in the Dumfries and Galloway Regional Peacetime Emergency Plan (U.K. Aviation, 1990). Reinforcements from Strathclyde and Lothian & Borders Constabularies arrived to help in the recovery. Military personnel from army bases across Scotland and England were called to assist in the effort. A temporary medical clinic was set up in the Lockerbie town hall. Throughout western Scotland, hospitals were placed on standby. Various agencies and volunteers provided for the welfare and support of survivors, Lockerbie's residents, and rescue workers.

In the early hours of the following morning it was clear there were no survivors. The rescue effort became one of recovering bodies. Lockerbie's town hall was turned into a makeshift morgue. Numerous helicopters were used to search for and recover aircraft wreckage (U.K. Aviation, 1990). Over the next few days, more than a thousand police and military personnel scoured the countryside searching for clues and victims. The degree of destruction made it difficult to determine an accurate death count. It was later learned that all 259 souls aboard Flight 103 perished along with eleven more on the ground. The explosion was the worst civil air disaster in the United Kingdom.

Investigation

Because the disaster occurred in Scotland, the Scottish were in charge of the investigation with the full cooperation from the U.S. government. In addition to the British Air Accident Investigation Branch, officials from various

American agencies joined the investigation, including the National Transportation Safety Board, the FAA, the FBI, and the Central Intelligence Agency, along with representatives from the Boeing Corporation, the Airline Pilots Association, and Pan Am. The town's school, Lockerbie Academy, served as the investigation's headquarters. Teams of experts covered each spot where wreckage was found.

Questions quickly arose as to whether mechanical problems caused the explosion. The Maid of the Seas, built in 1970, was the fifteenth 747 manufactured by Boeing. While the aircraft encountered mechanical difficulties through the years, it had received a major overhaul in 1987. Over a six-month period the plane's structure, engines, and landing gear had been checked. Pan Am indicated that one week prior to the explosion the aircraft had undergone a thorough routine base check. There were no signs of mechanical or structural problems (Watson, 1989).

Buried beneath the rubble investigators discovered the plane's two flight data recorders, but the recorders yielded little information. Investigators from the NTSB stated the CVR revealed normal flight-deck conversations until the tape ended abruptly. This suggested there was an instantaneous and total loss of power to the cockpit. An unidentified noise was heard at the end of the tape which was reminiscent of the cockpit recording retrieved from the 1985 Air India 747 explosion. Initial speculation as to why a 747 would just blow up in midair included a midair collision, a massive structural failure, or a bomb.

Though there was no immediate evidence of a bomb, investigators presumed early on that sabotage was the cause of the crash. The process of recovery and examination was slow and tedious. Investigators continued to search for fragments of the aircraft. Some items exhibited damage consistent with that near a detonating high explosive. Wreckage and victims were closely examined to determine the presence of explosives. On Christmas day, searchers discovered a shattered piece of luggage with a distinct pattern of rips and tears. The piece was taken to a weapons research laboratory where technicians examined the evidence. The following day officials announced the aircraft had been bombed.

The determination of a bomb as the cause of the crash completed the primary function of the accident investigation. It was now the responsibility of criminal investigators. A massive international criminal investigation by British and U.S. officials was immediately launched to find those responsible for downing Pan Am Flight 103. Joining Scotland Yard and the FBI were police agencies in Finland, West Germany, and elsewhere. The investigation extended into parts of Europe and the Middle East. By February, authorities had gathered more information. The bomb was in a suitcase loaded in Frankfurt and transferred to the doomed Boeing 747 in London. Reconstruction of the wreckage established the explosion occurred in the forward cargo hold. Investigators determined a Toshiba radio–cassette player concealing Semtex plastic explosives was placed into a luggage container positioned in the forward cargo hold. It was believed the bomber intended for the device to explode as Flight

103 flew across the Atlantic, removing all possible clues. The twenty-five minute delay at Heathrow, however, resulted in an explosion over Lockerbie, allowing investigators to gather sufficient evidence to identify the bomber.

Investigative Findings

For two years, investigators believed that the Popular Front for the Liberation of Palestine was responsible for the downing of Pan Am Flight 103; however, findings that surfaced during the summer of 1991 refuted these beliefs. New evidence connected the Flight 103 bombing to a bombing incident carried out by Lybia that destroyed a French airliner over Niger in 1989. It appeared that Lybian officials were behind the Flight 103 explosion, seeking revenge for the 1986 air raid of Lybia's capital, Tripoli, which killed thirty-seven people, including Lybian leader Moammar Gadhafi's daughter.

In September 1989, the FAA once again fined Pan American World Airways $630 thousand for repeatedly violating security rules. Security breaches in the pre-board screening of passengers and baggage and numerous weaknesses in security at Frankfurt and London were among the alleged violations. In comparison to fines assessed to other airlines for security violations, Pan Am's fine was relatively large. Two months prior to the bombing of Pan Am 103, the FAA had investigated the airline's security and recommended some changes, but the airline was not fined. Following the bombing, however, an intensive inquiry revealed Pan Am had violated a number of rules during a period when there were warnings of potential terrorist attacks (Cushman, 1989).

In May 1990, the President's Commission on Aviation Security and Terrorism published a report placing much of the blame for the Pan Am 103 bombing on the airline's dangerously flawed aviation security system. Moreover, the commission determined that the Flight 103 disaster may have been preventable. Of even greater concern was the finding that Pan Am's security was still lax for months after the bombing. The FAA was also criticized for being reactive where security was concerned, rather than proactive. The State Department was faulted for its failure to adequately inform victims' families. The following year, a Scottish study of the safety issues related to the Lockerbie disaster revealed similar findings. Both investigations assigned blame to Pan American World Airways and its lax security system for the Flight 103 disaster.

Victims' Families

At New York's JFK Airport, family members of Flight 103 passengers arrived only to learn of the fatal crash. The joy of the holiday season had suddenly turned tragic. Reporters and television cameras captured their hysterical responses. Families were ushered into a lounge and barricades were set up to shield them from prying cameras. In Detroit, members of "Flight 255—The Spirit Lives On," an organization of victims' families from the Northwest

Flight 255 crash, went to Detroit Metropolitan Airport to assist families. Within hours, some family members began traveling to Lockerbie to bring home their loved one's remains. Over the next few days, more family members followed. At Syracuse University, final exams were canceled in order to hold a memorial service for the students who had perished.

Two days after the crash, reports surfaced of a story out of Moscow about an anonymous threat received by the U.S. Embassy in Helsinki from a caller who said a Pan Am flight bound from Frankfurt to New York would be bombed. While the threat was considered a hoax, it was still communicated to Pan Am Airlines and the U.S. government. Government employees had the benefit of a warning that had not been given to the American public. The fact that Pan Am denied its passengers information concerning the threat enraged victims' relatives. This became an organizing point for the families. In February, relatives formed an organization, Victims of Pan Am Flight 103, for the purpose of demanding a thorough investigation and ensuring the prevention of a similar tragedy. A similar group was formed in Great Britain, the United Kingdom Families of Flight 103. Families wanted reasons for U.S. officials' failure to warn passengers of the bomb threat, information updates, and the return of their loved ones' belongings (Keen & Soda, 1989). By summer, the organization was more than 300 members strong and publishing a newsletter, picketing the Pan Am building, and lobbying the government for an independent investigation into the cause of the disaster (Horton, 1991). After months of opposing the idea, President Bush signed an executive order on August 4, 1989, creating the Presidential Commission on Aviation Security and Terrorism.

World Response

A number of nations were impacted by the bombing of Pan Am Flight 103. World leaders sent their condolences to Lockerbie. The morning after the crash, British Prime Minister Margaret Thatcher toured the wreckage site by helicopter and addressed the citizens of Lockerbie, expressing her shock and grief. U.S. President Ronald Reagan sent a note of condolence to city officials, as did Soviet President Mikhail Gorbachev (Horton, 1991).

Understandably, the bombing increased concerns about terrorism. A few weeks after the bombing, the *Los Angeles Times* reported an increase of uneasiness among flight crews (Dallos, 1989). Furthermore, an intense debate occurred over whether crews and passengers should be informed about sabotage threats (Dallos, 1989). Several large companies discouraged employees from flying U.S. airlines for trips abroad. Increased fear of flying due to terrorism threatened a crisis for the entire airline industry.

Industry Response

The confirmation of a bombing elevated security measures at major airports throughout the world and renewed concerns over the possibility of future attacks on U.S. carriers. The FAA immediately ordered U.S. airlines flying out of airports in Europe and the Middle East to tighten security. Britain also ordered increased security measures for flights by U.S. airlines. Airlines were expected to x-ray or physically inspect all baggage and to randomly search passengers (Phillips, 1989). An increase in security meant more annoyances and longer airport delays for passengers. Throughout the spring of 1989, concern about terrorism in the air remained a constant. Passengers continued to avoid U.S. airlines on overseas flights for fear of another bombing or a hijack attempt. Such fears threatened airlines' profitability, since international travel is much more lucrative than domestic air travel.

Media Coverage

The slow news period of December, the emotions surrounding the holiday season, and the possibility of a bomb all combined to magnify media coverage of the disaster. Media presence was almost immediate. In her book, *The Media and Disasters: Pan Am 103*, Deppa (1994) examined media response to the crisis, noting the disaster marked a turning point in media coverage of global happenings. Thirty minutes after the explosion the first reports of the disaster were broadcast. For the first time, a dramatic event unfolded "live" in living rooms across the world. Media from throughout the world poured into the tiny village of Lockerbie and positioned themselves at other key locations, including JFK Airport in New York, Detroit Metropolitan Airport, and Syracuse University. Reporters were relentless in their search for information. One reporter, pretending to represent Syracuse University, received a Flight 103 passenger list from Pan American Airlines. Once the list was broadcast, reporters actively sought out families and friends of the victims (Deppa & Sharp, 1991). This resulted in some relatives learning of their loved ones' deaths from television reports (Deppa, 1994). Initial reports speculated a mechanical or structural failure caused the explosion. After officials announced the cause of the explosion, media interest moved from the families to the bomb. Throughout the spring of 1989 media were present in Lockerbie, but by summer they had disappeared.

Television crews and photojournalists succeeded in recording the horrific results of the bombing by capturing the dramatic, painful, and shocking images which symbolized the tragedy of the event: the small community of Lockerbie engulfed in flames, the mother of a victim collapsing to the floor in hysteria at JFK Airport upon learning of the crash, the Maid of the Seas's mangled cockpit lying in a desolate Scottish meadow. The devastation of a terrorist act was effectively communicated to the world through these images.

Family members later recounted perceived abuses by the media which included privacy invasion, insensitivity, and rudeness (Deppa, 1994). Media were criticized for their tendency to report the sensational and failure to present accurate, clear, and honest information. Though families initially perceived the media as enemies, they eventually came to view them as allies who could assist the victims' survivors in promoting their political agenda. The feeling that they were being neglected by the U.S. State Department and Pan American Airlines further encouraged families to seek out media.

CRISIS COMMUNICATION:
AN ANALYSIS OF PAN AMERICAN'S COMMUNICATION

The day after the crash, Pan Am's stocks declined, but analysts predicted there would be a quick recovery ("Airline stocks dip," 1988). For the first few days, it appeared the crash would have little impact on Pan Am's level of bookings or flights ("Bookings unaffected," 1988). It soon became clear, however, that the Flight 103 tragedy would have long-term repercussions for the airline. In the weeks subsequent to the disaster, Pan Am's international traffic decreased. Following warnings given by companies to their employees in March 1989, travelers continued to avoid Pan Am and other U.S. airlines. Pan Am lost $437.1 million in 1989. In order to generate cash, Pan Am sold and leased back its aircraft and World Services unit ("Plaskett's persistence," 1991).

The pioneering airline was in a critical situation. Following the bombing of Flight 103, Pan Am was faced with four serious charges. First, victims' families alleged Pan Am had been cold and insensitive to them. Second, Pan Am withheld information from passengers concerning a threat. The airline had knowingly placed its passengers at risk. Third, Pan Am's security was lax, therefore the airline was not safe to fly. Fourth, Pan Am's flawed security system was to blame for the Flight 103 disaster. What follows is an analysis of Pan Am's efforts to address these threatening charges.

Immediate Response

At its world headquarters in New York, the company's executive offices were cordoned off (O'Rourke, 1993). Pan American activated its disaster plan upon notification of the explosion. The airline's most recent rehearsal of the entire plan was in 1982 (Deppa, 1994). Advertisements were quickly pulled. As families of Flight 103 passengers arrived at JFK Airport, they were met with a blinking "See Agent" on the arrival screen and immediately escorted to the Clipper Class Lounge which was sectioned off with barriers to isolate them from the press (Deppa, 1994). Telephone lines were provided for each family. Pan Am staff, along with volunteers from the Red Cross, clergy, and airport medical staff provided assistance to distressed families (Deppa, 1994).

At first, Pan Am was only able to say that radar controllers had lost contact with Flight 103, but they soon confirmed a crash had occurred. Pan Am "accommodated" the media by holding a press conference several hours after the accident (Deppa, 1994). An airline spokesperson provided reporters with an initial statement which contained limited information about the flight. Pan

Am executives indicated there were no survivors aboard the aircraft and there had been some casualties on the ground.

Pan Am refused to speculate on a possible cause of the crash. Unfavorable weather did not appear to be a problem. The 747's maintenance logs were provided and Pan Am answered questions regarding the aircraft. A spokesperson indicated the Maid of the Seas had recently undergone a major overhaul and was in excellent condition. When asked if there had been any kind of bomb threat, the airline denied there were any threats (Whitney, 1988).

The Issue of Victims' Families

Pan Am's handling of Flight 103 victims' families was perceived as ineffective. As victims' families and friends arrived at JFK airport, Pan Am indicated it was in the process of formulating a passenger list. According to the airline, there were some "people of note" on board. Initially there was confusion about the number of passengers on board, but the airline later verified the passenger count. The airline cautiously withheld the passenger list pending notification of victims' families, but a Pan Am employee released the list of Syracuse University students on board to an inquiring reporter (Deppa, 1994). That evening television stations in Syracuse broadcast the students' names.

Some relatives learned of their loved one's fate when they arrived at the airport, but many were notified by telephone. Pan Am told families it would keep them informed and assist them in any way; however, many family members later complained that the airline kept them in the dark. The airline established a special 800 number for relatives and friends, but because the number was broadcast throughout the world phone lines were jammed. Calls came in from everywhere. Family members in quest of information complained they could not get through to the airline. Because of difficulties, Pan Am was unable to confirm the passenger list until late in the evening, and the delay further increased the anguish for families. Some families reported Pan Am did not officially notify them of their loved one's demise until weeks after the crash. Others told of learning of a loved one's death from the television.

The company expressed its concern for victims' families by offering to house families at nearby hotels or fly them to Scotland. Airline employees from the company's Marketing Department were assigned to each family to help them deal with the situation. These employees, referred to as "buddies," functioned as liaisons between the family and the airline and offered information, counseling, and assistance in making arrangements (Deppa, 1994). Upon learning a bomb brought down Flight 103, families' grief turned to rage. In their minds, the airline was responsible.

The airline was portrayed as a cold corporate entity who lacked sensitivity and compassion where families were concerned and was basically negligent. Deppa (1994) tells of families' trauma when they viewed the return of their loved ones' remains. The fact that the coffins were treated as cargo was troubling and painful to many. From the families' perspective, the airline showed little respect. A few weeks after the crash, family members aligned themselves with the media and expressed their anger and frustration toward the airline, as well as the State Department. They stated that aside from the State Department issuing death notifications, the only communication they had received from the airline was information on how to arrange to receive victims' personal effects (Goldman, 1989). Because of legal constraints the airline limited its response, but denied it was insensitive and unresponsive to families. Pan Am explained it had attempted to be sensitive and responsive to the families' needs, "without being intrusive," and that it had communicated to the families through the buddy system (Deppa, 1994). The buddies, however, were perceived as inexperienced and unskilled in dealing with the difficult responsibility of assisting families. Furthermore, the buddies were considered by many families to be agents who wanted nothing more than to gather information for litigation purposes. Pan Am claimed airline representatives were present each time bodies arrived.

According to families, Pan Am's employees were sympathetic and helpful; however, the airline's management demonstrated little leadership. Pan Am's CEO, Thomas Plaskett, eventually made a public appearance eight days after the tragedy. In January, Plaskett, joined by Pan Am employees from locations throughout the world, attended a memorial service in Lockerbie. Numerous world dignitaries were present. Plaskett spoke, praising the hundreds of people who assisted with the disaster.

The Issue of a Bomb Threat

Initially, Pan Am denied receiving a warning of a possible terrorist attack. It was soon revealed that all U.S. air carriers had been informed of the Helsinki call. On December 23, the *New York Times* reported Pan Am had indeed been told of the threat (Cushman, 1988). A controversy soon arose over the public not being informed of threats to Pan Am flights. In an effort to minimize responsibility, the airline, along with the government, offered the excuse that the public had been denied the information for fear it would potentially create a crisis for the airline industry. Pan Am explained that the FAA's advisory stated that information conveyed to the airline and airport security personnel could not be disseminated without approval from the civil aviation security director ("Explosion aboard jet," 1988). This implied FAA policy prevented the airline from being open about the threat. Pan Am continued with its line of excuses by saying that upon receiving the warning, it took immediate action by increasing security. A Pan Am spokesman explained the airline considered the policy of "keeping security risks secret" necessary to heighten security. In other words, releasing information about the threat would have increased security risks. He claimed this view was not influenced by Pan Am's commercial interests (Cushman, 1988).

The Issue of Lax Security

Information that surfaced after the crash raised questions about Pan Am's security operations. Following the announcement that a bomb downed Flight 103, media reported that Israeli consultants hired in 1986 to advise Pan Am on security concluded that because of its inadequate security, the airline was highly vulnerable to a terrorist attack. Pan Am indicated that corrective action had been taken and that some of the report's recommendations had been implemented ("Cause of air crash," 1988).

In the months that followed the bombing of Flight 103, Pan Am found itself battling the public's fear of terrorism and the airline's reputation for lax security. From the public's perspective, the airline risked passengers' lives for financial reasons. Travel agents struggled to convince travelers Pan Am was a secure airline (O'Rourke, 1993). In order to counter this fear about security and reinforce its image as a secure airline, Pan Am attempted to refute evidence which suggested its security was inadequate. Pan Am developed a brochure which provided documentation about its security system. The brochure described and explained the airline's up-to-date security procedures and those present at airports worldwide. Brochures were distributed to travel agents and Pan Am ticket offices.

Pan Am also found itself having to respond to numerous corporations who discouraged their employees from flying U.S. airlines during the spring of 1989. The airline responded with an aggressive tactic. Pan Am initiated a letter-writing campaign. The letter from Pan Am's Plaskett, which was sent to hundreds of businesses, criticized companies for contributing to a wave of paranoia among travelers and claimed Pan Am was operating at maximum security levels. Plaskett noted foreign carriers were also targets of terrorist threats. The letter offered to have the airline's security chief meet with companies.

The Issue of Blame

Following the report from the President's Commission on Aviation Security and Terrorism, which assigned blame to Pan Am, Plaskett told the media he disagreed with some of the criticisms. Plaskett referred to Pan Am's efforts to right the wrong. He reminded reporters that while the report criticized the airline, it also conceded the airline's security was currently satisfactory (Phillips & Lardner, 1990).

EVALUATION OF STRATEGIES

The effectiveness of Pan Am's strategies was influenced by four factors: the severity of the disaster, the intentional nature of the act, Pan Am's knowledge of its flawed security system, and the airline's financial situation. The Flight 103 downing was horrific. A total of 259 persons on board the aircraft were killed along with eleven persons on the ground. The small community of Lockerbie was devastated. The bombing was an intentional act against the United States by an outside group. Innocent lives were claimed by a political act of violence. The fact that Pan Am was aware of its weak security operation increased the intensity of the crisis. The Israeli consulting firm hired two years earlier by the carrier to review its security system identified that Pan Am was highly vulnerable to a terrorist attack. The FAA had recently cited the airline for security violations. At a time when terrorism was at a high, Pan Am failed to ensure adequate security. Though the bombing was an external and intentional act, Pan Am was in the position to control security risks. The perception that Pan Am knew better and could have prevented the Lockerbie tragedy decreased the company's credibility. The fact that the airline was struggling financially raised questions as to whether Pan Am compromised safety for economic reasons.

Pan Am faced four charges following the bombing of Flight 103. First, the airline failed to adequately respond to victims' families. Second, it did not report the bomb threat to its passengers. Third, its security system was lax. Fourth, Pan Am was responsible for the Flight 103 tragedy. In general, the airline was ineffective in defending its image against these charges. Pan Am's defense to each of these charges is evaluated in the following discussion.

The Issue of Victims' Families

The analysis once again reveals the critical nature of family notification. That some families learned of their loss from television is, in itself, an unfortunate occurrence. This shows how difficult it can be for a company in crisis to maintain absolute control. While it appears the airline did everything humanly possible to assist families immediately after the crash, the chaotic nature of the situation hindered its efforts. The accusations made by family members about the airline's insensitivity may or may not be true. The point is, perception is reality. The airline's credibility was lessened following revelations of a bomb and the fact that Pan Am withheld information about a threat to passengers. From their perspective, Pan Am was responsible for the tragedy. Furthermore, Pan Am could not be trusted. This would account for families' suspicions about the airline's buddy system. Families viewed the buddies as spies whose sole purpose was to gather information for litigation. The families' perception of their treatment by the airline should have been better assessed by crisis managers.

In light of the severe nature of the crisis and the airline's weakened credibility, denying its insensitivity and unresponsiveness to families was a poor strategic choice. The company could not be believed. More appropriate strategies would have been to demonstrate concern and regret by correcting the problem and apologizing for the perceived insensitivity. Ingratiation strategies would reinforce efforts to make amends.

The importance of a chief executive's visibility in crisis is emphasized once again. Pan Am's CEO was not seen for days after the disaster. Plaskett's absence following the crash communicated a lack of concern and sympathy. Furthermore, as leader, his absence symbolized to many the greedy and uncaring nature of the airline. While Plaskett was likely grief stricken and felt a sense of responsibility, his absence suggested otherwise. It was important for families, as well as other stakeholders, to see that he shared in their grief. Plaskett's absence appeared to support the families' claim that the airline was insensitive and unresponsive. His appearance at a Lockerbie memorial service in January was much too late. Pan Am underestimated the symbolic role of leadership. On the other hand, the presence of Plaskett and the many Pan Am employees at the memorial service symbolized unity in a time of chaos.

The Issue of a Bomb Threat

Victims' families charged Pan Am was negligent in notifying its passengers about the bomb threat. Pan Am knew about the bomb threat and intentionally withheld information concerning the threat from its passengers. This suggested the company knowingly placed them at risk. The consequence of this act was extreme. In defending its image against this charge, Pan Am employed the strategies of denial and hedging responsibility. These were ineffective choices considering the severity of the situation. Pan Am initially denied receiving a warning of a possible terrorist attack. While this may have been a desirable strategy, it was a poor choice. When the truth about the threat emerged, Pan Am's credibility was damaged. The airline could not be trusted.

The fact that government employees were given the benefit of a warning conflicted with Pan Am's excuse that it denied the public information for fear of creating a crisis in the industry. The airline further explained the FAA placed restrictions on releasing security information. Pan Am's rationale for withholding critical information appeared self-serving. The airline claimed it increased security following the threat. Findings indicated this was not the case.

In light of the evidence, Pan Am should have accepted responsibility immediately and apologized. Legal ramifications, however, may have eliminated these strategies as options. Pan Am's image was not all that was at stake.

The Issue of Lax Security

Evidence suggested Pan Am's security was lax (Horton, 1991; Cushman, 1989; "Cause of air crash," 1988; Phillips & Lardner, 1990). In its defense, the airline employed the primary strategies of refuting evidence and aggression. These were poor strategic choices due to the overwhelming facts which indicated the company's security system was flawed. The airline contended it was operating at maximum security levels. It supported its contention by providing evidence and attacking its critics, accusing them of creating paranoia.

Media reported that following an extensive review in 1986, a consultant hired by the airline indicated Pan Am was extremely vulnerable to a terrorist attack. Though the airline responded to the findings, there was little improvement. The FAA had cited Pan Am for security violations only a few months before the Lockerbie tragedy. Furthermore, evidence which surfaced later indicated Pan Am's security was still lax for months after the bombing. The perception was Pan Am had compromised safety for financial reasons when international terrorism was at a high.

An effective strategic choice was to engage in genuine efforts to correct the problem and publicly identify the changes made.

The Issue of Blame

The findings of the President's Commission on Aviation Security and Terrorism assigned blame to Pan Am for the Flight 103 tragedy. Pan Am's attempt to respond to this charge was weak. Plaskett simply implied the problems had been corrected. The fact that Pan Am was held responsible for such a devastating tragedy required an attempt to win forgiveness. Plaskett did not atone for corporate responsibility. His response did not fit the damage done by the crisis nor did it provide closure to the crisis for victims' families.

EPILOGUE

In 1990 Pan Am shocked the industry when it entered a multimillion-dollar bidding war to acquire Northwest Airlines. A year later, however, Iraq invaded Kuwait and fuel prices escalated. Pan Am filed bankruptcy in January 1991. On December 4, 1991, Pan American World Airways stopped flying.

Many analysts contend that the Flight 103 tragedy expedited the inevitable demise of Pan American. The disaster was one in a series of blows that ended what once had been the U.S. government's chosen instrument for international aviation. Deregulation and the lack of a strong domestic route system were also factors contributing to its fall. The effects of the Pan Am bombing lingered long after the demise of the airline. In 1994, a Federal appeals court ruling required Pan American Airways to pay $19 million to families of three Flight 103 victims. The airline's insurer was expected to pay up to $500 million to other victims' relatives. Victims' families continue to await the trial of the two Lybians suspected in the bombing of Pan Am Flight 103.

CONCLUSION

The case of Pan Am Flight 103 strengthens a few of the lessons learned in earlier cases, including the symbolic role of management and the critical nature of responding to victims' relatives. Pan Am's crisis teaches three additional lessons to expand our understanding of crisis management and communication:

1. Because stakeholders' perceptions are directly linked to corporate image, a company must be sensitive to how stakeholders perceive corporate actions and responses during crisis.

2. Media coverage determines the significance and direction of a crisis and directly reflects upon an organization's image; therefore, crisis managers must understand journalistic processes in covering disasters.

3. A key to effective crisis management is developing a responsible corporate culture which values safety and is sensitive to the hazards of its operations.

Public perception of how a company handles a situation is highly significant. For stakeholders, the way in which they view a company in their minds is reality, even though the facts may suggest otherwise. The perceived inadequacy of Pan Am's response to victims' families along with the findings which indicated the airline failed to be truthful about a bomb threat and its flawed security system created the general perception of a company which was callous, careless, selfish, and uncaring and had compromised human lives for the almighty dollar. As a result of this perception, Pan Am lost credibility.

Stakeholders' perceptions of a company's credibility influence the perceived effectiveness of that organization's response to a situation. The more credible stakeholders believe a company to be, the more likely they are to accept the company's claims. While a company's credibility prior to a crisis is significant in influencing stakeholder perception, what the organization says or does during a crisis also influences its credibility. A failure to be open and honest with stakeholders will threaten a company's credibility. Pan Am lacked openness and honesty from the beginning. The airline failed to communicate honest human emotion and concern to victims' families; therefore, Pan Am was perceived as insincere. Withholding information about a bomb threat and failing to tighten its security system implied the company was more concerned with economy than safety. As a result of these actions, Pan Am lost the public's trust.

Because the believability of a company's actions and words is influenced by its credibility, companies must continuously strive to establish and maintain credibility during crisis. A loss of credibility lessens the effectiveness of strategic communication. The best approach is to provide open and honest responses which convey compassion and concern. A failure to be truthful is foolish, since the media will more than likely find out and the crisis will escalate. A genuine display of compassion and concern must be evident at the onset of a crisis. While a company is no doubt concerned and distressed about a situation, it must keep in mind how its responses are being perceived by others. Is the company successfully communicating what it intends to communicate? A company should also strive to be seen as a reliable and primary source of information by stakeholders. Withholding information suggests the company has something to hide and encourages media to seek secondary and less-reliable sources.

Stakeholder perception of the crisis and crisis organization is further deter-mined by media coverage. The way in which media depict the crisis and portray the crisis company, along with the depth and intensity of coverage, influ-ences stakeholder perceptions and reactions to the company in crisis. Media are frequently considered the antagonist in a crisis scenario. Pan Am's attitude of "accommodating" the media, for example, reflected its perception of media as adversary. Crisis managers must understand the value of media in crisis and the critical role media play. Media are a primary means through which a company communicates its message to relevant external stakeholders.

Because of media's highly influential role, a company must be prepared to take immediate control of the information flow in a crisis. Pan Am's failure to provide information in a timely way resulted in media focusing on victims' families' angry allegations. Other organizations have experienced similar consequences. NASA's failure to communicate openly with media after the Challenger explosion and its decision to impound press film from cameras located around the launch area raised questions about the organization (Brown, 1990). As a result of the information vacuum, rumors as to the cause of the explosion thrived.

Technology has increased the instantaneous and global coverage of crisis, placing additional pressure on those directly dealing with the crisis. A com-pany in crisis must be prepared to deal with an insatiable media. The bomb-ing of Flight 103 received worldwide coverage. Every crisis plan needs to factor in the potential global impact of crisis. Management's understanding of media processes and how they cover disasters is significant to effective crisis management and communication. A thorough understanding of media practices enables a company to predict media actions, allowing the company to plan appropriately. An organization's crisis management team must be pre-pared to develop a working relationship with media. This should be a primary feature of any crisis contingency plan.

As discussed in Chapter 3, an organization's culture can precondition a company to crisis. Certain values or attitudes present in a company may cre-ate unsafe cultures. The financial situation of a company, for example, may create internal pressures on its operations and the policies and procedures which effect safety factors. The result is a company that values economy over safety. Pan Am's inadequate security system appeared to be a consequence of its financial situation. While the company's initial thinking may have been that cutting back on security would save money, the eventual outcome was the total opposite. This was compounded by the public's belief that because Pan Am's security was weak the airline was not safe. Pan Am could have believed it was immune to a terrorist attack; however, in light of its history with terrorism that does not seem likely. Culture also played a significant role in the Challenger explosion. The Rogers Commission identified a variety of causes leading to the Challenger explosion, some of which directly resulted from NASA's culture. Historically, NASA had been an organization of risk taking, adventure, and heroes. It exemplified America's "can do" spirit (Brown, 1990). As a result of its successes and self-image, the events which led to the shuttle launch created an environment of overconfidence and complacency among the agency's membership. The Challenger explosion ultimately damaged the public's image of NASA.

While culture may precondition a company to crisis, it also influences its actions and decisions in a crisis situation. Following the Flight 103 disaster, Pan Am continued to deny it received a bomb threat and stated it had improved security following the crash. Considering the airline's claims were false, its response continued to demonstrate concern for its own position, rather than that of its customers. NASA was extremely slow in responding to the Challenger crisis. Five hours passed before the agency held a press conference. The delayed response in the early hours of the crisis reflected NASA's complacency and arrogance—they had not expected such an event (Brown, 1990).

Companies should be sensitive to the role culture plays in crisis. Crisis management occurs before a crisis takes place. Preventing or effectively managing and communicating in a crisis requires a culture which is highly responsive to safety and other factors which lead to crisis.

REFERENCES

Airline stocks dip in post-crash reaction. (1988, December 23). *USA Today*, p. B3.

Bookings unaffected by crash, airlines say. (1988, December 24). *New York Times*, p. 5A.

Brown, M. H. (1990). Past and present images of Challenger in NASA's organizational culture. In B. D. Sypher (Ed.), *Case studies in organizational communication* (pp. 111–124). New York: Guilford Press.

Cause of air crash has experts divided. (1988, December 26). *Chicago Tribune*, p. 1A.

Cushman, J. H. (1988, December 23). Pan Am was told of terror threat. *New York Times*, p. 1A.

Cushman, J. H. (1989, September 21). U.S. fines Pan Am for lax security on day of jet bombing. *New York Times*, p. 10A.

Dallos, R. E. (1989, January 14). Flying scared. *Los Angeles Times*, p. D1.

Denham, T. (1996). *World directory of airliner crashes*. Sparkford, Near Yeovil, Somerset: Patrick Stephens Limited.

Deppa, J. (1994). *The media and disasters: Pan Am 103*. New York: New York University Press.

Deppa, J., & Sharp, N. (1991, November). Under international scrutiny: Reaction of media targets. *American Behavioral Scientist, 35*, 150–165.

Explosion aboard jet confirmed. (1988, December 23). *Atlanta Constitution*, p. A1.

Goldman, J. (1989, February 7). Kin of victims on bombed jet demand new inquiry. *Los Angeles Times*, p. I14.

Heppenheimer, T. A. (1995). *Turbulent skies: The history of commercial aviation*. New York: John Wiley.

Horton, M. (1991). *The Lockerbie airline crash*. San Diego: Lucent Books.

Keen, J., & Soda, R. (1989, February 6). Flight 103 families demand answers. *USA Today*, p. 3A.

O'Lone, R. G. (1991, December 16). Pan Am pushed aircraft builders to advance transport state of the art. *Aviation Week & Space Technology*, pp. 34–35.

O'Rourke, R. J. (1993). Disaster at Lockerbie. In J. A. Gottschalk (Ed.), *Crisis response: Inside stories on managing image under seige*. Detroit: Invisible Ink Press.

Phillips, D., & Lardner, G. (1990, May 16). Laxity by Pan Am, FAA blamed in jet bombing. *Washington Post*, p. 1A.

Plaskett's persistence failed to overcome lack of capital. (1991, December 16). *Aviation Week & Space Technology*, p. 27.

United Kingdom Aviation Accidents Investigation Branch. (1990). *Report on the accident to Boeing 747-121, N739PA at Lockerbie, Dumfriesshire, Scotland on 21 December 1988*. Department of Transportation, United Kingdom.

Watson, R. (1989, January 2). An explosion in the sky. *Newsweek*, pp. 16–19.

Whitney, C. R. (1988, December 22). Jetliner carrying 258 to U.S. crashes in Scottish town. *New York Times*, p. A1.

Chapter 12

USAir Flight 427

The cases examined so far have illustrated how pre-crisis factors can complicate a company's efforts at crisis management and communication. A
company's poor image and weak financial status prior to a crisis, for example, may negatively influence stakeholder perceptions of that company's
actions and words during a major crisis. Crisis managers are wise to recognize the potential impact pre-crisis factors may have on managing crisis.

USAir's experience following the Flight 427 crash outside of Pittsburgh in
1994 further illustrates the significance of this point. From 1989 to 1994, USAir
suffered five fatal accidents, more than any other major U.S. carrier. USAir's
spate of crashes and its weak financial position prior to the Flight 427 disaster
increased the airline's difficulty in managing the post-crisis stage. This chapter
considers USAir's efforts to restore its image following the crash of Flight 427.

PRE-CRISIS

Deregulation in 1978 dramatically changed the world of aviation. Airlines
soon began expanding their route systems and forming competitive pricing
structures. Allegheny Airlines was one of many carriers that took advantage
of new opportunities brought on by deregulation. On October 28, 1979, Allegheny Airlines assumed a new identity to reflect its expanding network,
changing its name to USAir (USAirways, 1998). With its network extending
into Arizona, Texas, Colorado, and Florida during the early years of deregulation, the erstwhile regional airline had become nationally competitive with
the major carriers.

In its first few years, USAir was highly successful and profitable. The airline acquired new maintenance and training facilities, equipment, and, in 1982, Boeing 737s. Additional passenger gates were also constructed at the Greater Pittsburgh International Airport, a major USAir hub. By 1983, USAir was the operating subsidiary of its holding company, the USAir Group, Inc. Airline deregulation provided the impetus for a number of mergers. In 1987, Pacific Southwest Airlines and Piedmont Airlines became subsidiaries of the USAir Group, Inc. The following year Pacific Southwest, with its major West Coast route system, merged with USAir. Piedmont Airlines, the dominant carrier throughout the mid-Atlantic region, was integrated into USAir in 1989, creating the largest merger in airline history (USAirways, 1998). USAir was now the sixth-largest carrier in the United States. The airline gained Piedmont's international routes along with its hubs in Charlotte, Baltimore, Dayton, and Syracuse (USAirways, 1998). In the early 1990s, the airline expanded its international service and the USAir Shuttle began hourly service between New York and Boston and New York and Washington, D.C.

The acquisition of Pacific Southwest and Piedmont enabled USAir to maintain its position in an extremely competitive industry, but it did not come without difficulties. The merger of three airlines resulted in a diversity of experience and culture. While not necessarily bad, there was potential for confusion with regard to policies and regulations. This was especially critical to flight and maintenance-crew performance. In addition, the airline experienced labor problems, escalating equipment cost, and decreased on-time performance.

The late 1980s and early 1990s were difficult years for most domestic carriers. Analysts estimated USAir's losses totaled close to $2 billion between 1989 and 1994 (Morganthau, 1994). Subsequently, USAir reduced jobs and closed two major hubs. Some critics argued the airline was operating with a nonviable cost structure. USAir was spending 15 percent more than its competitors on labor costs (Cook, Hage, & Newman, 1994). British Airways, USAir's overseas partner, indicated it would not invest any more in the U.S. carrier until it significantly reduced its budget. As a result of the airline's vulnerability, low-cost rivals began invading USAir's lucrative bases in Baltimore and Charlotte. USAir responded by offering major fare reductions, further compromising its bottom line. At the beginning of 1994, USAir's chairman and chief executive, Seth Schofield, requested employees agree to a wage and benefit reduction as part of a $1 billion cost-cutting program. No agreement was reached.

Previous Accidents

In its first decade USAir went without a single fatality, but in 1989 the airline encountered what was the beginning of a streak of fatal accidents. On September 20, 1989, a USAir 737 crashed into New York's East River following takeoff from LaGuardia Airport, killing two persons: probable cause—

pilot error. On February 1, 1991, a USAir 737 struck a commuter plane while landing in Los Angeles, killing thirty-four persons: probable cause—air traffic control. On March 22, 1992, a USAir Fokker F-28 crashed into Flushing Bay during takeoff from LaGuardia, killing twenty-seven persons: probable cause—ice on the wings. On July 2, 1994, a USAir DC-9 on approach to Charlotte–Douglas International Airport crashed in a thunderstorm, killing thirty-seven persons (Cook, Hage, & Newman, 1994). Investigators focused on wind shear and pilot actions. As a consequence of these crashes, the airline had been placed under increased FAA surveillance.

CRISIS

USAir Flight 427, a Boeing 737, was a routine flight from Chicago to Pittsburgh, and then direct to West Palm Beach, Florida. Shortly after 6:00 P.M. EDT, on September 8, 1994, Flight 427 departed Chicago O'Hare for the approximately one-hour trip. On board were 127 passengers, many of whom were business commuters, and a five-member flight crew. The weather was clear from Chicago to Pittsburgh. On an easterly heading, USAir Flight 427 descended toward Pittsburgh International. Straight ahead of Flight 427, on the same flight path, was a Delta Boeing 727. A few minutes outside of Pittsburgh, Pittsburgh control directed Flight 427 to descend to 6 thousand feet. The first officer acknowledged the instructions and, along with the captain, proceeded with the landing checklist. At 7:00 P.M., the pilot radioed controllers that Flight 427 was on final approach at 6 thousand feet (Marshall & Davis, 1994). According to data retrieved from the flight recorder, minutes later the aircraft began to roll left, then right, and then it suddenly began a rapid descent. The pilots failed to regain control before the aircraft struck the ground. In a hilly and densely wooded area near the town of Aliquippa, Pennsylvania, six miles north of Pittsburgh International Airport, all 132 souls perished.

POST-CRISIS

Search and Recovery

Within minutes, emergency vehicles and personnel from Aliquippa, Hopewell, Pittsburgh, and other neighboring areas arrived at the crash site. Rescue workers immediately began extinguishing fires and searching for survivors, but it was soon apparent there were none. The scene, according to witness accounts, was gruesome. Carnage and aircraft parts were strewn throughout the heavily wooded hillside. Because of the speed at which the aircraft hit the ground, bodies were not intact and the aircraft had disintegrated.

The Green Garden Plaza Shopping Center near the crash site served as temporary headquarters for the initial response operations (Shaw, 1995). The shopping center quickly turned into chaos, with emergency vehicles crowding the plaza parking lot along with television vans and satellites. A triage site was established by teams of clergy and counselors who assisted family members, distressed witnesses, and workers. Food, drinks, and blankets were provided by the Salvation Army (Harr, 1996).

Local law-enforcement agencies, the Pennsylvania Air National Guard, and the U.S. Air Force Reserve worked to secure the area surrounding the crash site. Officials immediately closed all roads leading to the wreckage, backing up traffic for miles. The devastated area lured hordes of curious onlookers. Hours after the crash, six unauthorized people were arrested for attempting to get into the crash site. The following morning, workers began building a make-shift road through the wooded area which would enable investigators to haul in more sophisticated equipment.

The emergency response had quickly turned into a recovery operation. Workers performed the grisly task of collecting human remains and clearing the site. A temporary morgue was set up at the airport. Because of the highly traumatic nature of the recovery task, backup psychological support was provided. Early the following morning the NTSB go-team arrived, along with the FAA and the FBI. After assessing the crash area, the NTSB declared it a biomedical hazard site. This required workers and investigators to wear protective clothing, boots, and surgical and work gloves to perform their difficult assignment (Shaw, 1995). Upon leaving the site they were decontaminated. Ten days after the horrific disaster, all human remains and aircraft wreckage had been removed from the crash site, decontaminated, and released.

Investigation

The NTSB arrived early the morning after the crash and convened an organizational meeting. A command post was established at a nearby Holiday Inn. Progress meetings would be held every evening. Following the NTSB's arrival, the two black boxes were sent to the Safety Board's labs in Washington. Unfortunately, the cockpit voice recorder failed to provide any immediate answers. From the beginning, it appeared the investigation would be highly complicated. The NTSB referred to it as a "mystery crash" (Begley, Springen, Glick, & Hayer, 1994, September 19).

Three days after the crash, investigators had a better understanding of the circumstances associated with the accident, but were unable to identify a likely cause. Flight 427 had made an unexplained roll to the left and suddenly lost control, hitting the ground at more than 300 mph. The pilots were flying on autopilot at the time of the sudden dive. There were no weather complications or unusual bird activity (Beck, 1995). The captain and first officer were competent and highly experienced, and there was no evidence of a bomb. According to an NTSB spokesman, Flight 427's transmissions were regular up until something immediate and catastrophic happened. Throughout the on-site investigation, numerous theories were discussed, such as loose engine mounts and the improper engagement of the thrust-reverse actuator. The crash, according to investigators, was strikingly similar to the crash of United Flight 585, a Boeing 737, at Colorado Springs three and a half years earlier. The cause of that accident had yet to be determined by the NTSB. Investigators would consider similarities between the two accidents (Cook, Hage, & Newman, 1994).

A week after the disaster, the NTSB announced the on-site investigation was complete. Wreckage had been moved to hangars at a USAir facility for further examination, analysis, and reconstruction. The process of reconstruction would be a highly complicated task in light of the amount and size of the wreckage pieces. During the last on-site press conference, the NTSB indicated they had no particular theory as to the cause of the horrific crash. The fact that the Pittsburgh crash was USAir's fifth accident in five years prompted NTSB officials to gather in Charlotte a few weeks later to examine the carrier's maintenance and training procedures. In October, media reported the latest NTSB theory. It was possible that Flight 427 experienced wake vortex generated by the Delta Airlines Boeing 727, a heavier aircraft, which was about four miles ahead. Wake vortex refers to a rapidly rotating, high-energy mass of air, similar to a small tornado, which spins down from the wing tips of an aircraft (Smolowe, 1994).

In January 1995, a five-day public hearing into the crash of USAir Flight 427 was held in Pittsburgh (D. Phillips, 1995). There were still no obvious clues as to what caused the crash. The Safety Board discussed rudder control system malfunctions and wake turbulence. Testimony pertaining to various areas of the investigation was given by thirty witnesses from Boeing, NASA, USAir, the FBI, and the FAA. Transcripts from both the cockpit voice recorder and the flight data recorder were released.

One year after the crash, the investigation had become the most extensive and complex probe ever conducted by the NTSB (until the crash of TWA Flight 800). The investigation had centered on four specific areas: aircraft systems, aircraft performance, human performance, and sound spectrum analyses (E. H. Phillips, 1995). Though unusual, a second public hearing followed in November 1995. Witnesses testified as to the design and performance of the rudder power control unit.

The investigation into the crash of USAir Flight 427 has been one of the longest investigations in NTSB history. According to NTSB officials, the investigation was hindered by the lack of an enhanced flight data recorder aboard the aircraft (NTSB, 1997). The NTSB expected to issue a final report in 1998.

Families of Flight 427 Victims

A number of factors compounded the trauma for families. For example, obtaining information was a primary problem. Some family members complained of difficulty getting through to the toll-free number in the early hours following the crash. Once they got through, airline representatives were vague (Hoversten, 1995). When the NTSB convened its first public hearing in January 1995, families took the opportunity to express their feelings about the insensitive treatment they had received from USAir. As a result of their experience, they encouraged the government to appoint a "family advocate" to assist aviation victims' survivors.

Another issue concerned the remains of their loved ones. Because of the severity of the crash, there was great difficulty in identifying victims. Reports disclosed that families received only fragmentary remains of their loved ones, which further compounded their grief. A *Newsweek* article reported that a month after the crash USAir coordinated the burial of two symbolic coffins at a cemetery near the crash site and invited family members to attend. Families later learned the airline had buried hundreds of unidentified remains two weeks earlier (Beck, 1995). A support group of victims' families and friends, the "Flight 427 Air Disaster Support League," was later formed. In an effort to assist families, the group published a quarterly newsletter which contained information regarding the investigation and litigation.

Public Response

Despite the excellent safety record of the U.S. airline industry, the crash of USAir Flight 427 unearthed recurring concerns over USAir and airline safety in general. The debate over whether deregulation had impacted safety was once again a popular topic. Had the highly competitive industry forced airlines to cut corners on safety to save money? With its financial losses over the last few years, five accidents in five years, and two fatal accidents in two months, USAir was a prime candidate for suspicion. Some critics were quick to blame the airline for the accidents. Others attributed the airline's troubles to "really bad luck" (Stone & Davis, 1994). Federal officials contended USAir was a safe airline and there was no connection between the five accidents.

Following the crash, travel agents reported numerous USAir cancellations. A USAir spokesperson indicated that public concern was more severe following the Flight 427 accident than it had been with the airline's previous four crashes (Daly, 1994). To the flying public, USAir had become "US-Scare."

Media Coverage

Media were present within an hour of the crash. CNN began broadcasting pictures of the devastation. By dawn the following day, hundreds of reporters had invaded Aliquippa. Reports covered such topics as the extreme devastation of the crash, rescue and investigation operations, the striking similarity between USAir Flight 427 and the 1991 crash of a United Boeing 737 in Colorado Springs, airline safety, and USAir's alarming string of accidents.

In November, the *New York Times* published a stinging article on USAir, based on the findings of a two-month investigation (Frantz & Blumethal, 1994). The article raised a number of questions concerning the airline's safety operations. Graphs revealed that USAir's safety record had declined while other carriers' safety records had improved. Problems at the airline included deficiencies in its operations and training programs. According to the article, the FAA discovered forty deficiencies in the airline's operations and training programs in 1993. Contrary to what USAir had claimed following the Flight 427 crash, evidence suggested there were common causes among the accidents. Pilots had violated federal and airline regulations in at least two of USAir's five fatal accidents.

The article alleged the company compromised safety in order to save money (Frantz & Blumenthal, 1994). One frightening example revealed that a USAir maintenance supervisor had permitted a plane to fly when its warning system was not functioning because he wanted to save the company money. The report also cited frequent instances where USAir planes departed the gate without sufficient fuel. In one incident, a flight from Washington to Boston was forced to make an emergency landing because it did not have enough fuel. This was not an isolated incident. The article indicated that financial pressures and rapid growth had resulted in safety problems at the airline. Furthermore, management failed to effectively address safety issues. The article pointed out that the NTSB was examining USAir's questionable management culture as a possible cause for the airline's accidents. Evidence supported the image of USAir as an unsafe air carrier, and one more concerned about its bottom line than the safety of its passengers.

The *New York Times* article had a significant impact, escalating USAir's crisis. Newspapers throughout the country immediately jumped on the story, quoting the *Times*'s findings in subsequent articles. The FAA immediately responded to the *New York Times* report by stating that if it found any carrier's safety performance questionable, the carrier would be closed down. The FAA further indicated it had no plans to ground USAir and did not currently have an investigation in progress (Swoboda, 1994).

CRISIS COMMUNICATION:
AN ANALYSIS OF USAIR'S COMMUNICATION

For USAir, the crash of Flight 427 complicated an already critical situation. The tragedy, the deadliest since 1987, compounded the airline's questionable image. USAir was already losing money, struggling to keep its shareholders, and trying to maintain its passenger loads in the highly competitive U.S. air-travel market. Moreover, in five years the airline had experienced four fatal accidents, and two had occurred within a two-month period. When the Flight 427 accident happened, the memory of the Charlotte crash in July was still fresh. The day after the Flight 427 crash, USAir's stock fell 10 percent. Analysts and industry consultants were predicting the carrier would be forced to file Chapter 11 bankruptcy by the end of the year.

While USAir was contending with the immediate effects of the Flight 427 crash, it was simultaneously dealing with the developing image of an unsafe airline—an airline that compromised safety to save money. What follows is an examination of USAir's immediate response to the Flight 427 crash and its subsequent attempts to battle an "unsafe" image and regain public confidence.

Immediate Response

USAir immediately responded to the crash by implementing its crisis plan. An hour after the crash, the airline's operations were in full swing. Employees established bases at USAir's headquarters in Arlington, Virginia, and at its offices in Pittsburgh. Workers situated at the company's headquarters handled calls from the media and gathered critical information concerning the aircraft, the number of passengers, and maintenance and flight-crew records. According to the airline, it was able to notify all but two of the victims' families by the following morning (Schmit & Jones, 1994). In Pittsburgh, USAir assigned two employees to assist each family. Because the airline had convened a series of press conferences in Pittsburgh earlier in the day announcing its plan to improve business-class seating, numerous company managers were still present and immediately went to work. The following day, USAir's Chairman and CEO, Seth Schofield, returned to Pittsburgh.

The day after the crash, the airline was bombarded with questions concerning its safety record. USAir defended the safety of the airline and directly denied that there was any link between the five crashes of its planes. They all seemed to be isolated incidents. The company further denied that its financial difficulty had any bearing on the accidents. In a press conference discussing the crash, Schofield stated there was no association between the five accidents. He assured reporters that while the airline had undergone some stringent cost-cutting measures, there were no shortcuts with respect to airworthiness programs or training. Further, if he thought the carrier was unsafe, he personally would have grounded it until it was safe. A USAir assistant vice president expanded denial by suggesting that the airline was completely exonerated from blame for the Los Angeles crash, and that while the cause was still unknown in the recent Charlotte crash, investigators were focusing on weather.

Battling a Decline in Public Confidence

While most airlines experience a loss in the first few days following a major crash, they soon rebound. This was not the case for USAir. In the weeks following the Flight 427 disaster, USAir's sales continued to decline. The airline reported a third-quarter operating loss of $151.3 million (Velocci, 1994). The crashes in Charlotte and Pittsburgh were major contributors to its poor performance. Seventy-five percent of those losses occurred in September, following the crash of Flight 427.

With the lingering coverage of the Pittsburgh disaster, the airline's unusual string of crashes, and its financial struggle the public's perception of USAir continued to decline. In October the airline took aggressive action by initiating a public-relations campaign to convince air travelers about USAir's safety (Schmit & Overstreet, 1994). Letters from Schofield, discussing the carrier's safety record, were sent to thousands of USAir frequent fliers. Schofield's reference to the "USAir family" in his letter reinforced the positive nature of the organization. Airline executives visited hundreds of corporate accounts to convey the message that USAir was safe to fly.

Response to the *New York Times* Article

Following the article published on the front page of the *New York Times* (Frantz & Blumenthal, 1994), USAir became aggressive in its efforts to win back the confidence of the flying public. USAir reacted to the *Times* article by running a series of full-page ads addressing safety in over forty major newspapers nationwide. On the first day, papers published a letter from USAir's CEO, Schofield. The following day a letter appeared from the airline's pilots. On the third day, papers carried a letter from USAir's flight attendants and mechanics. These messages functioned to convince the public that the airline's flights were safe.

The letters employed three approaches: ingratiation, denial, and righting the wrong. In his introductory letter, Schofield created identification with readers by stating that the safety of air travel was vitally important to everyone: "We who are airline professionals know our system and our planes are safe. This is validated each and every day by federal regulators who fly with us, inspect our maintenance facilities and review our records" (Schofield, 1994). He stressed the positive aspects of USAir by referring to its employees as "airline professionals" and reminding the public that the FAA considered the airline's operations safe. The strategy of identification was also used in the letter from USAir's pilots: "To every USAir pilot, safety is the first priority. It is a commitment confirmed by everything that is meaningful to us: our passengers' well-being, our reputations, and our livelihoods" (Gauthier, 1994). The ad emphasized that safety was a value held throughout the organization.

The strategy of denial was not blatant, but rather implied when Schofield (1994) stated "our planes are safe." Though the airline directly denied accusations it was unsafe, it announced it would attempt to correct problems. Righting the wrong was demonstrated when Schofield announced two significant steps to assure the public of the "validity and integrity of our operating standards." First, the airline would hire a safety czar, Air Force General Robert

Oaks, to oversee the company's safety operations. Second, an aviation consulting group, PRC Aviation, would conduct a thorough and independent audit of USAir's flight safety operations and policies. The basic point of the message was that the airline was doing everything possible to ensure the safety of its passengers.

Following its newspaper ad campaign, USAir continued using the strategy of emphasizing the positive. In January 1995, the company took advantage of the press coverage of the NTSB Public Hearings in Pittsburgh and extended invitations to reporters to visit its maintenance and operational base for inspections and questions from the press (D. Phillips, 1995). Such an action demonstrated the airline's confidence in its level of safety and its concern over safety issues in general. In March, Schofield released the findings of the PRC Aviation safety audit. The consultant confirmed the airline was in compliance with Federal and airline regulations and was "being operated safely" (Quintanilla, 1995). The consultant offered thirty recommendations to improve safety. These findings once again reinforced USAir's contention that it was a safe airline. Schofield expressed the airline's future commitment to safety by stating, "PRC's findings, and its suggestions of ways that we can continue in the forefront of airline safety, give support to the airline and comfort to every traveler" (Quintanilla, 1995). He explained the audit would be used to revise and improve safety procedures.

EVALUATION OF STRATEGIES

Following the crash of USAir Flight 427, it was clear the airline would have to be aggressive in improving its deteriorating image to survive in a highly competitive industry. USAir's financial and accident history complicated its crisis management efforts after the Pittsburgh crash. From the public's point of view, the crash of Flight 427 raised the question as to whether USAir had even addressed safety issues following the previous four crashes. After all, with four accidents in five years the company should have been sensitive to safety issues. The impact of the crash in Charlotte combined with the crash in Pittsburgh resulted in the loss of $40 million in revenue during the third quarter (Bryant, 1995). Passenger traffic continued to decline during the months of October and November, resulting in a loss of $110 million in revenues for the fourth quarter (Bryant, 1995). The loss was primarily attributed to the crashes. The *New York Times* critical assessment of the carrier only compounded USAir's situation. For all of 1994, USAir lost $685 million, compared to a loss of $393 million the previous year.

USAir's general approaches of denial, ingratiation, and righting the wrong were appropriate choices to address issues affecting the company's image, though some were executed better than others. Assuming the airline had not skimped on safety, denial was a critical strategy. Immediately following the crash of Flight 427, USAir's questionable safety reputation became an issue with media and a concern among stakeholders. Perhaps if USAir had initially been more forceful and aggressive in denying accusations of lax safety caused by financial woes the company would not have incurred such dramatic losses in the third and fourth quarters. It was only after the *New York Times* article that the airline realized aggressive action was necessary. In many of the press conferences and interviews, USAir executives directly denied accusations that the airline compromised safety for financial reasons and that there was a clear link between its five crashes. While the approach was appropriate, executives would have been more effective in their efforts had they directly supported their claims with substantive evidence. Rather, they made general claims without support. Expanding denial would have strengthened their position. In defending itself against claims made in the *Times* article, USAir would have been more effective by directly addressing specific accusations. In light of declining public confidence in USAir's safety, ingratiation strategies were important. It was necessary for the airline to convey its concern over the public's concern about USAir's safety. Identification was needed to show that, like its customers, USAir cared a great deal about safety. This was clearly communicated in the newspaper ad campaign.

Initially, it seemed that by attempting to right the wrong USAir was contradicting its contention that the airline was safe. After all, if the airline was indeed safe, why would it suddenly need a safety czar and an audit? By using this strategy, USAir was not necessarily suggesting there were problems, but rather demonstrating its desire to enhance an already safe operation. This became apparent when Schofield presented the findings of the consultants' audit. While potentially risky, USAir's decision to have outside consultants perform an audit ultimately proved an excellent choice. Receiving confirmation from a legitimate external group enhanced the airline's safety operations. An emphasis on its positive aspects reinforced USAir's image as a solid company. Companies should, however, be sensitive to the fact that using the strategies of denial and righting the wrong in combination may be perceived as contradictory.

EPILOGUE

While the company's weak financial situation and string of crashes initially complicated its efforts to manage the crisis of Flight 427, USAir eventually succeeded in restoring its image. By December, traffic had almost returned to normal levels. The first-quarter results of 1995 indicated the airline was improving and, for the first time in seven years, USAir posted a profit for the third quarter. The airline indicated it expected to earn its first annual profit since 1988 (Quintanilla & McCartney, 1995). For USAir, it was finally the beginning of a financial turnaround.

CONCLUSION

We see a number of recurring themes and lessons in the case of USAir Flight 427. First, pre-crisis factors which are negative can increase the complexity of a company's crisis management and communication. USAir's weak financial history combined with an inadequate performance history lessened its credibility and supported the accusation that the airline was unsafe. Furthermore, it was alleged USAir compromised safety because of cost. As a result of USAir's situation, the debate over whether deregulation had impacted safety surfaced once again. What this teaches crisis managers is that they must recognize and anticipate the influence pre-crisis factors will have in the event of a crisis and plan accordingly.

As illustrated in Chapter 11, media coverage determines the significance and direction of a crisis and directly reflects upon an organization's image. For this reason it is critical that a company in crisis immediately take control of the situation by communicating promptly, openly, and adequately. It seemed USAir struggled to take control of the media situation from the beginning. The company's performance history and financial situation clearly influenced the media's line of questioning. When it was bombarded by questions from the press directly after the crash concerning the company's safety record, the airline was placed in a defensive position. Although USAir appeared open and honest with its communication when responding to questions concerning its four previous crashes and weak financial position, the fact that media continued to focus on the charges suggests the airline failed to convince them that its claims were true. Perhaps USAir would have been better able to control the crisis had it supplied more information concerning the company's accident history and financial position. Furthermore, in light of its accident streak USAir should have anticipated in its planning that in the unusual event of another accident the carrier's safety situation would likely become an issue. USAir would have been prepared at the beginning to identify and promote positive aspects of the company's safety system.

The cases in this book illuminate the difficulties airlines experience when responding to victims' families after a major air crash. That a company perceived as responsible for the death of a loved one could be sincere in its concern for those relatives left behind is clearly difficult for some victims' families to believe. This difficulty underscores the importance of a crisis plan which thoroughly recognizes and addresses the complexities of dealing with victims' and/or their families. Generally, their perception of a company's response to them must guide a company's actions. The airline industry and U.S. government demonstrated their concern about this issue with the passage of the Family Assistance Act. Hopefully, a neutral arrangement will resolve the difficulties airlines have encountered with a very sensitive aspect of crisis management.

A lesson that is demonstrated more clearly in this case is the importance of using sound evidence in persuasive claims. More specifically, a company whose credibility is in question due to pre-crisis factors must use sound evidence to support claims of denial when defending itself against accusations. USAir's weak financial position and performance history, along with the crash of USAir Flight 427, damaged the company's image and lessened its credibility. Again, the perception was USAir compromised safety to save money. Following the Flight 427 crash, USAir spokespersons continuously denied that there was a link between the five crashes or that the accidents were a result of the company's weak financial situation. In communicating to the general public, USAir failed to support its claims with sufficient evidence. Rather, the company made general statements concerning the importance USAir placed on safety. This was most evident in its series of ads addressing safety following the highly critical article in the *New York Times*.

Defensive claims fail to be persuasive when they are unsupported generalizations. Furthermore, a company with low credibility must use sound evidence to compensate for its weak credibility. Because the accusations waged against USAir were specific and detailed, the airline should have countered with a detailed response. In the end, strong evidence may have enhanced its credibility.

REFERENCES

Beck, M. (1995, September 11). Unsolved mystery. *Newsweek*, p. 48.

Begley, S., Springen, K., Glick, D., & Hager, M. (1994, September 19). The disaster detectives. *Newsweek*, pp. 26–27.

Bryant, A. (1995, January 28). USAir posts loss; crashes called a factor. *New York Times*, p. 33.

Cook, W. J., Hage, D., & Newman, R. J. (1994, September 19). The crash of flight 427. *U.S. News & World Report*, p. 30.

Daly, J. (1994, September 26). The fear of flying: A horrific crash rekindles the debate over air safety. *Maclean's*, p. 26.

Frantz, D., & Blumenthal, R. (1994, November 13). Troubles at USAir: Coincidence or more? *New York Times*, p. 1A.

Gauthier, P. J. (1994, November 22). Letter to travelers. *USA Today*, p. 9A.

Harr, J. (1996, August 5). The crash detectives. *The New Yorker*, pp. 34–55.

Hoversten, P. (1995, January 25). USAir crash victims' kin seek "advocate." *USA Today*, p. 7A.

Marshall, S., & Davis, R. (1994, September 9). Aftermath: There is no plane. *USA Today*, p. 3A.

Morganthau, T. (1994, September 19). The mystery of USAir flight 427. *Newsweek*, pp. 20–25.

National Transportation Safety Board. (September 8, 1997). Investigation Update: USAir Flight 427. *NTSB Website* [http://www.ntsb.gov/pressrel/970908.htm].

Phillips, D. (1995, January 26). Open hangars and a high profile. *Washington Post*, p. 11D.

Phillips, E. H. (1995, August 14). Baffled NTSB deepens probe of USAir crash. *Aviation Week & Space Technology*, pp. 28–29.

Quintanilla, C. (1995, March 20). Audit of USAir finds carrier operates safely. *Wall Street Journal*, p. 4B.

Quintanilla, C., & McCartney, S. (1995, October 19). Three airlines, even USAir, post profits. *Wall Street Journal*, p. B4.

Schmit, J., & Jones, D. (1994, September 12). How USAir coped with the crash. *USA Today*, p. 1B.

Schmit, J., & Overstreet, J. (1994, October 3). USAir: We're safe to fly. *USA Today*, p. 2B.

Schofield, S. E. (1994, November 21). Letter to travelers. *USA Today*, p. 9A.

Shaw, D. (1995, March). Flight 427: Lessons learned from a tragedy. *American City and County*, p. 50.

Smolowe, J. (1994, October 31). A bump in the sky: Did wake vortex contribute to the crash of USAir Flight 427? *Time*, p. 37.

Stone, A., & Davis, R. (1994, September 12). USAir taking a long, hard look. *USA Today*, p. 2A.

Swoboda, F. (1994, November 15). FAA vows to ground any airline found unsafe. *Washington Post*, p. 1D.

USAirways. (1998, January 8). USAirways: Historic milestones. *USAir Website* [http://www.usairways.com/company/profile/miles.htm].

Velocci, A. L. (1994, October 31). Major losses shake confidence in USAir. *Aviation Week & Space Technology*, p. 39.

Chapter 13

ValuJet Flight 592

While all airlines experience scrutiny and decreased passenger traffic following a major crash, ValuJet was particularly hard hit by the Flight 592 crash in
May 1996. ValuJet's pre-crisis situation not only led to crisis, but ultimately
compounded its efforts at post-crisis management and communication, as well
as created controversy about the FAA. The airline faced a serious credibility
problem, not because of its handling of the crash, but because of its rapid
growth and short history, a questionable corporate culture, and a series of
safety-related incidents.

The case of ValuJet Flight 592 reveals how organizational decision makers' and industry policy makers' failure to respond to glaring signs of an
impending disaster lead to tragic consequences. The events which occurred
prior to the crash suggest that ValuJet was extremely vulnerable to crisis.
Hindsight is always twenty–twenty; nevertheless, we can only assume the
disaster might have been avoided had the airline and the FAA readily acknowledged significant warning signs.

Crisis management begins in the pre-crisis stage. Once again, we see how
factors or conditions present in the pre-crisis stage can create a crisis and further
complicate management and communication efforts in the post-crisis stage.

PRE-CRISIS

After deregulation, new airlines were allowed to enter service and opportunities increased for carriers to offer lower fares and choose their routes. The
1980s witnessed airlines touting discount fares. Low-cost air travel benefited

consumers and encouraged an entirely new market of first-time flyers. After the collapse of Air Florida and People Express, it was questionable whether low-fare airlines would survive. But in the 1990s a new generation of low-cost, no-frills carriers emerged, offering cheap fares to new markets and forcing major airlines to reduce their fares. Low-fare airlines created a second tier among commercial carriers, saving consumers money and creating service in markets previously ignored or abandoned by the major carriers. Startups such as ValuJet, Reno Air, Kiwi International, and AirTran joined Southwest in entering larger markets to capture a bigger share of the passenger traffic.

ValuJet Airlines was one of the most successful startups in aviation history. Considered a darling of the Clinton administration, ValuJet exemplified government efforts to advance startups and reduce airfares. In a little over a year, Wall Street saw the airline's stock increase from approximately $3 in 1994 to almost $35 at the end of 1995 (Reed, 1996). Based in Atlanta, the airline began operations in October 1993, with two planes on eight routes between Atlanta, Jacksonville, Orlando, and Tampa. Under the leadership of Lewis Jordan, president of ValuJet and a former Continental executive, the carrier grew rapidly and in three years was flying fifty-one planes to thirty-one cities (Bynum, 1997). In 1995 alone, ValuJet netted an income of $67.8 million (ValuJet, 1997b).

Because of its no-frills approach, the carrier was able to keep its prices down. ValuJet offered one-way fares as low as $39. There were no meals, no reserved seating, no printed tickets, and no airline clubs or frequent-flyer programs. To the customer, ValuJet's allure was pricing consistency. The airline's marketing approach was one of traffic stimulation, rather than market share ("Low cost carriers," 1996). While other airlines focused on customer loyalty, ValuJet's focus was lower fares that would increase its clientele. Customers were typically those on a limited budget: students, seniors, families, and small-business owners (Schiavo, 1997).

A Questionable Corporate Culture

The idea behind ValuJet was to create a low-fare, no-frills, fun and friendly airline (Peyser & Hosenball, 1996). ValuJet's informal culture appeared to click with its employees and the public. Lewis Jordan was typically seen wearing golf shirts and khakis rather than the traditional business suit. The airline's playful culture was reflected through its rather unique logo, a grinning airplane. Known as "The Critter," the logo was painted across the airline's fleet of DC-9s. "Critter" also served as the carrier's official air traffic control nickname.

ValuJet's labor force was relatively inexpensive. Salaries were 50 to 70 percent of the industry average (Peyser & Hosenball, 1996). Low salaries, however, were supplemented by year-end bonuses based on annual profits. Pilots were paid only for the flights they completed, possibly influencing them to take unnecessary risks. ValuJet also saved money by purchasing only used or reconditioned DC-9s, some more than twenty-five years old. Nine of its fifty-one airplanes were bought from a Turkish airline. To increase its earnings, the carrier emphasized keeping the planes in constant service, often straining maintenance and compromising safety. ValuJet handled little of its heavy aircraft maintenance, farming out most of it, as well as some training and service functions, to various contractors. According to FAA records, ValuJet contracted with four private vendors in 1992, but by 1996 the carrier had spread its maintenance among fifty-six private contractors (D. Phillips, 1996a). The airline's heavy reliability on private maintenance vendors earned it the label of a "virtual" airline. By contracting out most of its maintenance, ValuJet lessened its control.

It appeared ValuJet had developed a culture that conflicted with safety. The airline's structure could not handle rapid growth. This became clear when ValuJet bid to contract with the Department of Defense, who in turn placed the airline under an intense review. Their findings revealed problems in numerous areas including management, personnel standards, quality assurance, maintenance, and training. As a result of the findings, the carrier did not receive a contract from the Defense Department.

Previous Incidents

In its three years, ValuJet encountered a number of mishaps. Emergency landings, overshot runways, and collapsed landing gear were common occurrences. In January 1994, Dulles Airport closed for two hours after a ValuJet DC-9 slid off an icy runway. A more serious accident occurred during June 1995, when an engine on a ValuJet plane taxiing down an Atlanta runway caught fire. The fire spread through the cabin, severely disfiguring a flight attendant. In January 1996, two planes slid off runways in Atlanta and Dulles after landing in bad weather, and in Nashville, a hard landing caused extensive damage to a DC-9. The following month in Nashville, a DC-9 tire burst after landing, and in Savannah another plane slid off the runway (Burch & Reed, 1996).

These incidents, along with the airline's rapid growth, forced the FAA to place ValuJet under an intense inspection program during the winter of 1996. Despite an extreme number of incidents, the airline had not come under public scrutiny. In the spring of 1996, ValuJet appeared to be flying high.

SabreTech Corporation

SabreTech was one of the contractors ValuJet used for line maintenance and heavy aircraft maintenance. In early 1996, ValuJet purchased three McDonnell Douglas airplanes. The planes were ferried to SabreTech's maintenance and overhaul facility in Miami for various modifications and maintenance. The tasks requested by ValuJet included the inspection of the three planes' oxygen generators to determine whether they had expired. SabreTech was then directed by the airline to replace all oxygen generators on two planes. Because of their hazardous nature when removed from an aircraft, generators require special handling and labeling for storage or disposal. Once removed from an airplane, plastic safety caps must be installed on generators not expended (NTSB, 1997). SabreTech began the process in mid-March of 1996 and completed it by May 5, 1996. The expired or near-expired oxygen generators were placed in five cardboard boxes and moved to a rack in a hangar. They were later taken to the ValuJet section of SabreTech's shipping and receiving hold area.

In early May, after being told to clean up the shipping and receiving area, a SabreTech stock clerk prepared the five boxes for shipment to Atlanta. On May 11, 1996, the five boxes of oxygen generators and three DC-9 tires were loaded into the forward cargo compartment of Flight 592 along with passenger baggage and U.S. mail. The boxes were labeled "Oxygen Canisters— Empty" (NTSB, 1997).

CRISIS

ValuJet Flight 592, a Douglas DC-9, departed Miami International Airport at 2:03 P.M. EDT on May 11, 1996, en route to Hartsfield International Airport in Atlanta. Originally scheduled to depart Miami at 1:00 P.M., Flight 592 was delayed by maintenance problems which occurred on the aircraft's preceding flight. Approximately seven minutes into the flight, the captain indicated electrical problems and requested to turn back to Miami. Seconds later there were reports of fire on board the aircraft. Ten minutes after takeoff the airplane crashed into the Everglades. Reports by witnesses fishing from a boat nearby indicated they saw a low-flying airplane with its nose dropped downward strike the ground, and then a massive explosion and vibration with a huge cloud of water and smoke (NTSB, 1997). On board, two pilots, three flight attendants, and all 105 passengers were killed.

POST-CRISIS

Search and Recovery

Recovery operations for Flight 592 were an intimidating process. The impact area, identified by a crater 130 feet long and 40 feet wide in the mud and sawgrass, contained fragments of the aircraft submerged in approximately seven feet of water (NTSB, 1997). Access was a major problem. Airboats and helicopters were used to reach the crash site. Rescue efforts were hampered by a swamp of flammable fuel, snakes, alligators, and sawgrass. Heat, humidity, mosquitoes, and thunderstorms further complicated the process of the firefighters, paramedics, and police. A recovery area for the victims was established on a track of dirt road a half-mile from the crash. As darkness fell, the search continued with airboats equipped with floodlights (Garcia, Cavanaugh, Driscoll, & Reed, 1996).

The search for survivors was called off the day after the crash and efforts focused on the recovery of bodies and wreckage. A primary challenge was how to safely conduct the search and deliver equipment to the crash site. U.S. Navy sonar equipment was used to gauge the depth of the submerged debris (Garcia et al., 1996). Divers, covered by boots, gloves, masks, and life vests worked in teams of five while sharpshooters were staged nearby to protect them from snakes and alligators (Cauvin & May, 1996a). Wreckage was gathered by hand and moved by airboat to a nearby levee for decontamination (NTSB, 1997). It was later transported to a hangar for examination.

The recovery effort was a tedious process. More than a week later only 25 percent of the wreckage had been recovered. Two days after the crash the flight data recorder was discovered. Two weeks later, the cockpit voice recorder was found. The first of June saw only 50 percent of the wreckage retrieved and twenty-four victims identified. At the time, the recovery was the longest and costliest effort in U.S. aviation history. In the end, approximately 75 percent of the wreckage was recovered and 68 of the 110 persons on board Flight 592 were identified (Viglucci, 1996; NTSB, 1997).

NTSB Investigation

The day after the crash the NTSB go-team began their investigation. Parties to the investigation included the FAA, ValuJet Airlines, SabreTech Corporation, McDonnell Douglas Aircraft Company, Pratt & Whitney, the Association of Flight Attendants, Scott Aviation, the FBI, the Research and Special Programs Administration, and the National Air Traffic Controllers Association (NTSB, 1997). Teams were formed in the areas of operations, structures, systems, powerplants, maintenance, aircraft performance, hazardous materials, survival factors, meteorology, air traffic control, and human performance (NTSB, 1997).

Three days after the crash, the NTSB indicated they were exploring the possibility that old chemicals used to release oxygen stored in fifty to sixty bottles in the cargo hold may have triggered an explosion that caused the crash. Investigators indicated that when installed in the seating areas the canisters are relatively safe; however, they can be hazardous when stored in the cargo hold (Lantigua & May, 1996). As the recovery and investigation continued, attention focused on the oxygen canisters and ValuJet's safety practices. A week after the crash, the NTSB indicated there were twice as many canisters on the aircraft as initially believed. In addition, the canisters were loaded in cardboard storage boxes and there were no plastic safety caps on the canister triggers. It was believed that the fire aboard the DC-9 which broke out immediately after takeoff was caused or accelerated by the old oxygen canisters. Furthermore, ValuJet was not authorized to carry them as cargo. In July, the investigation of ValuJet Flight 592 was delayed by yet another investigation: the crash of TWA Flight 800.

NTSB Public Hearing

A public hearing convened in Miami during November 1996. At the hearing, the president of SabreTech stated that the packaged oxygen-generating canisters aboard ValuJet Flight 592 were not labeled as hazardous material. According to NTSB documents, employees of SabreTech told investigators the canisters were sitting in a stock room at SabreTech in Miami when a stock clerk decided to send them back to ValuJet in Atlanta. The employees believed the requirements for packaging the canisters had been met, but as it turned out the special safety caps were mistakenly listed as installed and the canisters mislabeled as empty.

Probable Cause

Following its investigation and analysis of findings, the NTSB adopted the final report of the ValuJet Flight 592 accident on August 19, 1997. The cause of the crash resulted from a fire initiated by the actuation of one or more oxygen generators which were improperly carried in the aircraft's cargo compartment. The Board attributed the probable cause to SabreTech's failure to properly prepare, package, and identify unexpended chemical oxygen generators before presenting them to ValuJet for transport; ValuJet's failure to properly oversee its contract maintenance program to ensure compliance with maintenance, maintenance training, and hazardous materials requirements and practices; and the FAA's failure to require smoke-detection and fire-suppression systems in class-D cargo compartments (NTSB, 1997).

Contributing factors included the FAA's failure to adequately monitor ValuJet's heavy maintenance programs and responsibilities and to respond to the potential hazards of chemical oxygen-generator fires. ValuJet's failure to ensure contract maintenance employees complied with the airline's "no-carry" hazardous materials policy and received proper hazardous materials training was also cited as a contributing factor. Recommendations addressed ValuJet's oversight of its contract heavy-maintenance facilities as well as the FAA's oversight of the airline and its contract maintenance facilities (NTSB, 1997).

Victims' Families

Relatives of passengers who rushed to the ValuJet desk at Miami International Airport were immediately escorted to an auditorium by company officials where counselors were present to assist (Garcia et al., 1996). There was some confusion with the passenger manifest. ValuJet failed to record one victim, another passenger was listed under a supposed alias, and a third name was a man who had purchased a ticket for a friend (Cavanaugh, 1996). The fact that such mix-ups could occur during a period of heightened security raised questions.

As the days passed, family members grew impatient with the lack of news of their loved ones and lobbied officials to see the accident site. Four days after the crash, family members were taken to the crash site where they placed wreaths of flowers on top of the water (Garcia et al., 1996).

The Grounding of ValuJet

At the time of the crash, the FAA was conducting a 120-day special emphasis review of ValuJet. The crash prompted the FAA to expand and intensify its ongoing review of the airline. Daily inspections forced the airline to halve its number of daily flights. It was soon discovered that ValuJet's accident rate was higher than all but one low-cost carrier studied by the FAA. From May 12 to June 10, approximately sixty FAA aviation inspectors conducted over 2 thousand inspections on ValuJet's overall operations. (The FAA indicated this was the equivalent of four years' worth of inspections in four weeks). Significant deficiencies in ValuJet's operations surfaced, particularly in its maintenance control system. In light of the findings, ValuJet was asked by the FAA to cease passenger-carrying operations until corrective actions could be taken. The airline complied and on June 18 ValuJet was grounded.

On September 30, ValuJet Airlines resumed operations with a substantially smaller fleet of aircraft which enabled the FAA to better monitor the airline's managerial capabilities and compliance with safety rules. Customers eagerly snatched up $19 introductory fares and the airline booked 1,400 passengers in the first three hours of taking reservations (Bynum, 1997). By December 1996, ValuJet was in trouble again after it sold 15 thousand tickets without the FAA's approval. In January 1997, the FAA was once more reporting problems with the airline's safety.

Industry Repercussions

The crash of ValuJet Flight 592 reverberated throughout the airline industry, placing the U.S. air-transport business under intense scrutiny. Public and government attention focused on numerous issues; foremost were those concerning low-cost airlines. The worry was that cost cutting compromised safety. Could ValuJet, as well as other low-cost carriers, simultaneously maintain safety standards and keep costs as low as possible? Furthermore, there were concerns about the FAA. The public long believed the FAA was responsible for policing airline safety, but they now learned the FAA was also responsible for promoting the airline industry. Was the FAA, with its present structure, capable of regulating so-called "virtual airlines," who farm out their maintenance, training, and many other activities?

ValuJet's maintenance operation illuminated problems in the FAA's inspection and certification system. Reports indicated the FAA had notified ValuJet prior to the crash of concerns that the airline's culture prevented it from operating at a high level of safety. Yet despite the FAA's concerns the airline was not shut down. It appeared the FAA was not prepared to properly monitor and control airlines which conducted their business without any kind of central control or monitoring. The FAA's dual role of regulating safety and promoting air travel was conflicting.

In the first few days after the crash, both the Secretary of Transportation, Federico Pena, and FAA Administrator, David Hinson, appeared on television proclaiming ValuJet and other discount airlines safe to fly. Reassuring the flying public about ValuJet's safety, Secretary Pena stated he had flown the airline himself. As the inspection of ValuJet continued, however, the FAA began to change its position. Following the grounding of ValuJet, Secretary Pena stated at a news conference that "The FAA looked itself in the mirror. It found that organizational and management changes were needed" (Rosenberg, 1996). He further stated that the FAA should redefine its mission so there would be no questions concerning its priorities. The Clinton administration would request Congress to restrict the FAA's mandate to safety, eliminating its role in promoting the airline industry. Hinson admitted the FAA did not accurately assess the airworthiness of ValuJet prior to the crash and announced a tightening of FAA inspection rules (Rosenberg, 1996; "ValuJet crash prompts FAA shakeup," 1996). The FAA's top enforcement official would also be replaced.

At the end of June, aviation safety hearings were held before a House Transportation subcommittee. The hearings were an intense Congressional investigation of the FAA and the events leading up to the crash of ValuJet Flight 592. Those testifying included ValuJet President Lewis Jordan, the president of SabreTech, FAA Administrator David Hinson, and Inspector General Mary Schiavo of the Transportation Department (E. H. Phillips, 1996, July 1).

CRISIS COMMUNICATION:
AN ANALYSIS OF VALUJET'S COMMUNICATION

ValuJet had traded as a high-growth stock, but on Monday following the crash ValuJet's stock plummeted 23 percent (Reed, 1996). The airline also experienced a few cancellations from its passengers. ValuJet waived its no-refund policy. Because declines in stock and passenger bookings were common after fatal crashes, it was expected that it would pick up after a few weeks. The carrier claimed it had sufficient cash on hand to overcome problems.

Three weeks after the crash, ValuJet's stock had lost almost one-third of its value (Faiola, 1996). To further complicate the airline's position, three investors filed a lawsuit alleging ValuJet's executives misled investors into believing the carrier was safe. They sought compensation for the reduced value of their ValuJet shares. After the FAA announced it would ground the airline,

ValuJet shares plunged more than 50 percent ("Will ValuJet be able," 1996). In July, media attention on ValuJet faded and was redirected toward the TWA Flight 800 disaster. Following news in August that the company would fly again, stock went up 14 percent ("ValuJet sprucing up," 1996). As a consequence of its grounding, ValuJet reported a net loss for 1996 of $41.5 million compared to a net income of $67.8 million in 1995 (ValuJet, 1997a). For the first quarter of 1997, ValuJet reported a net loss of $18.5 million (ValuJet, 1997b).

Prior to the Flight 592 crash, the public perceived ValuJet as a successful, safe start-up company who offered desirable low fares to travelers. Following the crash, however, media reports and NTSB findings suggested otherwise. ValuJet was faced not only with the tragedy of Flight 592, but subsequent events resulted in two strong allegations being brought against the airline. First, stakeholders believed ValuJet was not a safe airline. ValuJet's performance history indicated consistent safety problems and because of this it was likely the airline was at fault in the Flight 592 crash. Second, NTSB findings suggested ValuJet shared in the blame for the Flight 592 crash. Because of its previous incidents and the FAA's ongoing inspection, safety factors should have been identified and controlled. Yet the airline failed to ensure SabreTech employees complied with airline policy. Critics argued the carrier's cost cutting had resulted in inadequate maintenance. The perception was ValuJet knowingly placed its passengers at risk. These charges plagued the airline for months after the crash.

This analysis considers ValuJet's response to these two allegations in the post-crisis period. Specifically, the analysis will focus on the airline's efforts to maintain its image in the year following the Everglades crash. Six points for analysis are identified: the Flight 592 crash, the FAA's interim findings, ValuJet's grounding, the Congressional hearings, ValuJet's return to the air, and the NTSB's final report. Each of these events required ValuJet to respond to the ever-present accusations of being an unsafe air carrier and being responsible for the Flight 592 disaster.

The Issue of Safety

The Crash of ValuJet Flight 592

Upon notification of the crash, ValuJet dispatched a team to Miami. Trained employees were assigned to each family to assist them with their needs and keep them updated on any developments. Advertisements were immediately pulled off the radio. Lewis Jordan spoke from Atlanta to express condolences: "Our thoughts and prayers and sincere emotion go out to the people onboard and their families, loved ones and friends. It's impossible to put into words how devastating something like this is to humans who care" (Garcia et al., 1996). From the beginning, Lewis Jordan addressed the issue of ValuJet's safety. In addition to conveying sympathy and concern over the tragedy, Jordan discussed the safety of the airline's maintenance procedures by outlining the different types of airplane checks ValuJet followed to maintain its aircraft ("Jet was up to date," 1996). This initial response created the impression ValuJet was a safe airline.

The following day, ValuJet released the passenger manifest which listed the 109 people aboard the plane. (It was later determined that there were 110 people aboard the aircraft. ValuJet had failed to account for an infant.) The fact that it was Mother's Day added an even greater tragic tone to the accident and Jordan drew attention to the tragedy's timing at a news conference in Miami: "Every human being in every seat of the airplane is a life and a loved one with stories to tell, with friends, with places to go. It's Mother's Day weekend, we know that" (Cavanaugh, Lantigua, & May, 1996). Such a statement emphasized the human side of the airline. Once again, Jordan defended the airline's safety record by describing the flight crew as extremely qualified and denied the plane had safety problems. According to Jordan, the list of ValuJet's previous incidents was not unusual and if the airline had any reason to believe the aircraft was unsafe, it would have voluntarily grounded the plane. Furthermore, the FAA would have grounded it. This suggested the industry's federal regulator believed the aircraft safe. Though Jordan's position was to deny the airline was unsafe, he stated if safety proved to be a factor the airline would take immediate action (Cavanaugh et al., 1996).

As the investigation progressed, more questions concerning the oxygen canisters and the safety of the airline arose. One week after the crash, Jordan, back in Atlanta, cautioned against misinformation and rushing to judgment. At a news conference the airline president hedged responsibility, stating, "I am not saying that ValuJet is faultless. I said I have seen no fault" (Cauvin & May, 1996b). The strategy now became one of pleading ignorance. ValuJet officials indicated the airline was not informed that there was hazardous cargo aboard the flight. Under considerable pressure because of increased regulatory scrutiny, ValuJet announced it was cutting its daily departures in half. Passengers would be reassigned to flights on another airline or receive full refunds (May & Cauvin, 1996).

As pressure mounted, ValuJet employed the tactic of ingratiation by placing an ad in the *Miami Herald* a week and a half after the crash, recognizing and expressing deep gratitude to local rescue workers, the NTSB, the Red Cross, the Salvation Army, as well as others on and behind the scenes (Merzer, 1996). By publicly acknowledging these individuals, the airline created a positive impression in the minds of its stakeholders. The strategy of ingratiation was followed by efforts to right the wrong. In late May, Jordan announced that retired Air Force General J. B. Davis and a team of experts would take on the role of safety czar at ValuJet. The general would have full independence, without limitation. The airline would repair every deficiency identified by Davis and his team.

FAA Interim Report

The FAA's inspection of the airline following the crash unearthed numerous safety-related problems. Findings indicated that ValuJet's practice of farming out maintenance created quality-control problems and overextended the FAA's limited inspection forces. In response to the growing pressure from the FAA, ValuJet would yet again offer corrective action by agreeing to withdraw its policy of contracting out maintenance work (D. Phillips, 1996a).

In an effort to counter the daily media accounts of ValuJet's shoddy maintenance, Jordan employed various strategies. Criticisms, according to Jordan, were based on misinformation. He stated the airline was being unfairly singled out by the press. Implying the airline was a victim would possibly elicit sympathy. He referred to his more than twenty years of experience in the industry and his ongoing efforts to promote safety, indicating that as the airline grew he only hired and promoted highly experienced individuals in safety-related positions (D. Phillips, 1996b).

Five days before the crash of ValuJet Flight 592 the FAA completed its preliminary special emphasis program report based on its 120-day inspection of ValuJet which began in February. The report contained descriptions of out-of-date manuals, inadequately trained crews, malfunctioning aircraft, a disregard for approved procedures, and repairs reported as complete when they had not been made (D. Phillips, 1996b). When initially asked about the report, Jordan was quoted by the *Washington Post* as saying, "It certainly does not sound like the way we want to do business" (D. Phillips, 1996c). Possibly caught by surprise, Jordan's strategy of pleading ignorance did little to reassure the flying public. It did, however, provide an additional point for criticisms.

Jordan later addressed the widely publicized interim findings of the FAA. He began by creating identification between the airline and its stakeholders, emphasizing the common value of safety: "Anything less than perfection where safety is concerned is unacceptable to ValuJet" ("ValuJet discusses," 1996). Jordan again attempted to elicit sympathy by portraying ValuJet as a victim because of its youth. "While the report includes findings that are, at first reading troubling, it is filled with many items typical of those that would be reported at any established major airline if it were subjected to this extreme level of in-depth inspection" ("ValuJet discusses," 1996). By suggesting established airlines had similar problems, ValuJet's president was attempting to distance the airline from the situation and minimize responsibility for the problems.

Jordan continued to identify the airline's efforts in correcting deficiencies when he said, "It is our policy to voluntarily and enthusiastically correct all legitimate findings immediately and to promptly implement any preventive measures that are indicated. While we have not had an opportunity to review completely the interim findings cited by the FAA, we believe that many of them have already been addressed" ("ValuJet discusses," 1996). By "welcoming" the intense FAA review, stating the airline would use their findings to enhance ValuJet's operations, Jordan attempted ingratiation. His acknowledgment of the FAA's findings reinforced the airline's willingness to cooperate. Jordan ended by saying, "There is no point too minor for scrutiny" ("ValuJet discusses," 1996).

The Grounding of ValuJet

The inspection of ValuJet revealed serious safety deficiencies. According to the FAA, the airline had not demonstrated an effective maintenance control system. On June 18, ValuJet complied with the FAA's request for a temporary shutdown. Following the grounding, ValuJet once again elicited sympathy by portraying the airline as a victim. Lewis Jordan claimed the FAA's decision to ground the airline had cost 4 thousand employees their jobs. The airline had begun its return-to-service plans and hoped to resume service in thirty days, but the final decision was out of Jordan's hands. ValuJet offered full refunds to customers whose flights were canceled by the grounding. Jordan stated, "We would not have chosen to be grounded as of today if everything had gone our way, but everything has not gone our way for quite some time, and we will work back from this" ("ValuJet crash," 1996). He indicated the airline had sufficient cash reserves.

Jordan called the grounding "unfair" since he was not given the opportunity to review and respond to the FAA's findings following the Flight 592 crash. He continued with the strategy of eliciting sympathy: "As every day unfolds and as the NTSB continues its investigation it becomes more and more and more clear that this is an accident that could have happened to any airline in the world and that ValuJet airlines is also a victim and ValuJet people are victims" ("ValuJet crash," 1996). The grounding prompted ValuJet employees to speak out about being badly treated by the media. A ValuJet attorney was quoted as saying that the airline had become the scapegoat amidst a political firestorm in Washington.

On June 21, Lewis Jordan appeared on ABC's "Nightline" with Ted Koppel. The late-night news show offered a format for Jordan to defend his airline. Koppel questioned the airline president as to why, in light of the FAA investigation which had been in progress, there were still numerous maintenance and safety problems. Jordan implied corrective action by saying that ValuJet was the most scrutinized airline in the world and that every occurrence would be addressed. He went on to say that it would make no sense to risk safety to save pennies. When asked if he would be willing to concede publicly about errors ValuJet made over the past year, Jordan stated "I cannot think of one at the moment. I would be happy to do it if I could."

During the grounding, which lasted fifteen weeks, ValuJet laid off most of its workers and hired a team of safety experts to improve its operations. In response to the consent order, ValuJet established a new engineering department to oversee its maintenance activities and new quality-control and planning departments. The carrier significantly decreased its number of maintenance contractors. These actions demonstrated the airline's efforts to correct its weaknesses and its determination to fly again.

Congressional Hearings

Toward the end of June, hearings were held before a House transportation subcommittee. The hearings served to illuminate problems with the low-cost carrier as well as the FAA. ValuJet continued to portray the airline as a victim in order to elicit sympathy. Jordan stated before the subcommittee that ValuJet was being unfairly scrutinized because of its size and youth. He argued that if larger airlines were similarly investigated, comparable problems would be found. The carrier, according to Jordan, should not have been grounded without the opportunity to respond to the FAA's findings. In the interest of fairness, Jordan asked Congress to encourage the FAA to remove the suspension of operations. Jordan questioned the reasoning of charges against himself and the airline: "I cannot understand the logic of how anyone could think the president of an airline would choose to do anything other than be the safest it could possibly be" (U.S. House of Representatives, 1996, June 25).

When the airline's weak safety record was brought up, Jordan dodged implications of responsibility. He acknowledged the deficiencies, but said they had to be placed in context. Jordan's excuse was ValuJet had provided good low-fare service to more than 10 million customers before it suffered an accident that was not its fault. In his testimony, Jordan redirected blame for the crash to SabreTech. He testified that SabreTech employees inspected the canisters, improperly labeled them, and failed to put safety shipping caps on the canisters. Jordan went on to say he was outraged by SabreTech's denial of responsibility. The shipment of oxygen generators was prohibited by the airline and no employee would have allowed them to be loaded had they been properly labeled: "It is my simple and straightforward contention that had those boxes been so marked, ValuJet would simply have not accepted them. They never would have been on the airplane and those 110 people would not have lost their lives" ("ValuJet CEO acknowledges," 1996).

Jordan admitted that ValuJet had committed violations that went beyond paperwork; however, the airline had begun correcting deficiencies. ValuJet employees demonstrated their loyalty to the airline during the Congressional hearings. Approximately 200 ValuJet employees rallied outside the Capitol and the White House, saying the airline was safe and offered necessary discount fares. This emphasized the airline's "family image" and employees' confidence in ValuJet's safety.

The airline also placed an advertisement in the *Washington Post*, proclaiming ValuJet a safe airline (ValuJet safety ad, 1996). Employing the strategy of ingratiation, the ad focused on ValuJet's pilots. Two ingratiation tactics were used, reinforcing company positives and identification. ValuJet's pilots were a positive point for the company. According to the ad, ValuJet's "pilot professionals" were highly experienced and knowledgeable. The ad specified the average experience of all its pilots as well as missions flown and prestigious honors earned by its pilots. ValuJet implied these highly professional people reflected the type of company they worked for. They would only fly for a solid, safe company. The ad states, "We'd like to tell you about ValuJet's pilot professionals, because we believe it will tell you something about the company they work for." Identification was demonstrated by the airline, implying safety was a concern for everyone. The fact that ValuJet's "pilot professionals" flew for the company suggested the airline was safe. Otherwise, these pilots would not risk their lives. The ad ends by stating safety was important to everyone at ValuJet: "Aviation safety always comes first with our pilots, and with everyone else who works at ValuJet. Our lives—as well as our livelihoods—depend on it."

At the end of June, ValuJet's Flight Attendants Union requested federal officials to remove Jordan and the airline's chairman, Robert Priddy, claiming the men were responsible for the airline's disastrous safety record. One member stated that when it came to safety management took a reactive position rather than a proactive one, thus a new management team was necessary for fundamental changes to occur in the airline. ValuJet responded by calling the request an "outrageous attempt to involve the government in labor relations" (McKenna, 1996).

Return to the Air

Corrective action was critical to ValuJet's plan to return to the air. In July, ValuJet submitted a plan with substantial operational changes to the FAA for resuming partial service. The plan indicated ValuJet would create an in-house organization to oversee all engineering and maintenance planning. It would upgrade its inspection oversight of maintenance contractors as well as improve maintenance training. The airline would shift to a more traditional compensation program. Prior to resuming service, the airline would conduct a thorough review of aircraft to ensure compliance with airworthiness directives. Jordan claimed the changes were appropriate for the airline at that particular point: "It is more important than ever that ValuJet function as an efficient, cohesive and strong organization with clear lines of responsibility and accountability these changes will provide" (Shifrin, 1996). These actions demonstrated an effort on the airline's part to correct its weaknesses and increase safety.

ValuJet continued to make changes to rebuild public confidence. In late August, Jordan stated, "We're confident as the most inspected airline in the world with the most cautious FAA this nation has ever seen, that ValuJet has a clean bill of health it can be very, very proud of" ("ValuJet sprucing up,"

1996). By the end of September, ValuJet had resumed operations. To win back customers, the airline offered $19 one-way fares between Atlanta and four other cities ("ValuJet set," 1996). ValuJet's site on the World Wide Web, with its memorable "Critter" mascot, exclaimed "We're Back!" Included among the links on the site was "Q & A with the Safety Czar." A message from Lewis Jordan stated ValuJet's safety operations had been approved and endorsed by the FAA and the Department of Transportation. He further emphasized the airline's determination to maintain a high level of safety: "And I want to give you my personal assurance that ValuJet and its employees have done, and will continue to do, everything in their power to provide you with affordable air travel that is comfortable, reliable, and above all—safe." Safety and competency were themes woven throughout the various links, which included ValuJet planes, pilots, maintenance, and airfares ("ValuJet's back!", 1996, September).

The Issue of Blame

ValuJet clearly stated its position prior to the approval of the NTSB's final report. The airline employed the strategy of redirecting blame. During the NTSB's public hearings in November, a ValuJet maintenance chief indicated his company accepted blame; however, he insisted it was the responsibility of SabreTech to properly prepare the canisters with safety caps and package the shipment. The FAA's failure to prevent SabreTech's incompetence should not be overlooked. The following spring, ValuJet requested permission from a county judge to make SabreTech a defendant in a lawsuit filed against ValuJet by a Flight 592 victim's relative ("ValuJet accuses," 1997).

In August 1997, the NTSB held a meeting to discuss the final report. ValuJet did not send a representative. At the meeting, the Safety Board indicated the airline had failed to monitor SabreTech's work adequately. One Board member responded that it was ultimately the responsibility of the airline to assure aircraft airworthiness. ValuJet later accused the Board member of having undermined the work of the Safety Board and being anti-ValuJet throughout the investigation. Once again, the airline was portrayed as a victim.

The airline maintained its strategy of redirecting blame to SabreTech. ValuJet maintained its workers believed the oxygen generators were empty when it accepted them for shipment. Though it had no direct evidence, ValuJet alleged that SabreTech employees deliberately mislabeled the cartons for shipment aboard Flight 592, even though they knew the canisters could be dangerous. If the boxes had been properly labeled, they never would have been placed on the aircraft. The airline urged investigators to review the statements ("ValuJet says," 1997). In an effort to bolster its claims, the airline released excerpts of interviews by the FAA investigators with SabreTech employees.

SabreTech responded by calling the charges "preposterous," pointing out that Federal investigators found the airline knowingly carried hazardous materials at least six times in 1996. SabreTech's attorney stated that it was simply the "hysterical rantings" of an airline about to be cited as a contributor to the cause of the Flight 592 crash.

EVALUATION OF STRATEGIES

Evaluating the effectiveness of ValuJet's defense requires determining whether the company chose the right strategies to address the allegations and considering whether the strategies were used effectively. It is necessary to consider factors which influenced the effectiveness of ValuJet's response: severity of the crisis, evidence pointing to blame, and past performance history. The crash of ValuJet Flight 592 was extremely severe—110 people were killed. Findings indicated ValuJet shared in the blame for the crash. Furthermore, the crash could likely have been avoided. In addition, evidence suggested ValuJet's safety performance was weak.

The Issue of Safety

In the immediate aftermath of the Flight 592 crash, little evidence questioning ValuJet's safety record had been made public. Nevertheless, Jordan felt it important to address the safety issue in his initial press conferences. His early strategy of denying safety problems seemed appropriate in light of the available evidence. At the time, no cause had been determined. To suggest that the aircraft, had it shown problems, would have been grounded by both ValuJet and the FAA strengthened and clarified Jordan's claim. As time passed, media reports revealed the questionable nature of the airline's safety operations as well as its prior mishaps. The fact that the FAA had placed ValuJet under an intense inspection program only a few months before the Flight 592 crash underscored the questionable nature of the airline's safety operations. Investigators' findings further indicated ValuJet had contributed to the crash by failing to oversee SabreTech employees and allowing the placement of improperly packaged oxygen canisters in the aircraft's cargo compartment. Data clearly supported the claim that there were serious safety problems at ValuJet. In light of the evidence, the strategy of denying the airline was unsafe and trying to minimize the airline's responsibility for its safety problems by hedging responsibility were inappropriate strategies.

Before the devastating crash, ValuJet was considered a remarkable start-up company that offered reasonable fares for those on a limited budget. Because of its popularity among consumers and the government, ingratiation was a good approach. Identification proved a significant tactic. ValuJet created identification between the airline and its stakeholders by emphasizing the common value of safety. The ad placed in the *Washington Post* emphasizing the safety of ValuJet was a good idea; however, it would have been more effective had it focused on the company's "maintenance professionals" rather than the airline's pilots. After all, it was the company's maintenance that was in question. The airline's actions to correct safety problems reinforced its efforts at identification. The company seemed to be saying, "Safety is important to all of us, therefore we're correcting safety weaknesses."

The damaging evidence made efforts to right the wrong critical. Appointing a safety czar and decreasing the number of maintenance contractors were logical responses. In particular, reducing the number of maintenance groups directly addressed a specific problem. The company's stakeholders needed reassurance that steps had been taken to improve the situation and eliminate or avoid future problems. The FAA's decision to allow ValuJet to resume operations confirmed the airline had indeed improved its situation. As time passed, however, it appeared the company was not firmly committed to its efforts in righting the wrong. Three months after ValuJet returned to the air, the FAA was once again reporting safety violations by the airline. ValuJet's own actions undermined its strategy of righting the wrong. The airline clearly lacked sincerity and it was questionable as to whether it truly valued safety. Righting the wrong appeared an effort to convince Federal regulators and the public of ValuJet's safety.

The strategy of eliciting sympathy seemed self-serving. Jordan argued that ValuJet was a victim because it was young and a low-cost carrier. He further generalized that if other major carriers were scrutinized to the same degree, similar problems could be found. Jordan failed to identify specific examples to support this serious and general claim. Moreover, it did little to reduce public concerns about the overall safety of air travel. Eliciting sympathy was an ineffective strategy because of the overwhelming evidence suggesting ValuJet was responsible for its own problems.

ValuJet was not effective in addressing the charge that it was an unsafe airline. The strategies of denial, hedging responsibility, and eliciting sympathy were poorly chosen considering the overwhelming negative evidence. It seemed ValuJet was more concerned about staying in the air than accepting responsibility for safety problems and doing what was right. The strategies of ingratiation and righting the wrong were well chosen, but inadequately executed. Under the circumstances, ValuJet should have primarily focused genuine effort on the strategy of correcting problems. Ingratiation tactics would be a secondary strategy to reinforce the primary strategy of righting the wrong.

The Issue of Blame

Redirecting blame to SabreTech was a poorly chosen strategy to address the charge that ValuJet shared in the blame for the crash of Flight 592. Because ValuJet contracted with SabreTech to perform maintenance, there was a clear association between the airline and the maintenance company. It was ValuJet's responsibility to oversee SabreTech's work. Because NTSB findings indicated ValuJet shared responsibility for the crash, it was necessary for the airline to accept responsibility in order to receive forgiveness from stake-holders. The airline would have been wise to publicly identify actions it would take to prevent a recurrence of the problem.

EPILOGUE

A costly three-month shutdown, extreme regulatory inspections, and an exceptionally slow return to service resulted in the carrier operating at a loss. A year after the crash, ValuJet was flying fewer planes to fewer places and strug-gling to return to profitability. During the summer of 1997, the Air Travelers Association, Inc. came out with its first biannual Airline Safety Report Card (1997), reviewing the safety performance of the worldwide airline industry. The Report Card assigned numerical grades of 0 to 100 and letter grades A to F, based on flights and fatal accidents. Among twenty-nine U.S. carriers, ValuJet was ranked last, the only U.S. airline graded F (Air Travelers Association, 1997).

Despite all efforts, its lack of a long-standing and loyal customer base com-bined with an unsafe image devastated the airline. In an effort to distance itself from a tarnished image, the airline announced in July 1997 it would merge with Orlando-based AirWays, Corp., parent company of AirTran Air-ways. In September, ValuJet began operating under the name of AirTran Air-lines, along with a new logo (a script teal "a"), a new slogan ("It's something else") and a new dual-class seating system. AirTran would maintain ValuJet's discount pricing while adding new amenities for business travelers ("Revamped ValuJet," 1997).

CONCLUSION

ValuJet's experience following the crash of Flight 592 reinforces a number of lessons learned in the preceding cases. These lessons illustrate the role of corpo-rate culture in crisis, the influence of pre-crisis factors on crisis management and communication, and the consequences of crisis for industry stakeholders.

There is a direct relationship between a company's culture and crisis. ValuJet's culture increased its susceptibility to a major accident. The airline grew quickly in its first few years. By offering consistent low-cost prices, the company lured many customers on tight budgets. But what contributed to ValuJet's success also contributed to the company's failure. ValuJet kept its prices down through a no-frills approach, low salaries, and keeping used and reconditioned DC-9s in constant service. As it grew, the airline came to rely heavily on contract maintenance. By contracting out most of its maintenance, ValuJet lessened its control over safety operations. The company's policy of paying pilots for only those flights completed created the potential for unnec-essary risks. It seems ValuJet's culture was one which conflicted with safety.

Despite the numerous mishaps with its flights, the Department of Defense's refusal to contract with the company because of problems, and being placed under an intense inspection program by the FAA, ValuJet failed to recognize and respond to its critical safety situation. Even after the Flight 592 crash, ValuJet seemed to have difficulty accepting the fact that safety was a real problem. Once again, we see how corporate culture can compromise safety. A responsible corporate culture that values safety and is sensitive to the hazards of its operations is critical to crisis prevention and effective crisis management and communication.

The importance of understanding how pre-crisis factors can increase the complexity of a company's crisis management and communication is implied within this case. ValuJet's initial positive image and credibility was damaged by evidence which emerged during post-crisis, suggesting the company's success was partially due to questionable pre-crisis practices. The airline had been in an enviable position as a result of its rapid growth and success. Following the Flight 592 crash, what was previously viewed as a positive suddenly became a potentially negative issue. ValuJet's low prices attracted the cost-conscious flying public, but at what cost did the company offer low prices? Could ValuJet maintain safety while simultaneously keeping costs low?

A crisis can resonate throughout an industry, implicating organizations, creating chaos, and threatening legitimacy. As a result of the Flight 592 crash, a number of industry stakeholders came under fire. Low-cost carriers in general were questioned for their ability to maintain safety standards. The FAA was criticized and scrutinized for its failure to effectively monitor virtual airlines, as well as for its conflicting role of safety regulator and air-travel promoter. Department of Transportation officials were chided by media for their awkward reactions to the accident. And SabreTech shared in the blame for the crash. Because one organization's crisis can impact an entire industry, every organization should be prepared to handle the consequences associated with a crisis event.

The case of ValuJet teaches two additional lessons concerning crisis communication:

1. A company that makes false denials risks further damage when evidence revealing the truth surfaces.
2. A company's actions must match its statements.

Though it seems human instinct is to deny fault, a company will experience significant damage when the truth eventually emerges. Not only will it be damaged by the act in question, but by the fact it lied about it (Benoit, 1995). When a company is placed under a microscope by various agencies and the media, information will be discovered. Evidence which surfaced as a result of post-crisis investigations indicated serious safety deficiencies in ValuJet's operations. Nevertheless, the carrier contended it was a safe airline and criticisms were based on misinformation. Following ValuJet's grounding, Lewis Jordan portrayed the company as a victim, stating that with the same degree of scrutiny similar problems would be found among major carriers. ValuJet's denials despite the overwhelming negative evidence increased media attention, worsening the situation and further damaging its image and credibility.

Clearly, for legal reasons admission of responsibility may not be possible. However, in defending image, accepting responsibility for wrongdoing and attempting to make amends can initiate a mending process. Benoit, Gullifor, and Panici's (1991) examination of Ronald Reagan's response to the Iran–Contra affair indicated the president's denial of knowing about the arms sale negatively affected his popularity. Following the release of the Tower Commission Report, he admitted making a mistake. His popularity improved. In an analysis of AT&T's response following a break in New York City's long distance service in 1991, Benoit and Brinson (1994) argued that by accepting responsibility, AT&T successfully improved its image.

The second lesson is that a company's actions must not contradict its statements. More than likely, a company will fail to convince stakeholders of its sincerity in improving conditions by simply discussing corrective and/or preventive actions. In order to be successful, it must back up its words with appropriate and genuine actions. ValuJet claimed it corrected weaknesses and improved safety during its grounding; however, reports of safety violations three months after it returned to the air conflicted with the company's claim. It seemed ValuJet was not sincere in its commitment to safety, further damaging its credibility. A company's actions must complement its statements. Perceptual errors on ValuJet's part may have resulted in an incorrect analysis of the situation and, ultimately, unwise decisions.

REFERENCES

Air Travelers Association. (1997). *Airline safety report card, 1.* Washington, DC: Air Travelers Association.

Benoit, W. L. (1995). *Accounts, excuses, and apologies: A theory of image restoration strategies.* Albany: State University of New York Press.

Benoit, W. L., & Brinson, S. L. (1994). AT&T: Apologies are not enough. *Communication Quarterly, 42,* 75–88.

Benoit, W. L., Gullifor, P., & Panici, D. (1991). Reagan's discourse on the Iran–Contra affair. *Communication Studies, 42,* 272–294.

Burch, A. D. S., & Reed, T. (1996, May 12). Safety problems spark parked ValuJet review. *Miami Herald* [http://www.herald.com/crash/docs/valujet.htm].

Bynum, R. (1997, May 11). Year after crash, ValuJet struggles. *Louisville Courier-Journal,* p. E4.

Cauvin, H., & May, P. (1996a, May 14). Hunt for remains moves at a crawl. *Miami Herald* [http://www.herald.com/crash/docs/crmain3.htm].

Cauvin, H., & May, P. (1996b, May 17). Ever-bigger pieces of plane recovered. *Miami Herald* [http://www.herald.com/crash/docs/crmain17.htm].

Cavanaugh, J. (1996, May 17). Passenger list problems caused painful doubts. *Miami Herald* [http://www.herald.com/crash/docs/005902.htm].

Cavanaugh, J., Lantigua, J., & May, P. (1996, May 13). Little debris, no bodies, no cause: Recovery of victims could take days. *Miami Herald* [http://www.herald.com/crash/docs/crmain2.htm].

Faiola, A. (1996, June 1). Turnover, lawsuit add to ValuJet woes. *Washington Post*, p. C1.

Garcia, M., Cavanaugh, J., Driscoll, A., & Reed, T. (1996, May 11). Jet crashes near Miami. *Miami Herald* [http://www.herald.com/crash/docs/crmain.htm].

Jet was up to date on safety checks, says CEO. (1996, May 11). *CNN Interactive* [http://www.cnn.com/US/96...sh/press.conf/index.html].

Lantigua, J., & May, P. (1996, May 15). Clues start to mount in jet's fatal plunge. *Miami Herald* [http://www.herald.com/crash/docs/001503.htm].

Low cost carriers, an American dream. (1996, May). *InsideFlyer* [http://www.insideflyer.com.c...domestic/may96/cover.htm].

May, P., & Cauvin, H. (1996, May 18). Big pieces of airliner are sought. *Miami Herald* [http://www.herald.com/crash/docs/crmain18.htm].

McKenna, J. T. (1996, July 8). ValuJet investigators uncertain pilot donned oxygen masks. *Aviation Week & Space Technology*, p. 32.

Merzer, M. (1996, May 21). Crash probe goes high-tech. *Miami Herald* [http://www.herald.com/crash/docs/042743.htm].

National Transportation Safety Board. (1997, August 19). *Aircraft Accident Report: ValuJet Airlines Flight 592, DC-9-32,N904VJ, Everglades, Near Miami, Florida, May 11, 1996* (NTSB/AAR-97/06). Washington, DC: National Transportation Safety Board (NTIS No. PB97-910406).

Peyser, M., & Hosenball, M. (1996, May 20). Death in the 'Glades. *Newsweek*, p. 31.

Phillips, D. (1996a, June 8). ValuJet to overhaul maintenance. *Washington Post*, p. A1.

Phillips, D. (1996b, June 10). As upstart ValuJet grew, so did FAA's anxieties. *Washington Post*, p. A1.

Phillips, D. (1996c, June 11). ValuJet procedures called inadequate. *Washington Post*, p. A1.

Phillips, E. H. (1996, July 1). ValuJet hearings focus on FAA oversight. *Aviation Week & Space Technology*, pp. 29–32.

Reed, T. (1996, May 14). Passengers bookings drop off after crash. *Miami Herald* [http://www.herald.com/crash/docs/032957.htm].

Revamped ValuJet begins service under new name. (1997, September 24). *CNN Interactive* [http://cnn.com/TRAVEL/NEWS/9709/24/valujet.presser/].

Rosenberg, C. (1996, June 19). FAA shakeup of own ranks aim at safety. *Miami Herald* [http://www.herald.com/crash/docs/crasha619.htm].

Schiavo, M. (1997). *Flying blind, flying safe*. New York: Avon Books.

Shifrin, C. A. (1996, July 15). ValuJet to change operations, seeks August restart. *Aviation Week & Space Technology*, pp. 42–43.

U.S. House of Representatives. (1996, June 25). Text of House Aviation Safety Hearing—Part 8. CNN Specials. Transcript Number: 950133760.

ValuJet. (1997a). ValuJet, Inc. *PR Newswire* reports first quarter 1997 financial results. [http://www.prnewswire.com/com/cgi-bin/stories.pl?ACCT=105&STORY=/oracle/dbtmp/108678&EDATE=].

ValuJet. (1997b). ValuJet, Inc. *PR Newswire* reports fourth quarter and year-end 1996 financial results. [http://www.prnewswire.com/cgibin/stories.pl?ACCT=105STORY+/oracle/dbtmp/68418&EDATE=].

ValuJet accuses subcontractor of negligence in fatal crash. (1997, April 12). *CNN Interactive* [http://cnn.com/US/9704/12/valujet/index.html].

ValuJet CEO acknowledges "deficiencies." (1996). *CNN Interactive* [http://cnn.com/ US/9606/2...et.hearing.pm/index.html].

ValuJet crash prompts FAA shakeup, new rules. (1996, June 18). *CNN Interactive* [http://cnn.com/US/9606/18/faa.presser/index.html].

ValuJet discusses interim FAA report. *PR Newswire*. (1996, June 11). [http:// www.prnewswire.com/cgi-bin/stories.pl?ACCT=105&STORY=/oracle/dbtmp/ 35910&EDATE=].

ValuJet safety ad. (1996, June 25). *Washington Post*, p. 15.

ValuJet says contractor caused Florida crash. (1997, August 15). *Louisville Courier Journal*, p. A16.

ValuJet set for takeoff. (1996, September 30). *CNN Interactive* [http://www.cnn.com/ US/9609/30/valujet/index.html].

ValuJet sprucing up, scrubbing down for return to air. (1996, August 30). *CNN Interactive* [http://www.cnn.com/US/9608/30/valujet.future/index.html].

ValuJet's back! (1996, September). ValuJet Airlines online [http://www.valujet.com].

Viglucci, A. (1996, June 11). Search called off in ValuJet crash. *Miami Herald* [http:/ /www.herald.com/crash/docs/crash612.htm].

Will ValuJet be able to come back financially? (1996, June 21). CNN Inside Business. Transcript Number: 950132992.

———————————————

Chapter 14

Lessons from the Airline Industry

Organizational crises differ according to types, associated characteristics, stakeholders, issues, and consequences. While every crisis situation is unique, focusing on one industry and one form of crisis has illuminated consistent factors and issues that are critical when determining strategic communication. The cases examined in the previous pages suggest that following a major airline disaster an airline may have to contend with issues concerning inadequate responses, victims' relatives, blame, irresponsibility, and airline safety. When threatened by these issues, a company must engage in defensive communication strategies. The cases further suggest the effectiveness of strategic communication in a crisis situation is influenced by pre-crisis conditions that characterize the airline in question and the industry, corporate culture, stakeholders' perceptions and involvement, uncertainty as to cause, and media coverage.

The unpredictable and complex nature of crisis makes it difficult to fully comprehend the multiple problems associated with its management and communication. In an effort to increase our understanding of crisis and the implications for strategic communication, this book was grounded in two assumptions. First, crises must be viewed in terms of phases. Second, crises are best understood from a system perspective.

Crisis management is a continuous process of recognizing and responding to factors associated with a potential or actual crisis and its resolution. Process implies organizational crises progress through phases. When considering crisis in terms of phases, crisis managers are in a better position to recognize the numerous factors which influence the onset of crisis, management, com-

munication, and resolution. An initial understanding of these factors is fundamental when planning for crisis.

The cases in this book were examined according to three phases: pre-crisis,
crisis, and post-crisis. Pre-crisis, a developmental or warning stage, is the point
where the conditions which can lead to a crisis accumulate. Some organizations,
like airlines, are more prone to crisis because of their highly vulnerable nature.
These companies exist in what has been referred to as a perpetual pre-crisis
stage. In some situations, a warning sign may not be recognized or may even
be absent. Effective crisis management requires organizations to constantly
monitor their internal and external environments in order to stay aware of the
threatening signs and symptoms. Recognizing these warning signs may prevent a crisis occurrence. Furthermore, the cases in this book show how pre-
crisis conditions influence efforts at crisis management and communication.

The primary impact of a crisis is experienced in the crisis stage. This stage
is initiated by a triggering event, such as an accident. The post-crisis stage, a
period of recovery and self-assessment, may present opportunities or additional negative effects. Investigations, audits, media revelations, criticism, and
blame typify the post-crisis stage. The length of each phase varies due to the
issues which emerge, the complexity of the situation, and the overall time
frame for resolution.

The airline industry has demonstrated an effective approach to controlling
pre-crisis factors which lead to crashes. Through a thorough and objective
accident investigation by an independent board which functions to identify
probable causes, safety has improved and airlines and the industry are in a
better position to recognize critical factors which lead to accidents and subsequently manage the pre-crisis phase.

A crisis cannot be fully understood in isolated parts; therefore, a systemic
perspective should be the crisis manager's paradigm for viewing the situation. Certain factors develop relative to a particular phase of crisis. Each phase
of crisis and its associated factors will then impact the other. Thus, crisis
factors are interdependent, influencing one another and ultimately impacting
the entire crisis situation. For example, an organization's actions, choices,
and credibility in the pre-crisis phase will not only determine whether or not
a crisis is avoided, but may further influence stakeholder perception of a
company's response to the situation and the issues which arise in the post-
crisis stage. The cases of Northwest and USAir illustrated how negative pre-
crisis factors (image, financial situation, performance history) can increase
the complexity of a company's crisis management and communication.

In the crisis stage, a company's immediate response to the event may result
in residual or lingering effects which then affect issues or perceptions in the
post-crisis phase. TWA's and Pan Am's responses to victims' families became major public issues for the companies to deal with during the post-
crisis phase. Once a crisis is resolved, a company reenters a pre-crisis phase.
If a crisis is not effectively resolved in the post-crisis phase, issues or events

may resurface, creating additional pre-crisis conditions and potentially triggering subsequent crises.

A crisis can resonate beyond the organization in crisis, impacting an entire industry. An airline crash jolts not only the airline, but its effects may touch other airlines, manufacturers, and the FAA, as well as other industry groups. The crash of American Airlines Flight 191 ultimately prompted the grounding of DC-10s, which in turn threw the industry into confusion. Stakeholders outside the industry, including victims, their families, and the general public, will be affected. Stakeholders come together to resolve a situation which affects them all to varying degrees. Consequently, an organization's crisis may be exacerbated by the involvement of various groups. As observed in the American, Delta, and Northwest cases the issue of blame often ignites battles among groups attempting to counter the effects of liability. Stakeholder involvement will likely influence the dynamics of a crisis.

Crisis managers who carefully observe and comprehend the scope and dynamics of a crisis situation are in a stronger position to manage, communicate, and ultimately control the crisis. Conversely, crisis managers who have a single focus or tunnel vision are in a weaker position to control the crisis. The interdependent nature of crisis factors, as well as their relationship to the organization, must be understood. Only then can appropriate actions and effective communication strategies be identified.

LESSONS LEARNED

In many ways, the airline industry provides a model for those in other industries seeking to understand and prepare for crisis as well as effectively manage and communicate in crisis. Although the airline industry maintains a remarkable safety record, an air carrier's natural vulnerability to an accident requires that airlines be crisis-prepared. Most airlines have developed thorough plans that they can immediately set in motion, but no plan is flawless. Unexpected complications often result from unforeseen circumstances.

The case studies illuminate how specific factors associated with a crisis can positively or negatively influence crisis management and communication. While the focus of this book is solely major airline crashes, those responsible for crisis management and communication in other industries can benefit from the lessons taught and learned by airlines in the heat of crisis. What follows are lessons regarding crisis management and communication.

Lesson 1: *A key to effective crisis management is developing a responsible corporate culture which values safety and is sensitive to the hazards of its operations.*

An organization's underlying assumptions, beliefs, attitudes, and values affect organizational practices, which in turn influence whether a crisis occurs and how well it is resolved. Events leading up to crisis, for example, may accumulate as a result of a company's culture. Pan Am and ValuJet clearly demonstrated how corporate culture can precondition a company to crisis. These cases revealed how misplaced priorities and a complacent attitude toward safety can lead to crisis. Corporate culture further influences a company's actions and decisions in a crisis situation. Prevailing corporate attitudes affect how the company responds to both the crisis and stakeholders.

Recognizing the role corporate culture plays in crisis is an important step toward effective crisis management. Crisis managers must be extremely sensitive to how the company's beliefs and values influence actions before or during crisis. A culture that is perceptive and responsive to risks should be encouraged. While a responsible culture does not necessarily ensure a crisis will be avoided, it will likely influence appropriate actions.

Lesson 2: *Crisis planning reduces some of the uncertainty associated with managing a crisis; however, crisis managers must anticipate the challenges of applying a rational plan to an irrational situation.*

Crisis planning provides managers with a tool to more effectively deal with a crisis situation by defining the company's philosophy, approach, and actions. This plan is then adapted to an organization's particular crisis situation. While planning reduces some of the uncertainty associated with crisis management, it rarely takes into account all the factors which can complicate a crisis situation. A crisis plan cannot fully prepare a management team for surprise, uncertainty, threat, extreme emotions, the involvement of many individuals and groups, and other unexpected circumstances.

Preparing for these complicated situations involves clearly identifying the company's philosophy for handling the crisis. A broad view of crisis is more effective in determining effective responses than a narrow view of the situation. Furthermore, because a crisis can threaten the legitimacy of an entire industry, groups associated with a particular industry should be prepared to handle the consequences associated with a crisis.

Lesson 3: *An organization in crisis must communicate from the beginning that it is in control and concerned about the situation.*

In any crisis situation, the goal is to control and manage the crisis, the message, and the communication. Stress, threat, uncertainty, time pressures, and other factors challenge a company's ability to effectively control the situation. There are some basic approaches companies should take in an effort to establish and maintain control in a crisis. Control may be established by communicating promptly, openly, honestly, and adequately. To do otherwise only compounds the situation. A delayed response allows media to gain control of the situation and creates the impression a company is disorganized or does not care. Failing to communicate openly and sufficiently may result in rumors. The case studies highlight the importance of promptly and accurately notifying victims' next of kin and releasing names of victims as a critical aspect of crisis management. A company that is dishonest in its disclosures risks further damage when evidence revealing the truth surfaces.

Control also involves determining what message the company wants to send. Companies must communicate with one voice to avoid contradictions and inconsistencies. It must be viewed as a reliable source of information. An organization in crisis must show compassion and concern through its actions and words. Control may be maintained by applying a clear philosophy on how the company should approach the crisis. Effective responses are significantly influenced by a company's sound philosophy and concrete objectives. The importance of recognizing the symbolic role of executive management was noted throughout this book.

Lesson 4: *A company must be sensitive to stakeholder perceptions of corporate actions and responses during crisis.*

Public perceptions of air-travel safety is critical to the airline industry. When a major crash occurs, the general safety of the airline and industry may be of public concern. Stakeholder perceptions are at the heart of strategic communication. The perceptions of stakeholders must be closely considered to fully understand the situation and determine appropriate responses to defend a company's image. To modify stakeholders' perceptions, a company in crisis must know how its actions and words are being perceived by stakeholders.

The way in which a company is perceived in the pre-crisis phase tends to shift to the crisis and post-crisis stages. The cases illustrated how stakeholder perceptions of an organization's credibility influenced the perceived effectiveness of that organization's response to a given situation. If a company's initial credibility was highly positive, this often provided a halo effect during the crisis, making its actions and statements more believable. Conversely, a lack of initial credibility complicated strategic efforts. Since credibility weighs heavily on stakeholder perceptions of a company's responses, companies in crisis must strive to establish and maintain credibility.

Effective communication is audience centered; therefore, an organization must understand stakeholder views. A company must identify its relevant stakeholders, being sensitive to both unintended and diverse groups, and determine approaches for dealing with various groups. Media may also influence the direction of a crisis by influencing stakeholder perceptions. The way in which media depict the grief and tragedy of an event, for example, will directly reflect upon an organization's image.

Lesson 5: *Media coverage determines the significance and direction of a crisis and directly reflects upon an organization's image; therefore, crisis managers must understand journalistic processes in covering disasters.*

In general, media influence crisis through the information they report, the way they depict the crisis and portray the company in question, and the amount and intensity of coverage. As a consequence of the instantaneous and global nature of crisis coverage, additional pressure is placed on a company. The critical role of media requires an organization to recognize their value and cooperate as much as possible. Understanding their process and developing a rapport with media can be helpful to an organization in handling this extremely critical dimension of crisis.

The case studies underscored three important points concerning communicating with the media. First, because media are highly influential, a company in crisis must be prepared to immediately take control of the situation by being open and providing sufficient and accurate information in a timely way. To do otherwise creates the perception that the company is uncooperative, not in control, or trying to hide something. Second, a highly defensive spokesperson will likely prompt negative media coverage. Finally, when engaging in defense strategies, it must be understood that battling issues publicly will increase media attention and likely do little for the organization's image.

Lesson 6: *When defending its position or image, a company's strategic communication choices must be determined in light of the unique crisis situation.*

Effective communication enables a company to control and manage the crisis, protect the company's long-term corporate interest and public image, and ultimately maintain public confidence. Communication which is ineffective may only create additional confusion. A company in crisis must communicate internally to its employees and externally to relevant groups, including media, government, victims and their families, industry stakeholders, and the concerned public. Corporate culture directly influences how a company will communicate in crisis. Subsequent to a crash, an airline may be charged with blame, irresponsibility, or inadequacy. Strategic communication is necessary to manage the crisis situation.

Determining appropriate and potentially effective responses involves considering significant factors which define the specific crisis situation. Crises differ according to type, complexity, stakeholders, evidence of blame, liability, issues, cause, degree of uncertainty, and threat, as well as other significant factors. The complexity of each crisis examined in this book was determined by the critical issues which emerged, the intensity and length of media coverage, and the threat to the company's situation. Because combinations of these factors created unique crisis situations, no one single communication strategy was effective across all situations. While a standardized communication strategy for crisis communicators has no place in crisis, there is one rule which applies to all situations: Speak with a credible and unified voice. Speaking with one voice creates the perception that the company is in control.

A company's effort at strategic communication will be constrained by various factors unique to the situation. In other words, situational constraints control crisis communication efforts by influencing both the source and receiver of a message. Constraints can be both positive and negative. They may provide opportunities or liabilities for a company attempting to defend its position or restore its image in a crisis. Constraining factors include the company's image, performance history, financial status, and initial response to the crisis; the crisis location; involved groups such as victims and/or their families, politicians, manufacturers, government agencies, and unions; industry status; liability; media; uncertainty; time; and corporate culture.

Managers must identify and understand how the various constraints which characterize a particular situation will influence the organization's image and strategic communication. The cases examined reveal a number of constraints, both positive and negative, which influenced the effectiveness of strategic communication.

When its position or image is threatened, an organization must engage in defense strategies to influence the public's perceptions of responsibility for a tragedy or impressions of the organization itself (Benoit, 1995; Coombs, 1995). In this book, five general strategic communication options were considered which provide a guideline for responding to various issues associated with crisis. Strategic alternatives are those which deny responsibility, hedge responsibility, ingratiate, make amends, and elicit sympathy. Companies may choose to use a single strategy or a combination of strategies. While multiple strategies may reinforce one another, it is critical that these strategies do not contradict one another (Benoit, 1995). The cases suggest a number of considerations for effective strategic communication.

First, strategies of denial (direct denial, expand denial, redirecting blame, and aggression) should obviously be used when an organization is not responsible for the charges made. However, a company that falsely denies it is responsible for an action risks severe damage, as observed in the Pan Am case. When the facts are uncovered the organization will encounter severe damage to its credibility. Although honesty may be the best policy, in crisis organizational liability may prevent an organization from being candid with its communication. Strategic communication then becomes a legal issue.

In general, strategies of denial are more effective when the organization has a high level of credibility. The company is supported by a strong image, performance history, and financial status. Furthermore, denial tactics are more effective when available evidence clearly supports the company's claims. When the source of blame is unclear, denial strategies can also be effective. For example, following the Delta investigation the NTSB deliberated whether the microburst wind shear or pilot error was the single probable cause of the Flight 191 crash. The Board's difficulty in determining a probable cause provided Delta an advantage in arguing its position.

Denial is considered ineffective when general claims are made without support, when existing evidence strongly suggests otherwise, and when a company's performance history and financial situation are questionable. In other words, denial is ineffective when there are no data, or weak data, to support the claim of denial. Strategies of denial are less effective when a company is constrained by a weak prior image and financial situation. Denial is seen as an attempt to offset liability. When addressing allegations of blame, aggression in the form of an attack is negatively perceived and serves to compound an already critical situation. For example, in the Northwest and American cases, the airlines' use of aggression was perceived as being more concerned with liability than safety. Redirecting blame had a boomerang effect: More attention was ultimately drawn to the company doing the redirecting. Furthermore, redirecting blame is considered ineffective when used by organizations with a weak image and financial situation, or when the company receiving blame is directly associated with the company directing blame.

Second, strategies which hedge or evade responsibility (excuses, scapegoat, plead ignorance, refute evidence) are effective when supported by a company's strong performance history. In some instances, the situation lends itself to such strategies. For example, providing excuses and pleading ignorance are more effective in situations where there is a high level of uncertainty as to cause. These strategies are ineffective when available evidence does not support such strategies or when strategies conflict with available evidence and when the company's performance history and financial situation are weak. When a company is constrained by a weak performance history and financial position, scapegoating creates the impression that the company is more concerned over liability than safety.

Third, strategies which ingratiate (accentuate the company's positives, create identification, positively acknowledge others) are not observed in cases that deal with the issue of blame. This would suggest that airlines are more concerned with the issue of liability than image. Ingratiation, however, proves an important strategy when dealing with the issue of airline safety. It is important for companies to convince the flying public that they care about safety. Emphasizing safety as a common value through the strategy of identification is critical. Strategies of ingratiation are particularly effective when the airline has a strong prior image. Ingratiation strategies are less effective when the company's prior image is weak. While credibility is generally considered necessary to support the ingratiation effort, USAir's experience suggests this is not always the case. Though the airline's image prior to the crash of Flight 427 was weak, the company's use of ingratiation appeared effective. Perhaps this was because of the high level of uncertainty over the cause of the crash. There was no clear evidence that the airline was responsible for the crash.

Fourth, in responding to the issue of blame, strategies which make amends (apologize, remunerate victims, right the wrong) are necessary if an organization's objective is to repair image. It appears, however, liability constrains the use of this option. Righting the wrong is an important strategy for airlines, particularly if the company's action is responsible for an accident. This strategy is ineffective when efforts to correct the situation are not sincere, as in the case of Pan Am. The company indicated that it was tightening its security, but evidence later revealed this was not true. Pan Am further damaged its credibility.

Fifth, eliciting sympathy is generally seen as a self-serving strategy. Only ValuJet was observed to use this strategy in responding to the issue of the airline's general safety. ValuJet's use of eliciting sympathy was ineffective because of the overwhelming evidence suggesting the airline was responsible for its own troubles.

Perhaps the most important lesson learned from the cases in this book relates to future outcomes. The airline industry teaches us how an industry can come together in a crisis and, with effective management and communication, reveal truths about its processes for the purpose of improving conditions to prevent future recurrences.

REFERENCES

Benoit, W. L. (1995). *Accounts, excuses, and apologies: A theory of image restoration strategies*. Albany: State University of New York Press.

Coombs, W. T. (1995, May). Choosing the right words: The development of guidelines for the selection of the "appropriate" crisis-response strategies. *Management Communication Quarterly, 8*, 447–476.

Selected Bibliography

Andriole, S. J. (Ed.). (1985). *Corporate crisis management*. Princeton, NJ: Petrocelli Books.

Benoit, W. L. (1995). *Accounts, excuses, and apologies: A theory of image restoration strategies*. Albany: State University of New York Press.

Benson, J. A. (1988). Crisis revisited: An analysis of strategies used by Tylenol in the second tampering episode. *Central States Speech Journal, 39*, 49–66.

ten Berge, D. (1990). *The first 24 hours*. Cambridge, MA: Basil Blackwell.

Cushing, S. (1994). *Fatal words: Communication clashes and aircraft crashes*. Chicago: University of Chicago Press.

Deppa, J. (1994). *The media and disasters: Pan Am 103*. New York: New York University Press.

Fink, S. (1986). *Crisis management: Planning for the inevitable*. New York: AMACOM.

Gottschalk, J. A. (Ed.). (1993). *Crisis response: Inside stories on managing image under siege*. Detroit: Visible Ink Press.

Gouran, D. S., Hirokawa, R. Y., & Marz, A. E. (1986). A critical analysis of factors related to decisional processes involved in the Challenger disaster. *Central States Speech Journal, 37*, 119–135.

Janis, I. L. (1982). *Groupthink: Psychological studies of policy decisions and fiascoes*. Boston: Houghton Mifflin.

Komons, N. A. (1984). *The Cutting air crash: A case study in early federal aviation policy*. Washington, DC: U.S. Department of Transportation, Federal Aviation Administration.

Lagadec, P. (1993). *Preventing chaos in a crisis*. London: McGraw-Hill.

Littlejohn, R. F. (1983). *Crisis management: A team approach*. New York: American Management Association.

Martin, D. (1990). *The executive's guide to handling a press interview*. Babylon, NY: Pilot.

Meyers, G. C. (1986). *When it hits the fan: Managing the nine crises of business.* New York: Mentor.

Pauchant, T., & Mitroff, I. (1992). *Transforming the crisis-prone organization: Preventing individual, organizational, and environmental tragedies.* San Francisco: Jossey-Bass.

Pinsdorf, M. K. (1987). *Communicating when your company is under siege.* Lexington, MA: Lexington Books.

Pinsdorf, M. K. (1991). Flying different skies: How cultures respond to airline disasters. *Public Relations Review, 17,* 37–56.

Ray, S. J. (1997). Investigating commissions as external advocates: The National Transportation Safety Board and the airline industry. In J. D. Hoover (Ed.), *Corporate advocacy: Rhetoric in the information age* (pp. 170–186). Westport, CT: Quorum.

Schein, E. H. (1985). *Organizational culture and leadership.* San Francisco: Jossey-Bass.

Seeger, M. W. (1986). The Challenger tragedy and search for legitimacy. *Central States Speech Journal, 37,* 147–157.

Seeger, M. W., Sellnow, T. L., & Ulmer, R. R. (1998). Communication organization and crisis. In M. E. Roloff (Ed.), *Communication Yearbook* (pp. 231–276). Thousand Oaks, CA: Sage.

Shrivastava, P. (1987). *Bhopal: Anatomy of a crisis.* Cambridge, MA: Ballinger.

Index